New Casebooks

POETRY

WILLIAM BLAKE Edited by David Punter
CHAUCER Edited by Valerie Allen and Ares Axiotis
COLERIDGE, KEATS AND SHELLEY Edited by Peter J. Kitson
JOHN DONNE Edited by Andrew Mousley
SEAMUS HEANEY Edited by Michael Allen
PHILIP LARKIN Edited by Stephen Regan
PARADISE LOST Edited by William Zunder
VICTORIAN WOMEN POETS Edited by Joseph Bristow
WORDSWORTH Edited by John Williams

NOVELS AND PROSE

AUSTEN: *Emma* Edited by David Monaghan
AUSTEN: *Mansfield Park* and *Persuasion* Edited by Judy Simons
AUSTEN: *Sense and Sensibility* and *Pride and Prejudice* Edited by Robert Clark
CHARLOTTE BRONTË: *Jane Eyre* Edited by Heather Glen
CHARLOTTE BRONTË: *Villette* Edited by Pauline Nestor
EMILY BRONTË: *Wuthering Heights* Edited by Patsy Stoneman
ANGELA CARTER Edited by Alison Easton
WILKIE COLLINS Edited by Lyn Pykett
JOSEPH CONRAD Edited by Elaine Jordan
DICKENS: *Bleak House* Edited by Jeremy Tambling
DICKENS: *David Copperfield* and *Hard Times* Edited by John Peck
DICKENS: *Great Expectations* Edited by Roger Sell
ELIOT: *Middlemarch* Edited by John Peck
E. M. FORSTER Edited by Jeremy Tambling
HARDY: *Jude the Obscure* Edited by Penny Boumelha
HARDY: *The Mayor of Casterbridge* Edited by Julian Wolfreys
HARDY: *Tess of the D'Urbervilles* Edited by Peter Widdowson
JAMES: *Turn of the Screw* and *What Maisie Knew* Edited by Neil Cornwell and Maggie Malone
LAWRENCE: *Sons and Lovers* Edited by Rick Rylance
TONI MORRISON Edited by Linden Peach
GEORGE ORWELL Edited by Byran Loughrey
SHELLEY: *Frankenstein* Edited by Fred Botting
STOKER: *Dracula* Edited by Glennis Byron
STERNE: *Tristram Shandy* Edited by Melvyn New
WOOLF: *Mrs Dalloway* and *To the Lighthouse* Edited by Su Reid

DRAMA

BECKETT: *Waiting for Godot* and *Endgame* Edited by Steven Connor
APHRA BEHN Edited by Janet Todd
SHAKESPEARE: *Antony and Cleopatra* Edited by John Drakakis
SHAKESPEARE: *Hamlet* Edited by Martin Coyle
SHAKESPEARE: *King Lear* Edited by Kiernan Ryan
SHAKESPEARE: *Macbeth* Edited by Alan Sinfield
SHAKESPEARE: *The Merchant of Venice* Edited by Martin Coyle
SHAKESPEARE: *A Midsummer Night's Dream* Edited by Richard Dutton
SHAKESPEARE: *Much Ado About Nothing* and *The Taming of the Shrew* Edited by Marion Wynne-Davies
SHAKESPEARE: *Romeo and Juliet* Edited by R. S. White
SHAKESPEARE: *The Tempest* Edited by R. S. White
SHAKESPEARE: *Twelfth Night* Edited by R. S. White
SHAKESPEARE ON FILM Edited by Robert Shaughnessy
SHAKESPEARE IN PERFORMANCE Edited by Robert Shaughnessy

(continued overleaf)

SHAKESPEARE'S HISTORY PLAYS Edited by Graham Holderness
SHAKESPEARE'S TRAGEDIES Edited by Susan Zimmerman
JOHN WEBSTER: *The Duchess of Malfi* Edited by Dympna Callaghan

GENERAL THEMES

FEMINIST THEATRE AND THEORY Edited by Helene Keyssar
POSTCOLONIAL LITERATURES Edited by Michael Parker and Roger Starkey

New Casebooks Series
Series Standing Order
ISBN 0-333-71702-3 hardcover
ISBN 0-333-69345-0 paperback
(outside North America only)

You can receive future titles in this series as they are published by placing a
standing order. Please contact your bookseller or, in case of difficulty, write to
us at the address below with your name and address, the title of the series and
the ISBN quoted above.

Customer Services Department, Macmillan Distribution Ltd
Houndmills, Basingstoke, Hampshire RG21 6XS, England

New Casebooks

ROMEO AND JULIET

WILLIAM SHAKESPEARE

EDITED BY R. S. WHITE

palgrave

First published 2001 by
PALGRAVE
Houndmills, Basingstoke, Hampshire RG21 6XS
and
175 Fifth Avenue, New York, N.Y. 10010
Companies and representatives throughout the world

PALGRAVE is the new global academic imprint of St. Martin's Press
LLC Scholarly and Reference Division and Palgrave Publishers Ltd
(formerly Macmillan Press Ltd).

ISBN 0-333-74780-1 hardback
ISBN 0-333-74781-X paperback

This book is printed on paper suitable for recycling and
made from fully managed and sustained forest sources.

A catalogue record for this book is available
from the British Library.

Library of Congress Cataloging-in-Publication Data
Romeo and Juliet / edited by R. S. White.
     p. cm. – (New casebooks)
   Includes bibliographical references (p.) and index.
   ISBN 0-333-74780-1 – ISBN 0-333-74781-X (pbk.)
    1. Shakespeare, William, 1564–1616. Romeo and Juliet. I. White,
R. S., 1948–II. Series.

PR2831 .R64 2000
822.3'3–dc21   00–053059

10   9   8   7   6   5   4   3   2   1
10   09 08 07 06 05 04 03 02 01

Printed in China

For
Marina and Alana

Contents

Acknowledgements ix

General Editors' Preface xi

Introduction: What is this thing called love? R. S. WHITE 1

1. 'Death-marked love': Desire and Presence in *Romeo and Juliet* 28
   LLOYD DAVIS

2. The Name of the Rose in *Romeo and Juliet* 47
   CATHERINE BELSEY

3. Romeo and Juliet: Love-Hatred in the Couple 68
   [Le couple amour-haine selon *Roméo et Juliette*]
   JULIA KRISTEVA

4. The Ideology of Romantic Love: The Case of *Romeo and Juliet* 85
   DYMPNA C. CALLAGHAN

5. 'The Murdering Word' 116
   KIERNAN RYAN

6. Baz Luhrmann's *William Shakespeare's Romeo + Juliet* 129
   BARBARA HODGDON

7. The Servants 147
   BERTOLT BRECHT

8. *Romeo and Juliet*: The Nurse's Story   152
   BARBARA EVERETT

9. Eloquence and Liminality: Glossing Mercutio's
   Speech Acts   166
   JOSEPH A. PORTER

10. *Romeo and Juliet's* Open Rs   194
    JONATHAN GOLDBERG

Further Reading   213

Notes on Contributors   220

Index   222

Acknowledgements

The editor and publishers wish to thank the following for permission to use copyright material:

Catherine Belsey, for 'The Name of the Rose in *Romeo and Juliet*', *Yearbook of English Studies*, 23 (1993), 26–42, by permission of the Modern Humanities Research Association; Bertolt Brecht, for 'The Resistible Rise of Arturo Ui' from *Bertolt Brecht: Collected Plays,* Vol.6, trs. R. Mannheim and John Willett (1976), pp. 352–5 by permission of Methuen Publishing Ltd; Dympna C. Callaghan, for material from 'The Ideology of Romantic Love: the Case of *Romeo and Juliet*' from *The Wayward Sisters: Shakespeare and Feminist Politics*, ed. Dympna Callaghan, Lorraine Helms and Jyotsna Singh (1994), pp. 59–62, 71–88, by permission of Blackwell Publishers; Lloyd Davis, for '"Death-marked love": Desire and Presence in *Romeo and Juliet*', *Shakespeare Survey*, 49 (1996), 57–67, by permission of Cambridge University Press; Barbara Everett, for '*Romeo and Juliet*: The Nurse's Story', *The Critical Quarterly*, Summer (1972), by permission of Manchester University Press; Jonathan Goldberg, for 'Romeo and Juliet's Open Rs' from *Queering the Renaissance*, ed. Jonathan Goldberg (1994), pp. 218–35. Copyright © 1994 Duke University Press, by permission of Duke University Press; Barbara Hodgdon, for 'Baz Luhrmann's William Shakespeare's *Romeo and Juliet*', *Shakespeare Survey*, 52 (1999), by permission of Cambridge University Press; Julia Kristeva, for material from '*Romeo and Juliet*: Love-Hatred in the Couple' from *Tales of Love* by Julia Kristeva, trs. Leon S. Roudiez (1987), pp. 209–25, 233. Copyright © 1987 Columbia University Press, by permission of Columbia University Press; Joseph Porter, for 'Eloquence and Liminality: Glossing Mercutio's Speech Acts' in *Shakespeare's Mercutio: His History and Drama*

(1988), The University of North Carolina Press, pp. 100–21, by permission of the author; Kiernan Ryan, for 'The Murdering Word' in *Shakespeare, 3e* (2000), by permission of Palgrave.

Every effort has been made to trace the copyright holders but if any have been inadvertently overlooked the publishers will be pleased to make the necessary arrangement at the first opportunity.

General Editors' Preface

The purpose of this series of New Casebooks is to reveal some of the ways in which contemporary criticism has changed our understanding of commonly studied texts and writers and, indeed, of the nature of criticism itself. Central to the series is a concern with modern critical theory and its effect on current approaches to the study of literature. Each New Casebook editor has been asked to select a sequence of essays which will introduce the reader to the new critical approaches to the text or texts being discussed in the volume and also illuminate the rich interchange between critical theory and critical practice that characterises so much current writing about literature.

In this focus on modern critical thinking and practice New Casebooks aim not only to inform but also to stimulate, with volumes seeking to reflect both the controversy and the excitement of current criticism. Because much of this criticism is difficult and often employs an unfamiliar critical language, editors have been asked to give the reader as much help as they feel is appropriate, but without simplifying the essays or the issues they raise. Again, editors have been asked to supply a list of further reading which will enable readers to follow up issues raised by the essays in the volume.

The project of New Casebooks, then, is to bring together in an illuminating way those critics who best illustrate the ways in which contemporary criticism has established new methods of analysing texts and who have reinvigorated the important debate about how we 'read' literature. The hope is, of course, that New Casebooks will not only open up this debate to a wider audience, but will also encourage students to extend their own ideas, and think afresh about their responses to the texts they are studying.

John Peck and Martin Coyle
University of Wales, Cardiff

Introduction: What is this thing called love?

R. S. WHITE

With its volatile mixture of adolescent passion, lyrical poetry and poignancy, *Romeo and Juliet* has always been a favourite amongst Shakespeare plays for performance and on school syllabuses. Memorable film adaptations, particularly by Zeffirelli (1968) and Luhrmann (1996), and its 'inset' appearance in *Shakespeare in Love* (1998), have given it wider currency as part of international popular culture. Oddly enough, the only people who have neglected it, at least relative to their attentiveness to other plays, are Shakespeare critics, who have never quite accepted it as a 'mature tragedy'. This may be because the plot appears to be parodied in the 'Pyramus and Thisbe' presentation in *A Midsummer Night's Dream*, as though even the dramatist could not take it fully seriously. But it is also because *Romeo and Juliet* does not conform satisfactorily to the paradigm of Shakespearean tragedy which, until recently, has prevailed: the idea of character as destiny – the 'great man' undone from within either by an innate weakness or a fallible moral decision. Certainly, older critics applied this model, and they debated as solemnly as they do over Hamlet, Macbeth, Othello, Antony, and King Lear, whether the young lovers fully choose the tragic destiny that awaits them, or whether they are victims of fate. However, generally speaking the play was regarded as relying too much on accidental mistiming and external social conflict to give them complete autonomy or choice. The kinds of recent, 'issues-based' criticism represented in this volume have at last allowed a

1

range of new and interesting perspectives to illuminate the play and explain its power in fresh ways. This Introduction does not try to summarise the essays, but rather to provide a series of different contemporary contexts in which the play and the criticism can be read.

The phrase 'Romeo and Juliet' has become proverbial, two names fused into a single concept signifying a certain kind of love and a certain kind of tragic destiny. How often do we see newspaper headlines like 'Romeo and Juliet in Belfast', 'Romeo and Juliet in Bosnia', 'Romeo and Juliet double teenage suicide'? They refer to young lovers from 'different sides of the tracks', divided by their families who represent warring religious or ethnic groups or who disapprove for other reasons of their children's choices in love. They die for their love, either as a result of social persecution or in acts of self-destruction. Representing love at its most young, passionate and intense, they stand against or above family loyalties, restrictions of conventional everyday obligations and external violence – both glamorous and profoundly sad at the same time. Like *Tristan and Isolde, Romeo and Juliet* deals with a paradoxical fusion of love and death, *liebestod* or 'love-death'.[1] Italicised, '*Romeo and Juliet*', similarly, is not so much a play title as a social phenomenon. It may be unfair to hold Shakespeare responsible for the tragedy of teenage suicides somehow connected with popular songs composed for a film which utilises less than 50 per cent of his words, but such documented consequences today do suggest that there is something, in Kiernan Ryan's words (in essay 5), 'subversive and protesting' about the play.[2]

> The whole thrust of the tragedy is to question the legitimacy of a world whose law deprives men and women of unbounded love as surely as it deprives the poor of their right to the world's wealth.

To some extent, and with their particular differences, each piece in this book deals with an aspect of the play's subversive potential.

One of the main liberating characteristics beneath recent Shakespeare criticism is a refusal to accept either the authority of a single text or the authenticity of a single performance. Those who argue that there is no such thing as an authoritative text of *Romeo and Juliet* (or any other play), point out that we have no manuscript from Shakespeare's own hand and no printed text clearly 'authorised' by Shakespeare. There are three contemporary printed versions of *Romeo and Juliet*, each different in important aspects:

Quarto 1 (1597), Quarto 2 (1599), and the First Folio (1623, after Shakespeare's death).[3] Moreover, printed texts of Shakespeare's time are full of details which are clearly mistakes and need to be corrected by modern editors, each of whom, in turn, differs from the others in their 'corrections'. A quick check of just a few lines from each of the available editions today, such as Arden, Penguin, Oxford, Cambridge, Signet, Riverside, Bell, reveals that no two are identical, especially in punctuation but also often in the words. Furthermore, there is considerable evidence that the plays were constantly being revised, either by Shakespeare or somebody else in the company, to suit particular theatrical circumstances such as provincial tours[4] or changing laws of censorship.[5] Textual criticism, the activity of establishing an accurate text, used to be claimed as a 'scientific' discipline, but its practitioners nowadays accept that it can be just as plural and indeterminable as literary criticism.

Meanwhile, those who argue that there is no such thing as an 'authentic', or 'inauthentic' performance, point to the impossibility of recreating Elizabethan theatrical practices, the paucity of eyewitness accounts, the history which dates from the eighteenth century down to the present day of cutting or even rewriting texts for performance. They remind us of the limitations and opportunities of different stages (Shakespeare's Globe, proscenium arch, apron, theatre in the round) employed in different periods, and of the impact of new technology, whether it be theatrical or the invention of a whole new medium such as film. Therefore, performances and films reflect their own times rather than returning us to an 'authentic' experience. The most textually 'faithful' are often the most tedious and thus 'inauthentic'; creative adaptations can refresh and clarify our insight into the plays. Films give us a very immediate proof of this, because unlike performances in the theatre different versions can be compared with each other. Each generation rewrites Shakespeare for its own purposes, and film reflects box office intentions of appealing to the widest audiences possible. Such admissions of textual instability and the apparent infinitude of potential interpretations and performances would have been firmly opposed by critics just twenty years ago as abandoning the search for stable 'truth'. Nowadays, however, tolerance of such pluralism in turn seems to fit 'the truth' in a more appropriate way: *Romeo and Juliet* has observably worked in many different texts, performances, and contexts, and its effectiveness must largely derive from its capacity for recontextualisation.

All this gives critics a licence to read in plural and indeterminate ways. From the evidence of the essays in this book, the play can be read in more or less opposite ways (as well as many in between) – for example, as giving psychoanalytical insight into the emotional state of young love in an individual, or as showing that young love is not an internal emotion but a socially induced, collective, and conventional set of attitudes explainable by material and gender considerations. Throughout the twentieth century, criticism of *Romeo and Juliet* oscillated between these opposite poles. At one end lies psychoanalysis, with its belief in the individual *psyche*, and its assumption that all people are driven from within by universal, primal feelings that seek fulfilment and happiness but are more often than not thwarted, perverted, sublimated into other pursuits, or repressed. At the other pole lies cultural materialism,[6] which assumes we are driven from without by our circumstances, by chance meetings and random contingencies, by social and cultural attitudes which are unavoidable, by advertising, the sentiments of popular music, family conventions, and so on. At issue are the cherished but contradictory western notions of individualism and of universal human nature. It is significant that defenders of each pole, in their very different ways, deny freedom of choice in our emotional lives. One group asserts that we are compulsively driven and our destinies shaped by largely inherited or manipulated feeling states and expectations, the other that we are at the mercy of the very limited culture of which we have experience.

LOVE AND DESIRE

We hear and use the word 'love' every day in many different contexts and we seem to understand it in so many ways that it is hard to think of another single word defined so diversely, unless it is 'desire'. Love describes not only the passionate, physical and emotional attraction to another person and the parodically related *l'amour fou*, but also the achingly solicitous and patient feelings of a parent for a child, the determined symbiosis of elderly couples who light fires against loneliness and infirmity, the caring and frustrating attachment to a physically or mentally disabled relative, dependence on a deity (sacred love), or just the free and easy exchanges of intimacy between trusting companions. All but the first of these kinds of love involve some acceptance of limitations, sacrifice, commitments and provisionality, and they can strike us as admirable, inspiring, touching, poignant, or funny. 'Desire' semantically hovers between genuine need and superficial self-gratification. Its mirror-image is nostalgia, longing for the past as desire is a longing for the future, and we find both points of view in *Romeo and Juliet*. William Hazlitt, emphasising the youthfulness of the protagonists who are engaged in 'an idle passion between a boy and a girl', celebrates desire as a yearning for 'promised happiness' in the unknown future:

> They were in full possession of their senses and their affections. Their hopes were of air, their desires of fire. Youth is the season of love, because the heart is then first melted in tenderness from the touch of novelty, and kindled to rapture, for it knows no end of its enjoyments or its wishes. Desire has no limit but itself. Passion, the love and expectation of pleasure, is infinite, extravagant, inexhaustive, till experience come to check and kill it.[7]

He describes poetically the dismaying course followed by the play's action, 'from the highest bliss to the lowest despair, from the nuptial bed to an untimely grave'. But in emphasising the preciousness of youthful desire as something which exists entirely in hopes for the future, Hazlitt downplays the play's other perspective, that expressed by Friar Laurence, Juliet's Nurse, and Lady Capulet – the wariness of experience and the tinge of nostalgia created by hindsight, an altogether more kindly desire that these two young people should not waste their lives in hopes that can never unambiguously be realised. So radically multiple are the associations of 'love' and 'desire', that we find ourselves circling around an absent centre of meaning, an evacuation. To the very pertinent and honest question which might be asked of the mature by the young, 'Why do you not offer us reliable advice about love and desire, since our love-choices will affect us for the rest of our lives?' the only answer can be 'Because we don't know what they are'.

Of the kinds of love and desire on offer, one type above all has grabbed headlines, and here the popular, western associations of the word are inextricably linked with romantic love exemplified by Shakespeare's *Romeo and Juliet*. We are bombarded with popular songs, television soap operas, and glossy magazines, all telling us that love is for the young or the 'young in heart', that it is primarily physical, urgent, reckless, and ecstatic, and very likely doomed in one way or another. The flagging middle-aged, aware of nature's stealthy and purposeful abandonment of them, sometimes try to revive its secretive thrills by strategies of adultery. So specific and ubiquitous are the representations of adolescent love in the culture that a new word, 'limerence', was once coined (without conspicuous success) to differentiate it from other kinds of love.[8] In explaining 'young love', views range across a spectrum. At one end are those who say romantic love is purely instinctual, spontaneous, and felt on the body – other-centred and yet mutually satisfying. At the other end are those who say it is a mental construction so overwhelmingly endorsed by popular culture that we are all deceived into thinking it 'natural'. They say that it is not spontaneous but externally conditioned behaviour: it thrives on social disapproval or opposition, and is essentially narcissistic. Cooperative friendliness and unillusioned trust seem to be more solid grounds for compatibility. The latter group points to rising divorce rates as evidence of the untrustworthiness and self-centredness of romantic love as a basis for marriage, and also demonstrates that different cultures have quite different concepts of love.

An anthropologist, Helen Fisher, claims that there are three radically different centres in the brain which control three kinds of emotions which can coexist or exist independently of each other: libido (sexual desire), infatuation (fantasy), and attachment (enduring commitment).[9] The rare ideal is seen as all three in tandem. In fact, similar threesomes have been proposed by many analysts of love. The eighteenth-century philosopher David Hume thought it arose from 'the pleasing sensation arising from beauty; the bodily appetite for generation; and a generous kindness or good-will',[10] while psychologist Robert J. Sternberg proposes as its essential ingredients intimacy, passion, and commitment.[11] Cultural anthropology reveals that definitions of love differ from culture to culture. For example, in traditional Chinese society the only genuine kind of love acknowledged as such is attachment. Deference to parental guidance and concern for the welfare of children make submission to, and celebration of, libido and infatuation seem unthinkably selfish – so that not only *Romeo and Juliet* but also *King Lear* and *Othello* in their different ways become almost incomprehensible except as symptoms of western decadence.[12] Infatuation, especially, seems a phenomenon limited to western culture influenced by medieval courtly love conventions and refined in movies, advertisements and the cynical packaging of singers. On the other hand, Alan Macfarlane points out that it is only in industrial western societies that the emotional relationship between man and woman in marriage is considered a primary value system: in other cultures the pivot of the social structure is relationships between parents and children.[13] Courtship is seen as functional, and marriage as no big deal, except as a safe environment in which children can be born and grow up. As a different approach, it would not be difficult to construct an argument that from time to time in some countries and cultures, subservience to the state (or the church, when it had worldly power) has influenced personalised relationships in providing a dominant framework of thinking which is replicated in marriage ('lie back and think of England' is one parody of the dutiful wife's attitude to sex in Victorian England). Even within one culture, such as England's, amatory and sexual norms have changed quite radically over time. The idea of marriage partners as companions who are mutually supportive is relatively recent, and still changing in nuance as equal opportunity employment laws and childcare facilities become accepted as human rights. Equality in marriage may have scriptural authority in Paul's advice to men to 'love their wives as their own bodies' and in Matthew's 'one flesh', but these Gospel attitudes are not consistently proclaimed throughout the Bible, and the ways in which Paul and Matthew interpreted them seem patriarchal and condescending to women. It has been argued that it needed the Reformation to establish companionate marriage in Protestant countries. And, as several writers in this book demonstrate, love can mean different things to men and to women, to heterosexuals and homosexuals, to royal families and commoners (as the marital fate of Lady Diana Spencer was to demonstrate), to the old and the young.

The outcome, as Catherine Belsey points out in her erudite and beautifully written book entitled *Desire*, is that it is probably impossible to extricate ourselves from our own limited understandings on this issue sufficiently to find more general agreement:

> What if, after all, there is no stripped-down, basic sexuality, no simple animal or clinical experience outside our culturally induced expectations, hopes, anxieties, values? ... it would indicate that we in the West now could not, as an act of will, simply step outside the metaphysics of desire which is our cultural heritage.[14]

As Belsey points out in this volume (essay 2), this kind of radical questioning of what usually in the West is regarded as 'natural', leads us to wonder if love is only solipisistic, individual and lonely, rather than shared, and in so far as it is shared, whether it is a product of an agreed *language* where metaphors are understood literally, rather than of emotions and psychology. Belsey draws attention to the importance of naming in the play (Romeo is out of bounds for Juliet simply because he is named Montague), while Peter Conrad has pointed to a persistent line of imagery in the play focusing on spoken and written language. The Nurse, Conrad notes, is considered amusing by her exclusion from courtly language, and from her 'social betters', who 'love by the book; their feelings are textual'.[15] Gayle Whittier in a justly admired article shows how prominently the highly artificial conventions of Petrarchan sonnet-writing are implicated in the supposedly spontaneous effusions of love-language,[16] and one of Shakespeare's own characters, Proteus (whose name means 'changeable') in *The Two Gentlemen of Verona*, encourages the calculated and studied writing of sonnets and songs as a devious ploy in courtship.

If nothing else, it is clear that love, far from being a many splendoured thing, is not a single thing, and in fact it may not even be a 'thing' at all, but rather, as Mercutio mordantly suggests of the love connected with Queen Mab, a 'nothing', simply a dream. His spellbinding and strange lines in the almost hallucinatory digression on 'Queen Mab' add to the play, in their intense bitterness and Bosch-like imagery, a vision of love which is even more dangerous and socially disruptive than the lovers' experience, since it contains cruelty and mischief-making. In our own day, the skilful construction, commodification and selling of actors or singer / musicians as 'sex symbols' shows how depressingly easy it is for the media periodically to manipulate emotions and persuade people what they 'really want', whether it is the dreamy romanticism of Juliet, paradoxical confusion of Romeo, earthy sexuality of the Nurse, or the sharp masochism and sadism of Mercutio. Advertising is explicitly based on the cynical knowledge that people's needs and desires can be cleverly manufactured, and the fashion industry, for example, has the power rapidly to change even what is considered a desirable body-type or a beautiful face. *Romeo and Juliet* itself has been appropriated by a series of film-makers to reconstruct images of ideal teenage beauty: compare, for example, the impetuous and latin Olivia Hussey with Claire Danes's college-girl wonder and intellectualism, and Leonard Whiting with Leonardo DiCaprio, from the 1960s and 1990s respectively.[17]

Shakespeare himself gives many different narratives of love. *The Taming of the Shrew* sees courtship as altogether lacking in romance, and marriage as a power struggle resolved only by one partner being accepted as dominant, the other submissive. *Love's Labour's Lost* and *As You Like It* see love as a game-like test in adversity with its ultimate reward as marriage, *Othello* as a kind of compensation where each lover represents to the other the quality s/he lacks (or worse still, as based on simple possessiveness). *Twelfth Night* presents love as privation, repression and sacrifice (or on the other side, wordy self-indulgence), while *A Midsummer Night's Dream* and *Romeo and Juliet* see premarital love as an overwhelming, bewildering and compulsive emotional experience. It is difficult to escape the conclusion that Shakespeare regards courtship as a 'fantasy' stage of a relationship and that the fantasies quickly evaporate after marriage: Rosalind in *As You Like It*, replying to her lover's oath that he will love her forever and a day, says 'Say a day without the ever. No, no, Orlando; men are April when they woo, December when they wed. Maids are May when they are maids, but the sky changes when they are wives' (IV.i.138–41). Successful marriage, according to the view that seems to prevail in *As You Like It* as a whole, depends not primarily on passionate wooing (which is seen as a game of role-playing) but on subsequent adaptation to reality: a transition from infatuation to attachment, driven by a kind of willed decision to accept the other as different and likeable, helpful, friendly and compatible on a day-to-day level. Those who cling to the mythologies of high romance, like Othello, Romeo, and Juliet, come to grief for one reason or another.[18] Again, Rosalind in *As You Like It* provides a salutary reminder that the death-wish may more plausibly be a fantasy or a temporary stage in maturation, and never needs to be enacted:

> **Orlando** Then in mine own person I die.
> **Rosalind** No, faith; die by attorney. The poor world is almost six thousand years old, and in all this time there was not any man died in his own person, videlicet, in a love-cause. Troilus had his brains dashed out with a Grecian club, yet he did what he could to die before and he is one of the patterns of love. Leander, he would have lived many a fair year though Hero had turned nun if it had not been for a hot midsummer night, for, good youth, he went but forth to wash him in the Hellespont and, being taken with the cramp, was drowned; and the foolish chroniclers of that age found

it was Hero of Sestos. But these are all lies. Men have died from
time to time, and worms have eaten them but not for love.
(IV.i.87–101)

At the least, all the evidence suggests that Shakespeare agreed on,
and perhaps helped to naturalise, the idea that love is plural, contradictory and paradoxical, many things rather than one. *Romeo
and Juliet* raises and builds into its vision the free-floating diversity
of the word 'love' and of language in general. If we compare the
surrealism of Mercutio on love as fantasy, the Nurse on marriage as
including bawdy physicality, Juliet's parents on love as something
that will grow within an arranged marriage, and the Friar who cau-
tions against acting on ephemeral emotional states, we find even
within one play a surprising range of incompatible attitudes.

LOVE AND DEATH IN PSYCHOANALYSIS

One twentieth-century thinker who has had enormous influence over
literary criticism and Shakespeare studies is the psychoanalytical theorist Sigmund Freud. His successor, Jacques Lacan, is also frequently
cited by some literary critics. Whatever one thinks of this approach
to human behaviour, it has been highly significant in shaping popular
theories of love and desire, and it is represented in this book in the
essay by Julia Kristeva (essay 3).[19] Some background might make the
essay more accessible. Helen K. Gediman's *Fantasies of Love and
Death in Life and Art* is, in the words of its subtitle, *A
Psychoanalytic Study of the Normal and the Pathological.*[20] While
it focuses on the *liebestod* (love-death) in contemporary psychiatry
and in the *Tristan and Isolde* story, it has as much to say about
Romeo and Juliet. Gediman refers us to the classic work of Dennis
de Rougemont, *Love in the Western World,*[21] which 'holds romanticism responsible for the "fact" that happy love has no history in
Western literature',[22] and links this pessimism with 'the traditional
psychoanalytical view regarding romantic passion as an illness'. De
Rougemont speaks of love as 'twin narcissism' where two people
are 'in love with their love': or, as Gediman more prosaically
defines it, 'as a more or less transient fusion state in which libidinal
investment of the self is transferred to the object ... Self and object
are loved as one because both share a love for a commonly es-
teemed activity, feeling state, or object' (p. 20). The presence of narcissism is what marks off the 'Liebestod fantasy' form of love from

the more complicated versions of companionate love or attachment which can last through the degradations of time into old age, in which ego integrity has been achieved in the individual, and feeling is now invested through empathy with others rather than gratification of the self. In an apparently unaware echoing of Theseus's 'The lunatic, the lover, and the poet, Are of imagination all compact' (IV.i.7–8), Gediman writes, 'Twin narcissism is a term for fusion of self and object that is evocative of an early ego state common to infants, lovers, and some creative artists' (p. 20). John Donne, Shakespeare's contemporary, uses the rather grotesque image in describing lovers gazing into each other's eyes in 'The Ecstasy':

> Our eye-beams twisted, and did thread
> Our eyes, upon one double string.

Philip Sidney in *Arcadia* depicts the male lover as so closely iden-tifying with his beloved that he disguises himself as a woman, partly to gain access to her company since her father denies her male company, but equally to denote his commitment to her. This situ-ation is echoed in *Romeo and Juliet* when Romeo dons a mask to gatecrash the Capulet ball without detection. Romances and popular songs down through the ages attest to the simultaneous ab-sorption in the other, and the self-sustaining fantasy that marks young love, a total investment in believing that one knows com-pletely the other, because one is seeing only the self. Love as twin narcissism, requited or mutually shared love, is, according to Gediman and other psychoanalysts, a symptom of the infant's in-complete detachment from the mother, or a desire to return to infant identification with the mother, and is a step from symbiosis to individuation. The brevity and transience of such a state is de-scribed similarly in both *A Midsummer Night's Dream* (I.i.143–8) and by Juliet, in *Romeo and Juliet*:

> Although I joy in thee,
> I have no joy of this contract to-night;
> It is too rash, too unadvis'd, too sudden;
> Too like the lightning which doth cease to be
> Ere one can say 'It lightens'.
>   (II.ii.116–20)

By way of contrast, Shakespeare shows in *As You Like It* the slow testing and confirmation of an initial 'love at first sight', through lengthy courtship and complex role-playing (imagining, testing and accepting the other's difference), suggesting not only the transition to companionate love but also that marriage is a 'world-without-end bargain'[23] and can be an ever-changing, ever-deepening love affair which moves past infatuation and dreams.

The psychoanalytical model explains the actual or fantasised role of parental conflict, so important to the plot of *Romeo and Juliet*, as essential to the rite of passage which leads, with luck, from romantic love towards affectionate companionship, a more realistic, less fantasy-prone version of mutual attachment. The latter state is seen as less trapped in infantile recollection, less bound by the past, because it represents an overcoming of the past, a growing into individual choice without compulsive and emotional retreat to a childhood fantasy of twin narcissism. In order to achieve the transition, the lovers first need to remove from their line of light the shadow of the past as it is personified in parents, and there is an implication that even if obstacles don't exist we would need to create them. Portia in *The Merchant of Venice* must overcome 'the will of a dead father', even while she paradoxically fulfils the condition of that will, in order to marry. Gediman quotes Freud as saying 'that obstacles are normally required to heighten libido and "where natural resistances to satisfaction have not been sufficient men have at all times erected conventional ones so as to be able to enjoy love"' (p. 187). We should be suspicious of Freud's sweeping phrase, 'at all times' – there must surely be easier and happier ways to enjoy a sexual relationship between equals than the long and arduous course of defeating parents. And yet, Gediman continues,

> rejection, scorn, the deliberate placement of obstacles to romantic and sexual fulfilment, and a flirting with death, are well-understood as pathological variations of the raising of normal arousal thresholds, which we see in milder versions in normal love relationships. If a real or fictional level of parental opposition is not present, then sadomasochism may fulfil the function of creating an obstacle ... The lovers' self-imposed obstacles may also function as devices aimed at ensuring an unambivalent state of union.
>
> (p. 157)

In *Romeo and Juliet* the obstacle is both literally and metaphorically the family feud with its consequential veto on the lovers' union, but it is also the self-inflicted problem of Romeo's murder of Tybalt, and the more general sense of the psychological necessity of some obstacle or other which is prefigured in *A Midsummer Night's Dream*:

> **Lysander.**   Ay me! for aught that I could ever read,
>   Could ever hear by tale or history,
>   The course of true love never did run smooth ...
>   (I.i.132–4)

Another characteristic of 'limerence' or passionate, romantic love, as immortalised in works like *Romeo and Juliet, Tristan and Isolde* and Verdi's *La Traviata*, is double death as the inevitable and only destination guaranteeing immortality to the state of twin narcissism. Gediman again gives the psychoanalyst's explanation that the double suicide is a 'wish to have a child with death; it is a suicide with no suicidal intent, but where the wish to die in the arms of the beloved represents a wish to beget a child with the loved one, and at another level, a return to the mother's womb' (p. 64). Gediman quotes G. Zilboorg's 'The sense of immortality':[24]

> murder–suicide pacts, the drive toward death, always with the flag of immortality in hand, carried with it the fantasy of joining the dead or dying, or being joined in death. The latter is particularly prominent among the double suicides of lovers. There is hardly a primitive race which does not have a lovers' volcano (Japan), a lovers' waterfall (Bali) or a lovers' rock from which the lovers jump so that they may be joined in the beyond.

But we should be suspicious of the dubious anthropology in this passage. It really imposes western conventions and shows no knowledge of 'primitive races'. The proximity of love and death in the western mythology of romantic love has always interested not only writers but psychiatrists, ever since Robert Burton in his *Anatomy of Melancholy* (first edn, 1621) inserted sexual passion within his multifarious categories of 'melancholy' (equivalent to our pathological emotional states), the condition we find Romeo in at the beginning of the play when his love is for Rosaline.

The writings of Georges Bataille lie behind some of the psychoanalytical readings of *Romeo and Juliet*. He provides an extreme example of the thesis that desire is inherently transgressive and linked with violence. He speaks of 'the profound unity of these apparent opposites, birth and death':

> De Sade – or his ideas – generally horrifies even those who affect to admire him and have not realised through their own experience this tormenting fact: the urge towards love, pushed to its limit, is an urge toward death.[25]

Bataille is perhaps the thinker who most consistently sees desire as transgressive and neurotic, inextricably linked with taboos and death:

> Possession of the beloved object does not imply death, but the idea of death is linked with the urge to possess. If the lover cannot possess the beloved he will sometimes think of killing her; often he would rather kill her than lose her. Or else he may wish to die himself ... If the union of two lovers comes about through love, it involves the idea of death, murder or suicide. This aura of death is what denotes passion ...[26]

But a protest can be voiced against this general view. It sounds more like rape than the mutual desire between Romeo and Juliet, which surely is presented by Shakespeare as a desire to live and love, not to die. Bataille's approach to erotic love, encapsulated in Oscar Wilde's 'We always kill the thing we love' may have some relevance in interpreting Shakespeare's other tragedy of love, *Othello* (although here too we must not ignore the external pressures on the marriage from Iago), but it is problematical in being applied to *Romeo and Juliet*. The question which sharpens the distinction between psychoanalytical critics and cultural materialists is whether the lovers make an active choice for death or whether it is forced upon them only when all other options are made impossible. While the former 'pathologise' the young lovers and suggest that the destructive and tragic element lies within their mutual desire as a kind of unconscious but real choice, the latter suggest that the lovers do not seek death, that their love is healthy, and that external circumstances destroy the possibility of sustaining their love in life.

CULTURAL MATERIALISM AND SOCIAL CONFLICT

The general approach which is often called cultural materialism does not accept that literary and dramatic characters have an unrevealed inner or unconscious life which can be psychoanalysed. Instead, materialists insist that explanations for the narrative turns can be found in those social, political and economic conditions which are represented in the literary or dramatic work, and these should be seen in the light of the contemporary realities and prevailing ideologies in Shakespeare's world and also our own. 'Love is always, first and foremost, social', writes Dympna Callaghan (essay 4). The overarching external circumstance which sets in train the events leading to the deaths is the feud between the families of Montague (Romeo) and Capulet (Juliet), a feud so ancient that nobody recalls its genesis, and so widespread that it threatens civic disorder at any time. The young lovers try to escape the feud. Although they themselves continually see the obstacles to their peaceful love as an impersonal destiny or providence, in fact there is nothing inevitable or unchangeable about the family rivalry. Indeed, an optimistic reading of the end of the play suggests that the sacrifice of their death does in fact shake the patriarchs into burying the hatchet of enmity, and the end of the film musical based loosely on Shakespeare's play, *West Side Story*, powerfully creates this effect (although here the rivalry is between gangs rather than generations). The young lovers, in other words, are not being transgressive and certainly not desiring violence – rather they are asking to opt out of their forefathers' quarrels in order to live a contented and peaceful life together. This must be their simple aspiration and vision of the future. The deaths of Mercutio and Tybalt are related to the lovers only through the prior feud, and they turn on honour rather than love. Mercutio as Romeo's kinsman provokes Tybalt in defence of Romeo, and he is killed only because Romeo tries to break up the fight and inadvertently allows Tybalt to stab Mercutio 'under' his arm. Romeo, who had earlier tried to pacify and reconcile Tybalt, then kills him as an act of revenge for murdering his friend and cousin. This murder, not the love plot, is what makes Romeo into an outlaw to be hunted as a criminal. In turn, the deaths of Romeo and Juliet, both by suicide, are precipitated by tragic mischance – because Friar Laurence's letter miscarried, Romeo did not know Juliet was in an induced coma, and believing her dead he feels life is not worth living. Similarly, Juliet awakens to find Romeo literally dead, and believing life is not worth living without her new husband, she too kills herself. It is hard to find any evidence that shows love is intrinsically linked with violence and inevitable death.

Dympna Callaghan (essay 4) also resists the psychoanalytical tendency to internalise the tragedy as a consequence of transgressive love, this time from another materialist position, that of feminist politics. She points out that the roots of a Kristevan reading lie in Shakespeare's source, Arthur Brooke, who sees the deaths as punishment for the 'unfortunate lovers, thralling themselves to unhonest desire', but that Shakespeare has at least made this interpretation ambiguous if not irrelevant. What emerges is the 'profound injustice' at work, not the sense of 'proper punishment'. However, Callaghan's argument does not pursue this line for its own sake, but rather suggests from a feminist perspective that desire as it is represented in the play is restrictive for women and homosexuals, for the play contributes to the normalising of heterosexuality with its normative destination of the marriage institution. So powerful is Shakespeare's myth, coming at a time when western capitalism was reinforcing inequality, that it has deceived and brainwashed even women into thinking such values are benign and irresistible. Others, such as Joseph Porter,[27] and Jonathan Goldberg (essay 10) have argued a similar case in terms of the exclusion of same-sex love. There is, however, some irony in this critical approach. After exonerating the lovers of charges of transgressive love or of love which has within itself violence and potential self-destruction, these critics might be said to reprove the lovers for not being transgressive enough against the norms of their society, for allowing themselves to be deceived into believing their love is not a political construction inherited from their patriarchal society. It does seem somehow odd that like the psychoanalysts, materialists are capable of coming around to blaming Romeo and Juliet, or Shakespeare's depiction of them, for something. Even Brecht's piece, while its main intention is to make us question the universality of the story, is harsh on the lovers, turning them into spoilt, self-indulgent, aristocratic brats.

Bertolt Brecht's 'intercalary scene', 'The Servants' may seem a curious and perverse choice in this collection, since neither is it criticism nor does it use Shakespeare's play. But it does stand as a forceful example of cultural materialism and offers an interesting perspective on the play. He wrote the scene to help the actors playing Romeo and Juliet to clarify their own attitudes to the characters, and to build in some conceptual complexity into the social situation. Brecht drew his own theatrical inspiration and much of his theories of drama from what he called the 'epic theatre' of the

Renaissance, and especially from Shakespeare. He claimed to learn
from Shakespeare that a play should not lure or ambush spectators
into total empathy and should not emotionally manipulate audiences like a trick of illusion. People should bring their rational
minds and judgements into the theatre, and the play should allow
these to be freely exercised. To this end Brecht found continually in
each of Shakespeare's texts a subtext or a perspective that resists
emotional coercion into a single, simple response of either tears or
laughter: the effect is always complex and contradictory, and a play
can be directed and played in such a way that scenes which are
widely known to the point of cliché are suddenly defamiliarised or
'alienated', distanced in a way that makes us think rather than
simply 'emote'. His 'practice pieces' and 'intercalary scenes' are designed to make audiences self-aware and actively involved in
ongoing interpretation of the action. This, I take it, is the function
of criticism as well. 'The Servants' works in a way that makes explicit the connection between Ryan's linking of lovers and of the
poor through deprivation. The Apothecary might seem to trade in
deathly narcotics, but from another point of view he is a poor man
making a living in a society that sanctifies 'market forces': if rich
lovers need drugs, then he can supply them, in return for money to
feed his family. In fact in Brecht's Marxist view the connection is
deeply ironic – 'one man's meat is another man's poison'.
Aristocratic lovers who see their rebellion against their respective
families as heroic and romantic, in turn are perceived as self-
indulgently and irresponsibly failing to notice the adverse consequences of their actions for their social inferiors. Romeo and Juliet
callously ignore the rights of their servants to a love life, by giving
priority to their own. Brecht may have taken the germ of the idea
from a teasingly ambiguous statement by one of the 'servants' in
Shakespeare's play, Gregory's 'The quarrel is between our masters
and us their men' (I.i.18–22). Gregory's comment could mean that
the Montague masters and men stand together against the Capulet
masters and men, but it could equally mean that the masters stand
together against the men, in the sense that the servants become
hapless tools. It is quite likely Brecht, with his sharp insight into
class struggle, would pick up the second meaning. Samson's shrug-
ging ''Tis all one' (I.i.20) seems to concede the ambiguity in the
situation, and he goes on to gesture towards an equally nasty
conflict between men and women, also generated by the prior
'ancient quarrel'. A cultural materialist's reading of the play as a

whole would dwell on such details as Samson's casual condoning of rape, to suggest that everybody, in Verona society, Romeo and Juliet included, is a moral or physical casualty of the family feud which has generated civil brawls and meaningless violence. Such a didactic reading would find support in the Prince's angry summation:

> Where be these enemies? Capulet, Montague,
> See what a scourge is laid upon your hate,
> That heaven finds means to kill your joys with love.
> And I, for winking at your discords, too
> Have lost a brace of kinsmen. All are punished.
>   (V.iii.290–4)

Perhaps Brecht's scenes are merely an interesting footnote to the study of *Romeo and Juliet* but at least they serve to de-familiarise a 'sacred' text so that we can look at it afresh in the light of challenging and sometimes iconoclastic contemporary criticism.

Brecht's provocative scene is presented here partly to 'alienate' this most familiar of plays, inviting readers to exercise scepticism as well as emotional involvement in the action, thus enriching the effect, but also partly to illustrate a point about twentieth-century criticism that underpins the whole collection of essays. Two entirely opposed attitudes to literature's function are at issue. Cultural materialism argues that a work like *Romeo and Juliet* has endured because it constructs situations which allow us to *think* and to clarify rationally problems and issues of human behaviour in particular societies. Another argues that a play allows us to *feel*, to suspend our rational faculties and instead sympathise and to project our emotions into fictional characters who exemplify our own individual dilemmas. The first line of approach is Brecht's, the second is probably closer to the normative tradition of western criticism. But the second, taken a stage further, leads into psychoanalytical criticism, since if literature and drama are mimetic then they allow us to analyse characters as if they are 'people like us' with individual psyches. Taken together, the essays indicate different ways in which the play's subversiveness, in Ryan's sense, operates.

GENDER

Related to cultural materialism, perhaps as a subspecies, is gender theory, and this approach is pursued by some writers in this collection. Gender theory evolved from feminist criticism in the 1970s and onwards, which in turn looked back to at least two key texts, Mary Wollstonecraft's *A Vindication of the Rights of Woman* (1792) and Simone de Beauvoir's *The Second Sex* (1949). Although all definitions would be contested, the general assumptions behind the approach are first, that gender is central to issues of identity, social interaction, and power, and is therefore a valid critical concern; and secondly that it does not hinge on biological sex but on cultural meanings which society has attributed to women and men. It would not be difficult to trace the changes in this rapidly developing field by compiling a different selection of essays on *Romeo and Juliet*, all based solely on gender. One does not hear so often these days the 'essentialist' reading assuming difference between men and women, arguing that Juliet, for example, displays the 'essence' of femininity while Romeo behaves in a characteristically masculine fashion. This approach had dominated the field for many generations, and was argued in different ways by certain feminists who were interested in 'images of women'. Nor has the linguistic equivalent, that women speak and write differently (*écriture féminine*) from men been argued much in recent times, although again earlier critics discriminated between Shakespearean characters on the basis of gendered speech acts and style. One approach summoned up by the word 'patriarchy' dominated gendered readings in the 1970s and 80s, and *Romeo and Juliet* criticism certainly reflected this. The play, it was persuasively argued, is dominated by fathers, whose power over families is mirrored in the organisation of the state as a whole.[28] Arguments raged over Shakespeare's own stance, whether he tacitly accepts the inevitability of patriarchy by not showing it overthrown and by marginalising women as amusing, shrewish mothers or as passive victims; or whether he attacks its ideology and existence by showing the terrible human consequences in the loss of young life, especially Juliet's.[29] Sasha Roberts, in her splendid, short book on *Romeo and Juliet* which ideally should be read alongside this one (see 'Further Reading'), develops the principle of 'constructionism' which in the early 1990s was an important assumption behind criticism in general and gender studies in particular: the idea that literature does not transparently show or mirror 'life' or 'character' in a value-free way, but that it is an ideologically loaded construction with assumptions about gender and class. The gendered readings represented in this volume are typical of the pluralist style of 1990s gender studies.

Callaghan (essay 4), Goldberg (essay 10) and Porter (essay 9) all see in *Romeo and Juliet* both the observation and underwriting of a normative, 'mainstream' assumption in *Romeo and Juliet* that heterosexuality is 'normal', while finding enough also in the play to allow a more subversive reading which allows voices 'from the margins' to challenge the norm. Mercutio has always been seen as a figure given curiously intense characterisation by Shakespeare, and Goldberg in particular locates the intensity in his homosexual attachment to Romeo, a fact which makes Mercutio resent his friend's attraction to women and finally explains his early death as the necessary exclusion of his viewpoint from a play celebrating love between man and woman. In some cases subliminally and in others ostentatiously, filmed versions of *Romeo and Juliet* during the twentieth century have depicted Mercutio as gay.

FILM VERSIONS OF *ROMEO AND JULIET*[30]

Since many, if not most people these days encounter *Romeo and Juliet* in one film version or another, the argument for diverse and culturally relative readings of the play can be conveniently demonstrated by a brief history of the play's adaptation into the twentieth-century medium of film. It may seem a contradiction in terms to speak of 'silent Shakespeare', since we value language above all else in the plays, but it is arguable that in fact the golden age of Shakespeare as a popular force came in the period of silent cinema, particularly from 1900 to 1920, when there were dozens of films (often based on single episodes) made from titles by Shakespeare. This is a salutary reminder that his plays can operate effectively as narrative and spectacle, even without the spoken word. There were many silent versions of Romeo and Juliet on screen, and more often than not this particular play was not treated reverently but often as a burlesque apparently unworthy of the seriousness accorded to the other tragedies. Robert Hamilton Ball traces the deliberately hilarious treatments up to the 1920s.[31]

Since the invention of 'talking pictures' in the 1920s, there have been at least thirty screen versions of *Romeo and Juliet*, including ones from Italy, France, Egypt, Mexico, India, the USSR, Czechoslovakia, Spain, Brazil, Canada, and (if it can claim Baz Luhrmann) Australia. The statistic does not include some openly pornographic appropriations such as the Swedish film, *The Secret*

Sex Lives of Romeo and Juliet (1968), also called *Juliet's Desire*, and *Romeo and Juliet II*, nor the 1990s 'grunge' version, *Tromeo and Juliet*. But apart from the oddities, some stand out as demonstrating the special power of *Romeo and Juliet* in the cinema. They are fine and popular films in their own right, and have reached far greater audiences than any stage production can. In 1936 George Cukor directed a version which cast two heart-throbs of the middle-aged movie-goers of the time – Trevor Howard (aged 39) and Norma Shearer (aged 36) – while Mercutio was played by John Barrymore (aged 54) and Tybalt by Basil Rathbone (aged 42). They were the most famous movie actors of their time, but even on release (and more so now) they were regarded as too old for the roles. Presumably the film was made for audiences over 30, the generation with enough money to go to the cinema, and they would no doubt be comforted to feel that age did not wither them, nor did it preclude them from identifying with youthful passion. One film version which, in hindsight, looks rather tame and old-fashioned, was in its time innovative, and pointed to the future. Renato Castellani in 1954 directed *Romeo and Juliet* with the kind of close attention to visual detail that would mark Zeffirelli's version. Whereas previous versions had used sets elaborately built for the occasion, Castellani filmed on location in Italy and produced a work which has been described as 'extraordinarily rich and voluptuous, photographed in the golden remnants of the High Renaissance in Verona, Venice, and Siena, and with costumes by Leonor Fini that are derived from works of art by Piero della Francesca, Pisanello, Carpaccio, and Fiorenzo di Lorenzo'.[32] As well as carrying these painterly references, the outdoors setting brings burgeoning nature to the fore, not just as a visual spectacle but as a symbol for the young lovers' relationship to natural forces. By the 1960s a new function was given to Shakespeare in films. He could galvanise hearts and minds to rectify social injustices, and in the words of a very influential book's title, he became 'Shakespeare our Contemporary'.[33] Two quite remarkable adaptations of *Romeo and Juliet* in that decade illustrate the capacity of his texts to be aligned with a social conscience and progressive politics. *West Side Story* (1961) is a Hollywood musical, transferred from the Broadway stage. It employs no lines from Shakespeare but clearly is based on his play. Instead of setting the lovers against warring families, it places them in the context of violent gang warfare in the slums of New York. The Capulets are a Puerto Rican gang called the

Sharks, the Montagues are white American 'Anglos', the Jets. This version trusts Shakespeare's narrative but not his language, as if that language would falsify the almost documentary and social realist emphasis. Unlike earlier versions, the film demystifies Shakespeare in order to focus the narrative on contemporary social problems. It reflects the contemporary preoccupation with street hoodlums, anarchic youth violence, gang warfare, popular music and youth rebellion (James Dean, Elvis Presley). The violence is seen ironically as the result of failures of their absent parents to restrain and control (or even care – the only older people we see are the bigoted policeman and the isolated 'Doc' in the drugstore who is Shakespeare's Friar).

Franco Zeffirelli directed *Romeo and Juliet* on the stage, and later turned it into a film which was released in 1968 at the height of '60s youth revolution, student unrest, 'flower power' and calls for sexual freedom. He cast actors of 17 (Leonard Whiting, with Beatles haircut) and 15 (Olivia Hussey) respectively, and clearly angled his film at teenagers, the first wave of the baby boomers who already had commercial power and media glamour. The great debates of the times from their point of view were the so-called 'generation gap' (being misunderstood by parents), the issue of 20-year-old youths in some countries who did not have the vote being conscripted to fight a war in Vietnam created by their parents; and the emergence of a new ethic encapsulated in the phrase 'make love not war'. Zeffirelli consciously appeals to these debates, invariably on the side of youth, and he makes the tragedy turn on the fact that family conflict reflects intergenerational conflict between teenagers and their corrupted parents' generation. The film is perhaps the most didactic of the various versions: the lovers are seen as genuinely innocent victims, whose poignant deaths lead to ending the family feud.

Barbara Hodgdon (essay 6) entertainingly leads us through *Romeo and Juliet*, directed by the Australian Baz Luhrmann in 1997, who hired his old tutor, Professor David Frost at the University of Newcastle in Australia, as Shakespeare adviser for the film, a fate which must be the secret fantasy of all Shakespeare tutors. The version is as much of its time as the others, showing a 1990s youth subculture based on the availability of drugs and guns, enforced idleness of unemployment, a society apparently marked by callous indifference to emotions, contrasted with eruptions of manufactured festivity and spectacle like a Michael Jackson concert.

The vision adds up to a nihilism of the senses which is set against, and presumably caused by, corrupt, profiteering multinational corporations (the families are companies), seedy urban decay (Verona Beach looks like an abandoned film set), and the frustrations of a neglected generation. In some way each of the groupings is, in Porter's word, 'liminal' (essay 9): the Capulets are Latin American, the Montagues are Irish American, Mercutio and the Prince both black, and the setting is represented as a crucible of ethnic and class tension as befits Miami Beach which is both playground for the rich and first port of call for Cuban refugees. In such an array of marginalities, 'the centre does not hold', and indeed the film intentionally shows a society devoid of shared, community assumptions. There seems in the film, as presumably in its target audience, to be a confused yearning for religious symbolism but no spiritual heart, and the final scene in the church (a cathedral rather than a chapel, let alone a crypt), full of candles, flowers and operatic music, evokes the music of Madonna with its unique concatenation of religion and eroticism. Here, the older generation is cynical, wilfully unaware of the consequences of their feuds, and literally beyond the law. Romeo and Juliet are victims not only of an uncaring society and their own divided generation, but of the insatiable greed of news moguls who exploit 'human interest' stories such as teenage suicide – their narrative is framed in a typically disposable television news story. In its way Luhrmann's film is as didactic as Zeffirelli's, but because the picture it gives of society is so bleakly negative, and the watery moments of love between Romeo and Juliet are so rare, brief and naïve, the film tends to confirm a 'no hope' reading. The lovers die bewildered and frightened, and it seems that their fate matters to nobody, except as a quickly forgotten news item. As a minor issue, it is hard entirely to reconcile the film's general anti-consumerist ethic with the 'hard-sell' marketing of the film by Fox Studios as commodity, with its CD music, interactive CD Rom, official and unofficial websites, overpowering advertising, and so on. These aspects of the film, together with its eclecticism of settings, costumes and cultural groupings, its juxtapositioning of glamour, stylishness and seediness, perhaps justify the use of that overused word 'postmodern', and make the film a genuine symptom of a generation's anxieties.[34]

The climax of Luhrmann's film, with its circling paramilitaries, helicopters, and journalists outside the cathedral, whilst within its hushed and sacred space is played out, to the strains of Wagner's music from *Tristan und Isolde*, a joint suicide for love, makes another point about intertextuality. Versions of *Romeo and Juliet*, whether on film or stage or in the pages of criticism, work within certain conventions of their own. In this case, we find multi-layered references to familiar tropes, from romantic opera to films like *Bonnie and Clyde*, numerous romantic thrillers, and the nightly televising of real-life 'hostage sieges'. The points to be drawn are, first the inescapable influence of Hollywood tragedy of love on con-temporary versions of the play, and more intriguingly, Shakespeare's pervasive influence on Hollywood tragedy of love. In *Romeo and Juliet* he has made out of an earlier and unpromising source a true myth, the narrative of doomed young love, love in the face of parental disapproval or family / social conflict, which has embedded itself so deeply in our culture that we accept it as 'natural' and literally cannot see beyond its perimeters. The endur-ing and subtle cultural influence of|*Romeo and Juliet* not only proves that Shakespeare has always been a popular writer, but also unnervingly suggests that he may have even invented every genera-tion's version of its own popular culture.|

NOTES

Quotations are from *William Shakespeare: The Complete Works*, ed. Stanley Wells and Gary Taylor (Oxford, 1996), published on CD-ROM by Andromeda Interactive.

1. For a history of this idea, including a long chapter on *Romeo and Juliet*, see Maya C. Bijvoet, *Liebestod: The Function and Meaning of the Double Love-Death* (New York and London, 1988).

2. The main quotation is reprinted below (Ryan, essay 5), but the words 'subversive and protesting' occur in an earlier version of this essay by Kiernan Ryan: '*Romeo and Juliet*: The language of tragedy', in *The Taming of the Text: Explorations in Language, Literature and Culture*, ed. Wilie Van Peer (London and New York, 1989), pp. 106–20.

3. A Quarto was a printed edition of a single play printed on 'quarto' size paper, while the 'First Folio' was a larger, handsome volume in which Shakespeare's complete works were collected. The study of the rela-tionship between these different texts is highly specialised and need not be explained in detail here, but for the interested, more technical detail can be found in the essays by Alan C. Dessen and Jay L. Halio collected in Jay L. Halio (ed.), *Shakespeare's 'Romeo and Juliet': Texts, Contexts, and Interpretation* (Newark and London, 1995).

4. In a story again too long to be told here, different texts used to be explained as being either 'good' or 'bad' transmissions of a Shakespeare original, but nowadays it is widely accepted that they represent different versions, perhaps revised by Shakespeare or his company for different theatre venues.

5. New plays had to be inspected by the Master of the Revels who could insist on changes or deletions of politically sensitive material in plays, and there were some relevant laws, for example the 1606 Act which tightened the rules about what phrases and words were considered blasphemous.

6. See Ivo Kamps (ed.), *Materialist Shakespeare: A History* (London, 1995).

7. *Hazlitt's Criticism of Shakespeare: A Selection*, ed. R. S. White (Lewiston, Queenstown, Lampeter, 1996), pp. 133–42, 135.

8. Dorothy Tennov, *Love and Limerence: The Experience of Being in Love* (New York, 1979).

9. Helen Fisher, *Anatomy of Love: The Natural History of Monogamy, Adultery, and Divorce* (New York, 1998).

10 Alan Macfarlane, *Marriage and Love in England: Modes of Reproduction 1300–1840* (Oxford, 1986), p. 175.

11. Robert J. Sternberg, *Love is a Story: A New Theory of Relationships* (New York, 1998), p. x (referring to his earlier work).

12. See, for example, Yang Zhouhan, 'King Lear Metamorphosed', *Comparative Literature*, 39 (1987), 356–62, who compares two Chinese translations of *King Lear* and raises the particular problems of translating the word 'nothing', and how to adjust sympathy for Cordelia in a culture where 'Filial obedience is as absolute as paternal authority' (p. 358). See also the fascinating comparative anthropological study, 'Love and Limerence with Chinese Characteristics: Student Romance in the PRC', by Robert L. Moore, in Victor C. de Munck (ed.), *Romantic Love and Sexual Behavior: Perspectives from the Social Sciences* (Westport, CT, 1998), ch. 11: 'the reduced emphasis of the Chinese on romantic love [as a rationale for marriage] can be seen as merely realistic compared to the Western viewpoint' (p. 264).

13. Quoted Macfarlane, *Marriage and Love in England*, p. 174.

14. Catherine Belsey, *Desire: Love Stories in Western Culture* (Oxford, 1994), p. 33.

15. Peter Conrad, *To be Continued: Four Stories and their Survival* (Oxford, 1995), p. 58.

16. Gayle Whittier, 'The Sonnet's Body and the Body Sonnetized in *Romeo and Juliet*', *Shakespeare Quarterly*, 40 (1989), 27–41.

17. For some interesting approaches to romantic love from the cultural studies area, see de Munck (ed.), *Romantic Love and Sexual Behaviour* and Robert J. Sternberg, *Love is a Story: A New Theory of Relationships* (New York, Oxford, 1998).

18. Stephen Orgel in the section 'The marriage contract' in his article entitled 'Prospero's Wife' comments very pertinently on Shakespeare's presentation of courtship and marriage as quite separate states: 'The wooing process tends to be … not so much a prelude to marriage and a family as a process of self-definition' and '[Shakespeare] seems to have expressed his strongest familial feelings not toward children or wives but toward parents and siblings'. He also points out that Juliet's marriage at 14 in fact 'is unusual in all but upper-class families', a judgement supported by Barbara Everett (essay 8). Orgel's article first appeared in *Representations*, 8 (1984), 1–13, and is reprinted in this series of New Casebooks on *The Tempest*, ed. R. S. White (London, 1999), pp. 15–31.

19. Also see Jonathan Dollimore, *Death, Desire and Loss in Western Culture* (New York, 1998), pp. 102–16.

20. Helen K. Gediman, *Fantasies of Love and Death in Life and Art* (New York, 1995). Subsequent references cited by page no. in the text.

21. Dennis de Rougement, *Love in the Western World* (New York, 1956). De Rougemont also wrote *Love Declared: Essays on the Myths of Love* (New York, 1963).

22. Gediman, *Fantasies of Love and Death*, p. 18.

23. Shakespeare twice used this phrase to describe marriage, once in *Love's Labour's Lost* and again in Sonnet 57.

24. G. Zilboorg, *Psychoanalytic Quarterly*, 7 (1938), 171–9, 179.

25. Georges Bataille, *Death and Sensuality: A Study of Eroticism and the Taboo* (New York, 1962), p. 42.

26. Ibid., p. 20.

27. Joseph A. Porter, 'Marlowe, Shakespeare and the Canonization of Heterosexuality', *South Atlantic Quarterly*, 88 (1989), 127–47.

28. Coppélia Kahn, 'Coming of Age in Verona', *Modern Language Studies*, 8 (1978), 171–93, several times reprinted; Marianne Novy, *Love's Argument: Gender Relations in Shakespeare* (Chapel Hill, NC, 1984); Peter Erikson, *Patriarchal Structures in Shakespeare's Drama* (Los Angeles, 1985); Marilyn French, *Shakespeare's Division of Experience: Women and Drama in the Age of Shakespeare* (London, 1983).

29. On this debate, and indeed all shades of opinion within feminist criticism, see the useful and exhaustive book, *Shakespeare and Feminist*

Criticism: An Annotated Bibliography and Commentary, ed. Philip C. Kolin (New York and London, 1991).

30. For a brief but excellent history of performance of *Romeo and Juliet*, see Jill L. Levenson, *Shakespeare in Performance: Romeo and Juliet* (Manchester, 1987).

31. Robert Hamilton Ball, *Shakespeare on Silent Film: A Strange Eventful History* (London, 1968), pp. 217–18.

32. CD-ROM, *Cinemania 5* (Microsoft).

33. Jan Kott, *Shakespeare our Contemporary* (London, 1967).

34. For an aspect of this large area, see Timothy Murray, *Drama Trauma: Specters of Race and Sexuality in Performance, Video, and Art* (London and New York, 1997), esp. pp. 1–9, where Luhrmann's film is used to illustrate cultural 'traumatophilia'. I am grateful to Gail Jones for pointing out this essay.

1

'Death-marked love': Desire and Presence in *Romeo and Juliet*

LLOYD DAVIS

I

The action of *Romeo and Juliet* occurs between two speeches proclaiming the lovers' deaths – the prologue's forecast of events and the prince's closing summary. The vicissitudes of desire take place in this unusual period, after life yet before death. It is a kind of liminal phase in which social and personal pressures build to intense pitch before they are settled. Such liminal tension, as Victor Turner suggests, is the very stuff of which social dramas are made.[1] It figures a mounting crisis that envelops those observing and taking part in the unfolding action. At the same time, this temporal setting has a range of interpretative implications.

With the lovers' deaths announced from the start, audience attention is directed to the events' fateful course. The question is less what happens than how it happens. By framing the action in this way, the prologue triggers various generic and narrative effects. First, it establishes the play as 'a tragedy of fate' similar to Kyd's *The Spanish Tragedy*, which gives 'the audience a superior knowledge of the story from the outset, reducing the hero's role to bring into prominence the complex patterns of action'.[2] In turn, this generic marker initiates a compelling narrative, poised between pro-lepsis and analepsis, as opening portents of death are played off against background details and further intimations in the following scenes.[3] The tension between these hints and flashbacks fills the narrative with foreboding. The breakneck speed of events (in contrast to the extended time frame of Arthur Brooke's version, a few days as opposed to nine months)[4] sees the ordained end bear relentlessly on the lovers. They are caught between a determining past and future.

The narrative has a further generic analogue. Gayle Whittier suggests that the play develops through a contrast between sonnet lyricism and tragedy that is finally reconciled in death: 'the "spoken lines" of the Prologue predestine the plot of the play to be tragic from without, even as the spirit of Petrarchan poetry spoken by Romeo to Juliet finally necessitates their tragic deaths from within'.[5] What first appears as thematic conflict between two of the period's key literary modes makes way for a troubling similarity. The spirit of Petrarchism is revealed as tragically fatal and idealised romance collapses.

In this view, *Romeo and Juliet* stages the outcome of unfulfillable desire. Although it appears to reverse the erotic story told in the Sonnets, the dramatic narrative ends up paralleling the failing course of identity and desire which can be traced through those poems. There the poet reluctantly finds his desire shifting from the self-gratifying potential figured by the youth to the disarming dark lady, who offers instead 'a desire that her very presence at the same time will frustrate'.[6] This pattern initially seems to be inverted in the play – Romeo willingly renounces self-centred longing for Rosaline, Juliet tests and proves her self-reliance, both find true love in each other. However, their love ends in reciprocal death, with the Petrarchan images fatally embodied and materialised. The links between love and death unveil a dark scepticism about desire, despite bursts of romantic idealism. They convey a sense of futility and ironic fate which Romeo momentarily feels but is able to forget for a time, 'my mind misgives / Some consequence yet hanging in the stars / Shall bitterly begin his fearful date / With this night's revels' (I.iv.106–9).

Such scepticism appears in many subsequent literary and psycho-analytic conceptions, where possibilities of romantic union are queried.[7] These questions carry implications about self-hood and desire and about ways of representing them. In theories and stories of divorce or isolation, selfhood is not effaced but conceived as incomplete; as Barbara Freedman puts it, 'The denial of self-presence doesn't negate presence but redefines it as a distancing or spacing we always seek but fail to close'.[8] Characters cannot attain their goals, and the inability to claim satisfaction affects desire as much as selfhood. Proceeding from an uncertain source, desire remains 'predicated on lack, and even its apparent fulfilment is also a moment of loss'.[9] In this view, desire and presence are forever intertwined: 'Differantiated [sic] presence, which is always and inevitably differed and deferred, and which in consequence exceeds the alternatives of presence and absence, is the condition of desire'.[10] They forestall each other's wholeness yet continue to provide the self with images of consummation, contentment and victory – the curtsies, kisses, suits, livings and battles which Mercutio's dreamers envisage but cannot clasp, 'Begot of nothing but vain fantasy, / Which is as thin of substance as the air, / And more inconstant than the wind' (I.iv.98–100).

The recurrence of this viewpoint in fiction and theory suggests that *Romeo and Juliet* stages a paradigmatic conflict between ways of representing and interpreting desire. The play affects these possibilities by placing idealised and tragic conceptions of desire and selfhood in intense dialogue with each other. This dialogue continues to be played out in literary and theoretical texts since, as Alan Sinfield notes, notions of sexuality and gender are 'major sites of ideological production upon which meanings of very diverse kinds are established and contested'.[11] *Romeo and Juliet* informs and illustrates a cultural history of desire in which images of romantic fulfilment or failure carry great importance.

As well as being part of this history, Shakespeare's play has two other distinctive temporal features. First, as noted above, it unfolds over a charged time span. Time allows desire to be acted out but also threatens its fulfilment, by either running out or not stopping. This equivocal link affects desire's tragic course in *Romeo and Juliet*, 'as the time and place / Doth make against' the characters (v.iii.223–4).

Secondly, its depiction of desire reverberates with erotic tropes from earlier traditions – Platonic, Ovidian, Petrarchan, as well as popular sayings. These tropes are used by the characters to talk and think about relationships, but they are also challenged for not allowing the gap between self and other to be bridged. They are unfulfilling since it feels as if they belong to someone else; as

Astrophil puts it, 'others' feet still seemed but strangers in my way'.[12] The lovers are often dissatisfied with or unsure about the words of others. Their discontent grows from early dismissals such as Romeo's 'Yet tell me not, for I have heard it all' (I.i.171) and 'Thou talk'st of nothing' (I.iv.96), or Juliet's 'And stint thou, too, I pray thee, Nurse' (I.iii.60), to deeper disquiet over the inability of this language to match their experience: 'Thou canst not speak of that thou dost not feel' (III.iii.64); 'Some say the lark makes sweet division; / This doth not so, for she divideth us' (III.v.29–30). The corollary of their frustration with the language of others and of the past is the value they put on their own: 'She speaks. / O, speak again, bright angel' (II.i.67–8); 'every tongue that speaks / But Romeo's name speaks heavenly eloquence' (III.ii.32–3).

Like the lovers, the play also seeks to revise existing rhetorical conventions. It reworks these tropes into personal, tragic terms which underlie later literary and psychological conceptions. Hence, in addition to exemplifying Stephen Greenblatt's point that 'psychoanalysis is the historical outcome of certain characteristic Renaissance strategies',[13] *Romeo and Juliet* shows that these strategies develop in response to earlier discourses. The play's pivotal role in later depictions of desire stems from the way it juxtaposes historical and emergent conceptions.

These complex temporal and rhetorical effects are hinted at in the Prologue, which repeatedly sets past, present and future against each other. 'Our scene' is initially laid in a kind of continuous present, yet one that remains hanging between 'ancient grudge' and 'new mutiny'. Likewise, the 'star-crossed lovers take their life' in a present whose intimations of living and loving are circumscribed by 'the fatal loins' of 'their parents' strife'. As the birth–suicide pun on 'take their life' hints, sexuality is already marked by violence and death, its future determined by the past's impact on the present. The Prologue ends by anchoring the staging of 'death-marked love' in the here and now of the audience, who attend 'the two-hours' traffic of our stage'. It anticipates a successful theatrical conclusion, with the play's performance 'striv[ing] to mend' what the lovers 'shall miss' – a kind of closure that their desire cannot realise. In contrast to the simple linear Chorus to Act II, which culminates in the lovers' union, the rebounding moments of the Prologue displace consummation with death.[14]

A complicity between sex and death is well known in Renaissance texts. Its function in *Romeo and Juliet* is, however, distinguished by temporal shifts which define the characters' relations. While the lovers in a poem such as Donne's 'The Canonization' exceed worldly time and place, and their post-coital condition is eternally celebrated, in Shakespeare's play the links between past and present, social and personal, cannot be transcended. The intense oneness felt by the lovers appears to signify mutual presence, but such intersubjective moments are overlaid with social and historical pressures. The drama alternates between instants of passion, when time seems to stand still, and inevitable returns to the ongoing rush of events. This contrast is manifested not only in the characterisation and plot but in the interplay of underlying traditions, sources and tropes. The play reiterates and revises these conventions, confirming a conception of desire that speeds not to its goal but its end. In this conception personal presence can exist only as a transient, illusory sign of desire.

II

One of the main influences *Romeo and Juliet* has had on later depictions of love lies in its celebration of personal desire. The force of this celebration comes partly from its dramatic mode, staging the lovers' experiences for a 'live' audience. In the decades after the play was first performed, poetry (till then, the key romantic discourse) was changing from oral to written modes. Until the rise of the novel, drama remained the pre-eminent form for presenting love stories, and stage performance could give these tales the confessional tones which earlier forms of poetic recitation doubtless achieved. The Prologue enacts this shift by relocating the love sonnet in the drama, a move again underlined by the verse which the lovers will soon share in Act I, scene v.

On stage, the impact of the 'personal' can come across in different ways – through physical, verbal, even interpersonal performance. In *Romeo and Juliet* these forms of presence concentrate in the protagonists' unshakeable love. It seems to assume an essential quality which captures the 'diachronic unity of the subject'.[15] This unity underwrites numerous adaptations of and responses to the play, from elaborate stage productions, operas and ballets, to more popular versions such as the American musical *West Side Story* or the Australian narrative verse of C. J. Dennis's *A Sentimental Bloke*, whose colloquial tones add to the impression of true romance. For many audience groups, each of these transformations once again discovers the play's 'spirit', which surpasses local differences to reveal truths about desire and 'ourselves'.

The director's programme notes to a recently well-received production in Australia illustrate this kind of response. The mixed tones of confession and authority sway the audience to accept his views:

> My fascination with this play continues. Considerable research over the years has taken me twice to Verona and Mantua, but the conflict in Bosnia has brought the work urgently closer. I first considered a Muslim–Christian setting several months before the tragedy of Bosko and Admira ... A study of the text supplies no religious, class, nor race barriers between the 'two households' and this makes Shakespeare's vision all the more powerful. When differences are minimal, ancient grudges seem the more difficult to understand. Yet they remain with us today, passed on by our parents. It seems the one thing we teach the next generation is how to maintain rage and other forms of prejudices. Thus this work is as much about young people in the Brisbane Mall today as it is about the hot days in medieval Verona ... The human spirit, as portrayed by the 31 year old playwright, is a thing of wonder to be nurtured and treasured.[16]

The paradoxical effects of citing 'real' personal and political situations are first to detach the drama from its own historical concerns and then to efface the ideological grounds of the current crisis. The revelation of 'human spirit' triumphs over any tragic significance. Indeed, the play's freedom from material contexts testifies to its, its author's, and our affirming 'vision'. This viewpoint recalls Coleridge's claim that Shakespeare is 'out of time', his characters 'at once true to nature, and fragments of the divine mind that drew them'.[17]

Because it hides sexual, class and ethnic factors behind archetypal human experience, this sort of perception of Shakespeare's work becomes a target of materialist criticism:

> Idealised and romanticised out of all dialectical relationship with society, it [Shakespeare's work] takes on the seductive glamour of aestheticism, the sinister and self-destructive beauty of decadent romance ... this 'Shakespeare myth' functions in contemporary culture as an ideological framework for containing consensus and for sustaining myths of unity, integration and harmony in the cultural superstructures of a divided and fractured society.[18]

In relation to sexual issues, universal images of the personal in *Romeo and Juliet* can be seen as helping to naturalise notions of desire which reinforce an 'ideology of romantic love' in terms of 'heterosexualising idealisation' and the 'canonisation of heterosexuality'.[19] Personal romance and desire are revealed as authoritative codes which conceal and impose official sexuality.

The kinds of ideological impacts that the 'personal' registers may be intensified *or* interrogated by the generic effects of 'Excellent conceited Tragedie', as the Quarto titles announce. The combination of personal experience and tragic consequence can turn *Romeo and Juliet* into an account of contradictory notions of desire and identity, in line with Jonathan Dollimore's recognition that, notwithstanding traditions of celebration 'in terms of man's defeated potential', tragedy questions ideological norms.[20] The genre's ambiguous drift to 'radical' or cathartic ends sees the play assume a kind of meta-textual disinterestedness, distanced from final interpretations as it seems to reflect on how desire may be conceived and staged. This distance can be observed in the play's citing and reworking of tropes and conventions from existing discourses of love and romance. The intertextual traces reveal continuities and changes in the depiction of desire, keyed to social and historical notions of the personal and interpersonal.

Platonism is traditionally seen as offering a set of tropes that affirm selfhood and desire as forms of true being despite possibilities of loss.[21] In the *Symposium*, for instance, Socrates defines love as desire for what one lacks, either a specific quality or a lost or missing element of the self. Aristophanes goes so far as to image love as a 'longing for and following after [a] primeval wholeness ... the healing of our disseevered nature'. The *Symposium* deals with this incipiently tragic situation by redirecting desire to the heavens; in a comedic resolution, love's lack is fulfilled by catching sight of 'the very soul of beauty ... beauty's very self'.[22] Such vision provides the model for Renaissance Petrarchism.

This model is famously reproduced in Pietro Bembo's Neoplatonic paean to divine love at the close of Castiglione's *The Courtier*. He recounts 'a most happie end for our desires', as the courtier forsakes sensual desire for a wiser love that guides the soul: 'through the particular beautie of one bodie hee guideth her to the universall beautie of all bodies ... Thus the soule kindled in the most holy fire of true heavenly love, fleeth to couple her self with the nature of Angels'. This 'most holy love' is 'derived of the unitie of the heavenly beautie, goodnesse and wisedom', and in narrating its course Bembo himself undergoes an ecstatic loss of identity. He speaks as if 'ravished and beside himselfe', and emphasises that 'I have spoken what the holy furie of love hath (unsought for) indited to me'.[23] Speaking and experiencing true desire are related forms of self-transcendence, and Bembo can rejoice in the loss of selfhood.

Similar experience underpins the double structure of Edmund Spenser's *Fowre Hymnes*, first published in 1596, around the time *Romeo and Juliet* was written. The hymn in honour of earthly love characterises the lover as Tantalus, feeding 'his hungrie fantasy, / Still full, yet neuer satisfyde ... For nought may quench his infinite desyre'. This figure is recast in the corresponding hymn of heavenly love, where the poet renounces his earlier poems – 'lewd layes' which showed love as a 'mad fit' – for a lover linked to 'high eternall powre'.[24] In these instances, the lack or absence which motivates love is conceived positively, part of a spiritual response which lifts the lover beyond temporal identity. Through its philosophic or poetic utterance, the self is not destroyed but surpassed.

However, the link between lack and love can also affect selfhood less positively, even fatally. Classical texts again offer tropes and characters to Renaissance authors. Ovid depicts less drastic versions of desire and self-loss in the changes that Jove makes to pursue various nymphs. These can be read in varying ways – on the one hand, a carnivalesque switching of sexual roles for the sake of pleasure; on the other, a sequence of illusory identities that offers no final fulfilment. Though Jove's transformations bring different degrees of satisfaction, none is tragically oriented (at least for himself). In contrast, the tale of Narcissus sets desire and selfhood in irresolvable conflict. In Arthur Golding's 1567 translation of the *Metamorphoses*, Narcissus gazes into the pond to find that 'He knowes not what it was he sawe. And yet the foolishe elfe / Doth burn in ardent love thereof. The verie selfe same thing / That doeth bewitch and blinde his eyes, increaseth all his sting'.[25] His desire cannot be satisfied, and the attempt to do so pains and then destroys selfhood.

Opposing notions of genre, time and character underlie these figures of ecstasy and loss. Platonic and Neoplatonic transcendence is marked by timelessness and selflessness. It brings narration and character to an end, as the self enjoys eternal fusion with the other. In comparison, Ovidian images of disguised or deluded self-loss entail conflict within or between characters. These interactions rely on distinct, often opposed, figures who respond to each other through time. Their fates frequently impose eternities of lonely, unfulfilled selfhood.

Platonic images of true desire and identity are invoked in Shakespeare's comedies during the 1590s; but even there, as characters move to romantic union, they are usually questioned. The disguises, confusions and mistakes through which love's destiny is reached may suggest random or enforced effects that unsettle 'nature's bias'. In a less equivocal way, Shakespeare's use of Ovidian images of desire and selfhood tends to limit or foreclose positive readings, especially where narcissistic traces are discerned. This tendency takes place in both comic and tragic genres: 'Like Ovid's tales, Shakespeare's comedies never lose sight of the painfulness and the potential for the grotesque or for disaster wrought by love's changes ... If part of the Ovidianism of the comedies is their potential for violence and tragedy, it would seem logical to expect that Ovidianism to be developed in the tragedies'.[26] In *Venus and Adonis*, for example, the humour of the goddess's overweening desire and her beloved's petulance changes to grim consequence. 'The field's chief flower' (l. 8) is mournfully plucked, recalling Narcissus's end, 'A purple flower sprung up, chequered with white, / Resembling well his pale cheeks, and the blood / Which in round drops upon their whiteness stood' (ll. 1168–70). The characters have shared an ironic desire whose deathly goal was unwittingly imaged by Venus, 'Narcissus so himself forsook, / And died to kiss his shadow in the brook' (ll. 161–2). As noted / earlier, comparable effects occur throughout *Romeo and Juliet*, where moments of romantic union are disrupted by ongoing events that undercut their idealism. The mixed genres in these tales represent desire as a hybrid of the comic, tragic and ironic.[27]

Related images of threatening or incomplete desire and self-transformation are repeated through many sixteenth- and seventeenth-century texts, from the angst of sonneteers to Montaigne's musings in the *Apologie of Raymond Sebond* on 'The lustfull longing which allures us to the acquaintance of women, [and] seekes but to expell that paine, which an earnest and burning desire doth possesse-us-with, and desireth but to allay it thereby to come to rest, and be exempted from this fever'.[28] As most of these references suggest, this notion of erotic jeopardy is almost always tied to masculine conceptions of desire and selfhood. The pains of desire are indulged if not celebrated, and they may convert to misogyny, as in Hamlet's tirade against Ophelia or Romeo's charge that Juliet's beauty 'hath made me effeminate' (III.i.114).

This attitude echoes through Romeo's early laments about Rosaline. As Coleridge noted, he is 'introduced already love-bewildered':[29] 'I have lost myself. I am not here. / This is not Romeo; he's some other where' (I.i.194–5). Amid these tones of despair a self-satisfied note can be heard. The early Romeo is a 'virtual stereotype of the romantic lover',[30] whose role-playing brings a kind of egotistic reassurance. The lament for self-loss becomes proof of self-presence, a 'boastful positiveness',[31] with Romeo still to know the unsettling force of desire.

From this point, the play proceeds by exploring the limits of the Platonic, Ovidian and Petrarchan tropes. The seriousness of narcissistic absorption is questioned (underlined by Mercutio's quips at romantic indulgence);[32] yet the full consequence of desire is not realised in Platonic union but deferred to its aftermath. None of the conventional models can quite convey what is at stake in the lovers' story, and the discourse of desire must be revised.

III

Clearly, then, *Romeo and Juliet* invents neither tragic nor personal notions of desire. Both are strongly at work in Shakespeare's direct source, Brooke's *The Tragicall Historye of Romeus and Juliet* (1562): the threats to selfhood caused by love; the workings of 'False Fortune' and 'wavering Fortunes whele'; an intense desire that can be quenched 'onely [by] death and both theyr bloods'; time as tragic and ironic, first intimated in woe at Juliet's 'untimely death' and then gaining full significance as Romeus's man tells him 'too soone' of her end.[33]

While it reiterates these ideas, Shakespeare's play also develops and sharpens the connections among desire, the personal and the tragic. The lovers create new images of individuality and of togetherness in order to leave their worldly selves behind. Yet their efforts remain circumscribed by social forces. The ironic result is that the ideal identities the lovers fashion in order to realise their desire become the key to its tragic loss. Self-transcendence can be experienced but not as a kind of timeless ecstasy; instead it becomes entwined with unfulfilled desire.

The play personalises desire in ways which constantly alternate between idealism and failure. As Kay Stockholder notes, threats to desire are 'externalised' and the lovers consciously create 'a radiant world apart by attributing all inimical forces to surrounding circumstance'.[34] In this reordering of reality, desire becomes part or even constitutive of private, individual identity. Romeo and Juliet's love is secret from others and transgresses the roles imposed by their families. In *The Petite Palace of Pettie his Pleasure* (1576), George Pettie considered this opposition the key to the story: 'such presiness of parents brought Pyramus and Thisbe to a woful end, Romeo and Julietta to untimely death'.[35] In *A Midsummer Night's Dream* and *Romeo and Juliet*, resisting or contesting patriarchal authority allows a temporary move towards selfhood.

Through this contest, love appears to be one's own, yet both plays show the impossibility of holding onto it. The personal is as elusive as it is idealised, destined to slip back into constraining and distorting social forms. In retrospect, we may see this elusiveness prefigured in the lovers' first meeting, an intense bonding that occurs amid an elaborate ritual of masks and misrecognition. The symbolic means through which love must be expressed will prevent its consummation.[36] For the moment, however, love beholds a single object of desire, whose truth authenticates the lover and recreates both their identities: 'Deny thy father and refuse thy name, / Or if thou wilt not, be but sworn my love, / And I'll no longer be a Capulet ... Call me but love and I'll be new baptized. / Henceforth I never will be Romeo' (II.i.76–93).

The nexus between identity and desire is strengthened by the need for secrecy. Hidden and equivocated as the lovers move between private and public realms, secret desire endows selfhood with interiority and intention. It grants a depth of character, and even if its longings are not fulfilled inner experience is confirmed. Juliet's cryptic replies to her mother's attack on Romeo reveal private pleasure couched in pain: 'O, how my heart abhors / To hear him named and cannot come to him / To wreak the love I bore my cousin / Upon his body that hath slaughtered him!' (III.v.99–102). Like secret desire, the obstacles to fulfilment sharpen internal experience and give it a kind of sensuous reality: 'runaways' eyes may wink, and Romeo / Leap to these arms untalked of and unseen. / Lovers can see to do their amorous rites / By their own beauties' (III.ii.6–9).

This deep desire and selfhood develop in terms of intentionality – desire *for* someone, effected through imagination, speech and action. Desire marks the self as agent, and tragic desire portrays the onus of agency. It is felt sharply by Juliet before she takes the friar's potion, 'My dismal scene I needs must act alone' (IV.iii.19), and by Romeo as he enters the Capulet tomb 'armed against myself' (V.iii.65). In this sense, the play's depiction of desire is linked to representations of subjectivity that emerge during the sixteenth century. It reflects the important role that tropes such as the secret, with its social and personal disguises, have in discourses which are starting to inscribe both an inner self and the individual as agent.

Even as it invests in such notions of selfhood, at its most intense desire in *Romeo and Juliet* surpasses individual experience and re-alises an intersubjective union. The lovers re-characterise each other as much as themselves: 'Romeo, doff thy name, / And for thy name – which is no part of thee – / Take all myself' (II.i.89–91). Again this effect has generic analogues, as we see the lovers' discourse moving beyond single-voiced Petrarchism. They share exchanges which reveal 'not only the other's confirming response, but also how we find ourselves in that response'.[37] Unlike contemporary sonnet se-quences, which portray the poet by stifling the woman's voice (just as Romeo invokes and silences Rosaline), the play is marked by the lovers' dialogues. This reciprocity is epitomised by the sonnet they co-construct and seal with a kiss at their first meeting (I.v.92–105).[38] It is a highly suggestive moment, capturing the sepa-rateness of the lovers' world and speech from others, and also rewriting the dominant 1590s genre for representing desire. The sonnet is re-envoiced as dialogue, its meanings embodied in the cli-mactic kiss. At the same time, the heightened artifice of the scene in-timates its transience. The lovers start another sonnet but are interrupted by Juliet's garrulous nurse, who foreshadows the dire interventions of others. A further irony is also implied – as noted earlier, their union will be ended by events that literalise poetic tropes of love and death: Romeo really does die 'with a kiss' (V.iii.120), and Juliet falls in eternal sexual embrace, 'O happy dagger, / This is thy sheath! There rust, and let me die' (V.iii.168–9).[39]

The deaths verify the Prologue's vision of inescapable ties between sex and violence. Not only can the lovers not escape the eternal feud that frames them, they even play parts in it, responding impulsively, at the threshold of nature and nurture, to news of Mercutio's and Tybalt's deaths. For a moment their union bows under its violent heritage as each impugns the other: 'O sweet Juliet, / Thy beauty hath made me effeminate, / And in my temper

softened valour's steel' (III.i.113–15); 'did Romeo's hand shed
Tybalt's blood? ... O serpent heart, hid with a flow'ring face!'
(III.ii.71–3)

Other characters also link sex and violence, suggesting that the
connection has become naturalised and accepted. The Capulet servants joke aggressively about raping and killing the Montague
women (I.i.22–4). The friar parallels birth and death, 'The earth,
that's nature's mother, is her tomb. / What is her burying grave, that
is her womb' (II.iii.9–10), and is later echoed by Romeo, who calls
the Capulet crypt a 'womb of death' (V.iii.45). The friar also connects 'violent delights' to 'violent ends' (II.v.9), and the lovers'
suicides suggest a final fusing of love and death. Yet as different
interpretations maintain, this fusion's meaning may be tragic,
romantic, or both. The lovers are 'consumed and destroyed by the
feud' and seem to rise above it, 'united in death'.[40]

The final scene thus accentuates the connections among selfhood,
death and desire. It caps off the discourse of tragic desire announced by the Prologue – a tradition of failed love known through
numerous European novellas, the second volume of *The Palace of
Pleasure* (1567), and two editions of Brooke's *Tragicall Historye*
(1562, 1587). The action has thus had a doubly repetitive stamp,
not only replaying this oft-told tale but restaging what the Prologue
has stated. Foreknowledge of the outcome plays off against
moments of romantic and tragic intensity, and triggers a kind of
anxious curiosity that waits to see the details of the deaths – the
near misses of delayed messages, misread signs, plans gone awry.

Through this repetitive structure, the play affirms precedents and
conditions for its own reproduction as if anticipating future responses. Before ending, it even shows these possibilities being realised. The grieving fathers decide to build statues of the lovers, and
the prince's final lines look forward to 'more talk of these sad
things', in an effort to establish once and for all what desire's tragic
end might mean (V.iii.306). As Dympna Callaghan observes, the
play not only 'perpetuates an already well-known tale', but its
closure is predicated on 'the possibility of endless retellings of the
story – displacing the lovers' desire onto a perpetual narrative of
love'.[41]

Patterns of repetition weave through the play as well as framing
it. Characters constantly restate what has previously been staged –
in the first scene Benvolio explains how the opening brawl started,
and later he recounts details of Mercutio's and Tybalt's deaths and

Romeo's involvement; the Chorus to the second act reiterates the lovers' meeting; the Nurse tells Juliet of Tybalt's death; the Capulets and Paris echo each other's lamentations over Juliet's apparent death;[42] and lastly the Friar recaps the whole plot to the other characters after the bodies are found. These instances are part of the effort to explain the violent meaning of events, but as the prince's closing words suggest, something extra needs to be told, 'never was a story of more woe / Than this of Juliet and her Romeo' (V.iii.308–9). There is a sense that 'this' version of the story exceeds earlier ones. For all its repetition of tropes and narratives, in closing the play recognises and stresses a difference from precursors.

Other repetitive designs through the play are used to underline the tension between desire and death. Four meetings and kisses shared by Romeo and Juliet structure the romance plot. They are in counterpoint to four violent or potentially violent eruptions that occur between the male characters, especially involving Tybalt. A muted fifth interruption is provided by the presence of Tybalt's corpse in the Capulet crypt where Juliet and Romeo finally meet and miss each other. These turbulent scenes frame the romantic ones, unsettling the lyric and erotic essence which they seem to capture.

The repetitions and retellings connect with the representation of time in the play, imposing a destructive pressure between the weight of social and family history and personal longings. Social and personal time are opposed, and desire is caught between these conflicting time frames. Social time is frequently indexed through the play, in general terms such as the 'ancient grudge' and through the scheduling of specific events such as Capulet's banquet and Juliet's wedding to Paris. Against this scheme, the lovers' meetings seem to dissolve time, making it speed up or, more powerfully, stop and stand still, as the present is transformed into 'the time of love'.[43] The lovers seek to disregard time and death in their union, 'Then love-devouring death do what he dare – It is enough I may but call her mine' (II.v.7–8). Yet this passionate energy also drives the drama to its finale, and Romeo's words link their union and separation with death. The time of love confronts the passing of its own presence.

In various ways, then, *Romeo and Juliet* renovates tragic desire for the Elizabethans and for subsequent periods. In early scenes it evokes a narcissistic poetics of desire as self-loss and death but moves beyond that to stage a dialogic reciprocal presence. The reappearance of death then inscribes ineluctable external influences – the determinations of time and history which frame desire – and the impossible idealisation of self and other which passion seeks but fails to find. In this sense, Shakespeare's play marks a complex intersection between historical and emergent discourses of desire. First, in a period when modern institutions of family, marriage and romance are starting to appear, it translates Platonic, Ovidian and Petrarchan tropes of ecstasy and love into personal notions of desire. Next, it conceives desire as the interplay between passion, selfhood and death. And thirdly, its equivocal staging of love's death anticipates the tension between romantic and sceptical visions of desire that runs through many later literary and theoretical works.

It could be said that the play's symbolic bequest to these works is a notion of desire as lost presence. Though love continues to be celebrated as present or absent or present-in-absence in many texts (in different ways, Herbert's poetry and Brontë's *Wuthering Heights* come to mind), a significant line of literary works explores the interplay among desire, death and selfhood. Like *Romeo and Juliet*, these texts place desire in conflict with time, recounting moments of ideal presence whose future reveals they could never have been. This revision of desire begins with Shakespeare's later tragedies – *Hamlet, Othello, Macbeth* and *Antony and Cleopatra* – where one lover survives, though briefly, to feel the other's loss. It runs from the fallen lovers of *Paradise Lost* ('we are one, / One flesh; to lose thee were to lose myself' [9.958–9]), to the equivocal pairings at the end of Dickens's great novels or the images of foreclosed desire in Henry James's major phase. Its most poignant statement comes at the close of Scott Fitzgerald's *The Great Gatsby*:

> the green light, the orgiastic future that year by year recedes before us. It eluded us then, but that's no matter – to-morrow we will run faster, stretch out our arms farther ... And one fine morning –
> So we beat on, boats against the current, borne back ceaselessly into the past.

If *Romeo and Juliet* helps to initiate this tradition, it does so as the last tragedy of desire. For in these later texts the note is of melancholic rather than tragic loss: what hurts is not that desire ends in death but that it ends before death. The present then becomes a time for recounting lost desire, and the self's task is to try to hold the story together. 'The subject's centre of gravity is this present synthesis of the past which we call history', writes Lacan.[44] Like Romeo's last letter, this history reveals the 'course of love' (V.iii.286) to those who remain.

From Shakespeare Survey, 49 (1996), 57–67.

NOTES

[Lloyd Davis finds that in *Romeo and Juliet*, 'The links between love and death unveil a dark scepticism about desire, despite bursts of romantic idealism'. Desire is defined by a lack or loss, even when it is apparently fulfilled – if desire is genuinely fulfilled, it is no longer desire. This has implications for characterisation, since a person desiring is incomplete and requires the other for integration into the selfhood. Davis argues that the play's representation of desire as 'lost presence' has influenced later works and ways of thinking about desire, both sexually and more widely, but that *Romeo and Juliet* is so much a product of its own source and of the cultural moment of the 1590s that it should not be seen as by itself idealising this notion. In drawing on psychoanalytical theory as well as cultural materialism and an historical approach, Davis shows that these approaches need not be in conflict with each other, but that all can be used to illuminate Shakespeare's play. Quotations are from the single volume *The Oxford Shakespeare*, ed. Stanley Wells and Gary Taylor (Oxford, 1986).

1. Victor Turner, *Drama, Fields, and Metaphors: Symbolic Action in Human Society* (Ithaca, NY, 1974), pp. 40–1 and *passim*.

2. Brian Gibbons, Introduction, in *Romeo and Juliet* (London, 1980), p. 37.

3. On analepsis and prolepsis, see Shlomith Rimmon-Kenan, *Narrative Fiction: Contemporary Poetics* (London, 1983), pp. 46 ff.

4. Gibbons, Introduction, p. 54.

5. Gayle Whittier, 'The Sonnet's Body and the Body Sonnetized in *Romeo and Juliet*', *Shakespeare Quarterly*, 40 (1989), 27–41, p. 40.

6. Joel Fineman, *Shakespeare's Perjured Eye: The Invention of Poetic Subjectivity in the Sonnets* (Berkeley, CA, 1986), p. 24.

7. Two of the primary psychoanalytic texts are *Civilization and Its Discontents*, and *Beyond the Pleasure Principle*. A clear reading of this direction in Freud is offered by Jean Laplanche, *Life and Death in Psychoanalysis*, trans. Jeffrey Mehlman (Baltimore, MD, 1976): 'the death drive is the very soul, the constitutive principle of libidinal circulation' (p. 124). Related scepticism underlies Lacan's view of the link between desire and demand. Desire is dependent on demand, but

demand, 'by being articulated in signifiers, leaves a metonymic remainder that runs under it ... an element that is called desire': desire leads only to desire. See *The Four Fundamental Concepts of Psycho-Analysis*, trans. Alan Sheridan (New York, 1981), p. 154; compare Catherine Belsey's gloss of Lacan's view – 'desire subsists in what eludes both vision and representation, in what exceeds demand, eluding the demand for love' – in *Desire: Love Stories in Western Culture* (Oxford, 1994), p. 139.

8. Barbara Freedman, *Staging the Gaze: Postmodernism, Psychoanalysis, and Shakespearean Comedy* (Ithaca, NY, 1991), p. 110.

9. Belsey, *Desire*, pp. 38–9.

10. Ibid., p. 70.

11. Alan Sinfield, *Faultlines: Cultural Materialism and the Politics of Dissident Reading* (Oxford, 1992), p. 128.

12. *Sir Philip Sidney: Selected Poems*, ed. Katherine Duncan-Jones (Oxford, 73), p. 117. As discussed below, this first sonnet's turn to a seemingly authentic self is also made in *Romeo and Juliet*.

13. Stephen Greenblatt, 'Psychoanalysis and Renaissance Culture', in *Literary Theory/Renaissance Texts*, ed. Patricia Parker and David Quint (Baltimore, MD, 1986), pp. 210–24, p. 224.

14. 'But passion lends them power, time means, to meet, / Tempering extremities with extreme sweet' (2 Chor. 13–14). The Chorus, not included in first Quarto, is reprinted in the Arden edition (see n. 2).

15. Catherine Belsey, *The Subject of Tragedy: Identity and Difference in Renaissance* (London, 1985), p. 34.

16. Aubrey Mellor, 'From the Artistic Director', in Queensland Theatre Company Program for *Romeo and Juliet* (Brisbane, 1993), p. 3.

17. Samuel Taylor Coleridge, *Lectures on Shakespeare and Other Poets and Dramatists*, Everyman's Library (London, 1914), p. 410.

18. Graham Holderness, Preface: 'All this', in *The Shakespeare Myth*, ed. Graham Holderness (Manchester, 1988), pp. xii–xiii.

19. See Dympna Callaghan, 'The Ideology of Romantic Love: The Case of *Romeo and Juliet*', in Dympna Callaghan, Lorraine Helms and Jyotsna Singh, *The Weyward Sisters: Shakespeare and Feminist Politics* (Oxford, 1994), pp. 59–101; Jonathan Goldberg, '*Romeo and Juliet's* Open Rs', in *Queering the Renaissance*, ed. Jonathan Goldberg (Durham, NC, 1994), pp. 218–35; p. 227; and Joseph A. Porter, 'Marlowe, Shakespeare, and the Canonization of Heterosexuality', *South Atlantic Quarterly*, 88 (1989), 127–47. [All reprinted in this volume – Ed.]

20. Jonathan Dollimore, *Radical Tragedy: Religion, Ideology and Power in the Age of Shakespeare and His Contemporaries* (Chicago, 1984), p. 49.

21. Cf. Michel Foucault, *The Use of Pleasure*, vol. 2 of *The History of Sexuality*, trans. Robert Hurley (New York, 1990), p. 5 and *passim*.

22. *Symposium*, in *The Collected Dialogues of Plato*, ed. Edith Hamilton and Huntington Cairns (Princeton, NJ, 1985), pp. 193a–c, 211d–e.

23. Baldassare Castiglione, *The Book of the Courtier*, trans. Sir Thomas Hoby (London, 1948), pp. 319–22.

24. *Fowre Hymnes*, 'A Hymne in Honovr of Love' (ll. 197–203) and 'A Hymne in Honovr of Heavenly Love' (ll. 8–28), in *Spenser: Poetical Works*, ed. J. C. Smith and E. de Selincourt (Oxford, 79).

25. *Shakespeare's Ovid: Being Arthur Golding's Translation of the 'Metamorphoses'*, ed. W. H. D. Rouse (Carbondale, IL, 1961), book 3: ll. 540–2.

26. Jonathan Bate, *Shakespeare and Ovid* (Oxford, 1993), p. 173. Bate emphasises Actaeon as another figure of self-consuming desire (p. 19 and *passim*).

27. Cf. George Bataille's conceptions of eros as 'laughable', tragic and 'arousing irony', and of 'The complicity of the tragic – which is the basis of death – with sexual pleasure and laughter': *The Tears of Eros*, trans. Peter Connor (San Francisco, 1990), pp. 53 and 66.

28. Michel de Montaigne, *Essays*, trans. John Florio (London, 1980), vol. 2, pp. 192–3.

29. Coleridge, *Lectures*, p. 103.

30. Harry Levin, 'Form and Formality in *Romeo and Juliet*', in *Twentieth-Century Interpretations of 'Romeo and Juliet': A Collection of Critical Essays*, ed. Douglas Cole (Englewood Cliffs, NJ, 1970), pp. 85–95; p. 86.

31. Coleridge, *Lectures*, p. 103.

32. Joseph A. Porter emphasises that Mercutio's opposition is to romantic love not to sex: *Shakespeare's Mercutio: His History and Drama* (Chapel Hill, NC, 1988), p. 103.

33. Geoffrey Bullough, *Narrative and Dramatic Sources of Shakespeare*, vol. I (London, 1966), ll. 114, 210, 935, 2420 and 2532.

34. Kay Stockholder, *Dream Works: Lovers and Families in Shakespeare's Plays* (Toronto, 1987), p. 30. In *Love's Argument: Gender Relations in Shakespeare* (Chapel Hill, NC, 1984), Marianne Novy sees that the lovers' private world crystallises in the aubade of Act II, scene i (p. 108).

35. Bullough, *Sources*, vol. I, p. 374.

36. On the interplay among misrecognition, desire and the symbolic, see Catherine Belsey, 'The Name of the Rose in *Romeo and Juliet*', *Yearbook of English Studies*, 23 (1993), 126–42 [Reprinted in this volume – Ed.]; on the significance of the lovers being masked from each other, see Barbara L. Parker, *A Precious Seeing: Love and Reason in Shakespeare's Plays* (New York, 1987), p. 142.

37. Jessica Benjamin, *The Bonds of Love: Psychoanalysis, Feminism, and the Problem of Domination* (New York, 1988), p. 21.

38. Edward Snow suggests that the son registers 'an intersubjective privacy' that subdues 'sexual difference and social opposition': 'Language and Sexual Difference in *Romeo and Juliet*', in *Shakespeare's 'Rough magic': Renaissance Essays in Honor of C. L. Barber*, ed. Peter Erickson and Coppélia Kahn (Newark, NJ, 1985), pp. 168–92; p. 168; Novy contrasts this scene with the scene with the stichomythic exchange between Juliet and Paris at IV.i.18–38 (*Love's Argument*, p. 108).

39. On the love–death oxymoron, c.f. Whittier, 'Sonnet's Body', p. 32.

40. Coppélia Kahn, 'Coming of Age in Verona', in *The Woman's Part: Feminist Criticism of Shakespeare*, ed. Carolyn Ruth Swift Lenz, Gayle Greene and Carol Thomas Neely (Urbana, IL, 1980), pp. 171–93; p. 186. Marilyn Williamson regards deaths as alienating rather than uniting, 'Romeo's suicide fulfils a pattern to which Juliet is both necessary and accidental': 'Romeo and Death', *Shakespeare Studies*, 14 (1981), 129–37; p. 132.

41. Callaghan, 'Ideology', p. 61.

42. See Thomas Moisan, 'Rhetoric and the Rehearsal of Death: the "Lamentations" Scene in *Romeo and Juliet*', *Shakespeare Quarterly*, 34 (1983), 389–404.

43. Julia Kristeva, *Tales of Love*, trans. Leon S. Roudiez (New York, 1987), p. 213.

44. *The Seminar of Jacques Lacan*, Book I, *Freud's Papers on Technique 1953–1954*, trans. John Forrester (New York, 1991), p. 36. On literature and psychoanalysis as twin discourses of mourning and melancholia, see Julia Reinhard Lupton and Kenneth Reinhard, *After Oedipus: Shakespeare in Psychoanalysis* (Ithaca, NY, 1993), esp. pp. 32–3.

2

The Name of the Rose in *Romeo and Juliet*

CATHERINE BELSEY

I

Is the human body inside or outside culture? Is it an organism, subject only to nature and independent of history? Or alternatively is it an effect of the signifier, no more than an ensemble of the meanings ascribed to it in different cultures, and thus historically discontinuous? Or, a third possibility, is this question itself reductive, a product of our wish to assign unambiguous causes and straightforward explanations?

When it comes to sexual desire, our culture is dominated by two distinct and largely contradictory models, both metaphysical in their assumption that we can identify what is fundamental in human nature. One metaphysic proposes that sex is a matter of the body, originating in the flesh and motivated by it, however people might deceive themselves with fantasies about romance. The other holds that love is a marriage of true minds, and that sex is (or ought to be) the bodily expression of this ideal relationship. Both models take for granted a dualist account of what it is to be a person, a mind on the one hand, and a body on the other, one of them privileged, the two either in harmony or in conflict. This dualism is associated with the Enlightenment and the moment of its crystallisation is the Cartesian *cogito*.[1]

But in practice desire deconstructs the opposition between mind and body. Evidently it exists at the level of the signifier, as it imagines, fantasises, idealises. Desire generates songs and poetry and stories. Talking about it is pleasurable. At the same time, however, desire palpably inhabits the flesh, and seeks satisfaction there. Desire undoes the dualism common sense seems so often to take for granted.

The human body, we might want to argue in the light of our postmodernity, is subject to the imperatives of nature, but at the same time it does not exist outside culture. It owes to the differentiating symbol its existence as a single unit, with edges, limits. Psychoanalysis adds the presence of the symptom, evident on the body, the mark not of organic disease but of disorder at the level of the signifier, and psychoanalysis identifies the 'talking cure' as the disorder's remedy.[2] Desire, it urges, is an effect of difference, in excess of the reproductive drive. Furthermore, it knows itself as desire to the degree that it reads both the signifying practices of the body and the cultural forms in which desire *makes sense*. It is not possible to isolate the human body as natural organism, even methodologically: such a body would precisely not be human.

Romeo and Juliet is a play about desire. It is also a text poised on the brink of the Enlightenment, and it can be read, I want to suggest, as engaging with some of these issues, putting forward for examination in the process paradoxes that, for all the historical difference, a postmodern moment can find sympathetic. The bodies of the lovers are inscribed and, crucially, tragically, named. Their own account of love, while it displays a longing to escape the constraints of the symbolic order, reveals in practice precisely the degree to which it is culture that enables love to make sense. In *Romeo and Juliet* desire imagines a metaphysical body that cannot be realised.

II

Though there can be no doubt that Renaissance culture was profoundly and distinctively patriarchal, one sphere in which Shakespeare's women are perfectly equal to men is their capacity for experiencing sexual desire. Venus, Cleopatra, Portia in *The Merchant of Venice*,[3] and, of course, Juliet, are presented as sharing with their near-contemporaries, Alice Arden, the Duchess of Malfi, Beatrice-Joanna and Ford's Annabella, for example, an intensity of passion which is not evidently exceeded by that attributed to the men they love. These women are shown as subjects and agents of their own desire, able to speak of it and to act on the basis of it.

Meanwhile, Thomas Laqueur's *Making Sex* assembles persuasive documentation from the Greeks to the Renaissance of similar assumptions among European analysts of physiology and anatomy. Laqueur finds in this distinct sphere of knowledge, which is also, of course, a distinct discursive genre, what he calls the 'one-sex' model of the human body. The one-sex understanding of the body prevailed, he argues, until modern science redefined women and men as *opposite* and antithetical sexes. In the one-sex body the sexual organs are understood to be similarly distributed among men and women, though externally visible in men and internal in women. Thus the vagina commonly corresponds to the penis, the uterus to the scrotum, and so on. Laqueur is clear about the implications of this account for the understanding of erotic impulses themselves: both sexes were capable of intense sexual pleasure; both sexes experienced desire. Indeed, it was widely held that female pleasure was necessary to conception, and this was consequently seen as an important project of male sexual activity. Desire was not in any sense a masculine prerogative. On the contrary,

> The process of generation might differ in its nuances as the vital heats, the seeds, and the physical qualities of the substances being ejaculated differed between the sexes – but libido, as we might call it, had no sex.[4]

Some Renaissance physicians would have gone even further. Jacques Ferrand, for example, whose second treatise on lovesickness was published in Paris in 1623, argues that, being less rational than men, women are correspondingly more subject to violent erotic desires, and less able to resist their own impulses. A woman, according to Ferrand, 'is in her Loves more Passionate, and more furious in her follies, then a man is'.[5]

Laqueur does not, of course, imply that the one-sex body was the product of a less patriarchal culture. On the contrary, the male body represented the ideal of perfection; the female body, meanwhile, differed from it because women possessed less of the vital heat which pushed the sexual organs outwards. But the difference was one of degree, Laqueur insists, not kind. Women, less perfect than men, were in consequence less entitled to power and prestige.

But they were not men's opposite, passive and passionless where men were active and desiring. That antithesis belongs to a later epoch.

Renaissance medical knowledge is neither a source of the plays nor a guarantee of their meanings. It is too easily supposed that we can read off the true meaning of fictional texts from the other knowledges of the period, as if the culture somehow shared a single, homogeneous account of the world, and was in that respect simpler, less diverse than our own.[6] We should not now expect popular romance to depict the world in the same way as psychoanalysis, and even current pornography frequently takes precious little account of elementary anatomy. I invoke Laqueur's extremely valuable work here simply as additional evidence that it was possible in the sixteenth and seventeenth centuries to imagine female desire, and even to take it seriously.

But there are also significant generic differences between Renaissance anatomy and Renaissance fiction. In the medical treatises libido had no necessary moral implications: this was a knowledge which set out to record the world it found in the authorities and in experience. The drama, however, makes no attempt at value-free analysis. It cannot avoid showing the implications of the passions it depicts, and consequently it tends, whether incidentally or as its main project, to offer an assessment and evaluation of female desire. But the judgements it makes are by no means univocal or monolithic. As my examples suggest, desire may lead women into bad ways (*Arden of Faversham*, *The Changeling*); it may be radically misdirected (*'Tis Pity She's a Whore*); or innocent in itself but unfortunate in its consequences (*The Duchess of Malfi*); its moral status may be profoundly ambiguous (*Antony and Cleopatra*); it may be seen as lyrical but at the same time absurd (*Venus and Adonis*). But alternatively, desire reciprocated may be the foundation of conjugal marriage and (we are invited to assume) the nuclear family, as it is in Shakespeare's comedies. It was the Enlightenment, according to Laqueur, which insisted on the two-sex model of male and female bodies, the woman's lacking what defined the man's. And it was also the Enlightenment which tended to polarise male erotic activity and female passivity. Not until the nineteenth century was it established as a fact of nature that good women had no sexual feelings at all. The oppositional stereotypes of sexless virgin and voracious whore are not helpful in making sense of the work of Shakespeare and his contemporaries.

III

There was of course a convention, not that women should feel nothing, but that they should appear aloof in order to intensify male desire. This is the convention that Juliet unwittingly breaks when she declares her love at her window, only to be overhead by Romeo. It is quite late in their discussion, however, that she alludes, perhaps rather perfunctorily, to the proprieties of female behaviour: 'Fain would I dwell on form, fain, fain deny / What I have spoke, but farewell compliment!' (*Romeo and Juliet*, II.ii.88–9). The moment for observing the conventions has clearly passed, and propriety itself soon becomes matter for a teasing romantic overture on her part: 'If thou thinkest I am too quickly won, / I'll frown and be perverse, and say thee nay, / So thou wilt woo, but else not for the world' (II.ii.95–7).

At the heart of the play it is Juliet who speaks most eloquently and urgently to define, perhaps on behalf of both lovers, the desire experienced in the secret life of the body:

> Gallop apace, you fiery-footed steeds,
> Towards Phoebus' lodging; such a waggoner
> As Phaeton would whip you to the west,
> And bring in cloudy night immediately.
> (III.ii.1)

The opening imperative, in conjunction with the image of the pounding, burning hooves, suggests the speeding pulses and the impatient ardour of desire, as well as its barely controlled power, and the allusion to Phaeton which follows evokes the boy's failure to manage Apollo's unruly horses, and so implies a surrender of what remains of restraint. Juliet's speech is entirely explicit in its invocation of love performed, acted, possessed and enjoyed. Their wedding night will be 'a winning match / Play'd' between a symmetrically and reciprocally desiring couple 'for a pair of stainless maidenhoods' (ll.12–13). This necessarily clandestine love – perhaps the more thrilling because it is clandestine, because the fear of discovery intensifies the danger and the excitement[7] – is to be enacted in secret, in total darkness, and in silence:

> Spread thy close curtain, love-performing night,
> That [th'] runaway's eyes may wink, and Romeo
> Leap to these arms untalk'd of and unseen!

Lovers can see to do their amorous rites
By their own beauties.

(III.ii.5)

The (bed-)curtain of the dark is to exclude all outsiders, and the runaway god of love himself will close his eyes,[8] so that no one sees their union, not even the lovers. If 'see' is a metaphor (1.8), they are to be guided in the performance of their amorous rites by the beauty of each other's bodies. Love, the conceit implies, has no need of light, since its mode of 'seeing' is tactile, sensational. And the syntax here might lead us to suppose that if the lovers are 'unseen' by themselves as well as other people, so too, perhaps, the act is 'untalk'd of' by the lovers, since speech is also superfluous. Indeed, night is invited to obscure even the signifying practices of the virgin body: 'Hood my unmann'd blood, bating [fluttering] in my cheeks, / With thy black mantle' (ll.14–15). It is as if Juliet imagines the presence of the desiring bodies as pure sensation, sightless, speechless organisms in conjunction, flesh on flesh, independent of the signifier. A rose by any other name, she had earlier supposed, would smell as sweet (II.ii.43–4): the same gases, emanating from the same petals, striking the same nostrils, its physical being separable from the word that names it. The name, the signifier, and the symbolic order in its entirety are to be relegated to a secondary position, the place of the merely expressive and instrumental.

But these isolated, unnamed bodies (and roses) are only imaginary. The human body is already inscribed: it has no existence as pure organism, independent of the symbolic order in which desire makes sense. In the sixteenth-century text Juliet's imagined act of love is paradoxically defined in a densely metaphoric and tightly structured instance of signifying practice. The speech depends on invocations repeated with a difference ('Come civil night [. . .] Come night, come Romeo [. . .] Come gentle night' [ll.10, 17, 20]), framing an elaborate conceit in which the love-performing darkness both is and is not synonymous with Romeo himself, the lover who is ultimately to be perpetuated in little stars (l.22). The text specifies a wish in a tissue of formally ordered allusions, comparisons and puns, which constitute a poem, the zenith of signification, self-conscious, artful, witty. In order to bring before us its imagined bodies, the play here invokes a long poetic and rhetorical tradition, and in the process the lyricism which conjures up the act of love

necessarily supplants it too. Moreover, this is a set piece, an epithalamion, though it is spoken, ironically, not by the assembled wedding
guests, but by the bride herself, and in solitude.[9] What is enacted
within it is desire imagining its fulfilment, and not the event itself, nor
even any possible event. Love is inevitably performed within culture,
within, indeed, a specific culture: bodies do not exist outside the cultural moment which defines them, and experience cannot be identified
beyond the meanings a cultural tradition makes intelligible. What we
call a rose might take any other name, but if it were name*less*, outside
difference, who is to say that its smell would be 'sweet'? Here too a
whole cultural tradition underlies the recognition (re-cognition) of this
sweetness – and its association with love.

Romeo and Juliet is about desire. It is also one of Shakespeare's
most evidently formal, conventional texts. As Rosalie Colie points
out, the play draws on the traditions of Roman comedy, with its
young woman and two suitors, one of them approved by her father.
The garrulous nurse belongs to the same genre. Meanwhile, the
Prologues to Acts I and II are sonnets, and the lovers converse in
Petrarchan imagery. Mercutio, on the other hand, is an Ovidian
figure. When the lovers are together they perform in joint and reciprocal set pieces: first a sonnet (I.v.93–106) and then an *aubade*
(III.v.1–36). But there is no necessary contradiction, Colie proposes,
between convention and desire: on the contrary, the effect in the
text is precisely to naturalise the familiar forms. 'One of the most
pleasurable, for me, of Shakespeare's many talents, is his "unmetaphoring" of literary devices, his sinking of the conventions
back into what, he somehow persuades us, is "reality".' The
Petrarchan convention of love at first sight, she goes on to argue, 'is
here made to seem entirely natural [. . .] its conventionality forgotten as it is unmetaphored by action'.[10]

In this respect, Colie might have added, Shakespeare's text is no
more than a superlative instance of culture in general, which works
precisely by unmetaphoring the device and naturalising inherited
forms. There is no unmediated experience located entirely outside
the existing semiotic repertoire, though there are, as the play
demonstrates, unexpected deviations, juxtapositions, turns, and resistances. In the play Ovid disrupts Petrarch; comic form leads to
tragic denouement; choric narrative appropriates the lyric voice of
the sonnet. Culture imagines the symbol as truth, and 'proves' its
case by novelty, demonstrating that it is constantly possible to for-
mulate something new, surprising or unexpected.

In a brilliant discussion of the formality of *Romeo and Juliet* Gayle Whittier argues that the play shows how the inherited word declines 'from lyric freedom to tragic fact'.[11] She points out that the poetic mode in which Romeo falls in love precedes him, and that he longs to be the author of the lover he becomes. But in Whittier's account the narrative mode of drama displaces the abstract and timeless paradoxes of Petrarchan poetry. It endows the word with flesh, and in the process necessarily subjects it to time and death. Poetry, Whittier argues, is transcendent: love is referential. The bodies of the lovers exist in time, and confront death: the poetry which precedes them also survives them.

The argument is extremely convincing, and it is eloquently presented. If in the end I put a slightly different case, the distinction between us is perhaps no more than a matter of emphasis. I want to stress the degree to which the letter invades the flesh, and the body necessarily inhabits the symbolic. This above all is the source of the tragedy of *Romeo and Juliet*. Petrarch, their names and the word of the Prince ('banished') are all decisive for the protagonists, but the symbolic order is not external to their identities: on the contrary, it is exactly the element in which they subsist. On the other hand, they exceed it too. The body which it defines is not contained by the symbol, and desire seeks to overflow the limits imposed by the differential signifier.

IV

In recognising that the name of the rose is arbitrary, Juliet shows herself a Saussurean *avant la lettre*, but in drawing the inference that Romeo can arbitrarily cease to be a Montague, she simply affirms what her own desire dictates.

> O Romeo, Romeo, wherefore art thou Romeo?
> Deny thy father and refuse thy name;
> Or, if thou wilt not, be but sworn my love,
> And I'll no longer be a Capulet [. . .]
> 'Tis but thy name that is my enemy;
> Thou art thyself, though not a Montague.
> What's Montague? It is nor hand nor foot,
> Nor arm nor face, [nor any other part]
> Belonging to a man. O, be some other name!
> What's in a name? That which we call a rose
> By any other word would smell as sweet;

So Romeo would, were he not Romeo call'd,
Retain that dear perfection which he owes
Without that title. Romeo, doff thy name,
And for thy name, which is no part of thee,
Take all myself.

(II.ii.33–49)

Identity, the speech acknowledges, exists in the symbolic as the Name of the Father. Juliet imagines a succession of (im)possibilities: that Romeo should repudiate his father's name, or she hers; that he should be named differently; and finally that he should simply remove his name, as if it were extrinsic, separable from identity. In place of Romeo's name Juliet offers her 'self', implying that beyond their names, as beyond the name of the rose, the lovers could exist as unnamed selves. This move to transcend the signifier, however, the play at once makes clear, is precisely a contradiction. In offering to take what she urges *literally*, Romeo can only propose punningly to assume another *name*, to adopt a different location in the symbolic:

I'll take thee at thy word
Call me but love, and I'll be new baptiz'd;
Henceforth I never will be Romeo.

(II.ii.49)

But the signifier, however arbitrary, is not at the disposal of the subject. Romeo's name precedes him, makes him a subject, locates him in the community of Verona. It is not optional. Later Romeo will offer to excise his murderous name, but he cannot do so without killing himself:

O, tell me, friar, tell me,
In what vile part of this anatomy
Doth my name lodge? Tell me, that I may sack
The hateful mansion.

(III.iii.105)

Unlike hand or foot, Romeo's name is not something that he can lose and retain his identity, continuing to be the specific, differentiated Romeo that Juliet loves.

Jacques Derrida discusses the relationship between lovers and their names in his essay on *Romeo and Juliet*.[12] Lovers are prone to perceive the imaginary essence of the object of desire, to identify a 'self', a presence which subsists beyond the symbolic order, the 'dear perfection' of the loved one independent of the public and external name. This is the evidence of their idealising passion. A lover who might be expected to know better, the author of Jacques Derrida's sequence of postcards, also affirms something of this kind:

> you will never be your name, you never have been, even when, and especially when you have answered to it. The name is made to do without the life of the bearer, and is therefore always somewhat the name of someone dead. One could not live, be there, except by protesting against one's name, by protesting one's non-identity with one's proper name.[13]

Here too, the letter kills, we are invited to suppose, but desire gives life. The name is a trapping, inessential, inherited or given, a reminder that the individual's autonomy is always imaginary, the effect of a place allotted by others, by the family, by a whole culture.

But Derrida's amorous-philosophical text is not naïve (of course!). The name is dead because it is ancestral; it is dead because in differentiating the person that it names, it constitutes a reminder of all the other possible objects of desire, and the arbitrariness that singles out *this* one; and it is dead finally because it stands in for the person it names, and thus supplants the being who elicits so much intensity, intervening between the lover and the loved one. But there is no suggestion that it is possible to do more than protest against the imposed identity, to insist on non-identity with *that*, to refuse the imposition. Though it imagines it in an oxymoron ('I am calling you [. . .] beyond your name, beyond all names'),[14] 'the text does not in the end suppose that the person could exist independently, a free-floating essence beyond nomenclature, which is to say beyond difference.

Nor, indeed, is Shakespeare's text naïve. The name of Montague, imposed, ancestral, *is* Juliet's enemy, the text as a whole makes clear. If Romeo's non-identity with his name legitimates their love, the repudiated name returns, nevertheless, to ensure their tragedy. Even though his name is no part of the man Juliet loves, the play at once draws attention to the impossibility of discarding the name which differentiates him. Hearing in the darkness a voice reply to her musings, the shocked Juliet demands, 'What man art thou?' (l.52), and how else can Romeo indicate who he is but by refer-

ence to a name which precisely cannot be specified without identifying an opponent of all Capulets:

> By a name
> I know not how to tell thee who I am.
> My name, dear saint, is hateful to myself,
> Because it is an enemy to thee.
>
> (II.ii.53)

In the event, Juliet recognises his voice, a property of the lover like
hand or foot, or any other part, and promptly puts her recognition
to the test – by naming him:

> My ears have not yet drunk a hundred words
> Of thy tongue's uttering, yet I know the sound.
> Art thou not Romeo, and a Montague
>
> (II.ii.58)

The question of names recurs at intervals throughout Derrida's
'Envois' to *The Post Card*. The text is at least in part an engagement with Oxford philosophy and its distinction between 'use' and
'mention' ('Fido is my dog'; ' "Fido" is a possible name for a dog').
But this issue is part of a larger debate in Western philosophy concerning the question whether proper names have meaning. The
answer to this question has implications for our understanding of
the relationship between language and the world,[15] and this in turn
is the problem Derrida has addressed throughout his work. Proper
names imply that words may be no more than substitutes for
things, labels for the objects they refer to, without meaning in themselves. What, after all, does 'Smith' mean? If names have no
meaning, however, but only reference, what are we to say when the
name is Medusa, and the referent does not exist? And is 'Homer'
meaningless? Or does 'Homer' precisely *mean* the anonymous
author(s) of the *Iliad* and the *Odyssey*, who must have existed, but
probably not as Homer? If so, is meaning independent of what goes
on in the world, a matter of shared, inherited knowledge, which
may be false? Who does Homer's name belong to? To an individual? Or to a culture? What *gives* it its meaning?[16]

   The 'Envois' to *The Post Card* consists of a series of love letters
to an unnamed person, addressed poste restante 'because of all the
families' (p. 45). The epistolary form throws into relief the problems of 'communication', and the story of a passionate clandestine

love makes evident how much is at stake in the process of writing. The secret love letter is a paradigm case of the urgency and the impossibility of meaning as immediate, transparent, individual, exclusive *presence*. All language is subject to what Derrida calls 'the Postal Principle as differential relay' (p. 54). The message is always differed and deferred (differentiated), since the intervals and the distance, the delays and relays, separate the people it was designed to unite. Much of Derrida's love story concerns a critical, definitive, 'true' letter which fails to arrive. Instead it is eventually returned unopened, and remains for ever unread by the addressee, unopened by the sender, though it goes on to haunt the relationship, since its existence cannot be forgotten. This 'dead letter' is at once outside the living love affair and formative for it. In response to Lacan's account of *The Purloined Letter*, Derrida's text insists that the letter never arrives at its destination.

At the same time, *The Post Card* proposes, the letter can never ensure its own secrecy. However cryptic it is, however coded, designed exclusively for the recipient, if the message is intelligible, it is always able to be intercepted, read, misread, reproduced. Since it is necessarily legible for another, who does the letter belong to? To the sender, the addressee, or an apparently irrelevant unspecified third party, representative of the symbolic order in all its (dead) otherness? Their secret love does not belong exclusively to Romeo and Juliet. To the degree that it inhabits the symbolic, to the extent that it is relayed in messages and letters, even when the messages in question are those of the signifying body itself, love is tragically not theirs to control.

Derrida's text refuses to name its object of desire, the secret addressee of the love letters, though it plays with a succession of possible names (Esther, Judith, Bettina [pp. 71–3, 231]). It names others, however, who feature in the itinerary of the lover (Neil Hertz, Hillis, Paul, Jonathan, and Cynthia, and a woman who seems tantalisingly, comically, to be called Metaphysics [p. 197]). It thus keeps the reader guessing, about the identity of the beloved, and about whether the named and apparently non-fictional figures can be ruled out (p. 223). It names the writer, but only (punningly?) as acquiescent, as *j'accepte* ('this will be my signature henceforth [. . .] it is my name, that *j'accepte*' [p. 26]), leaving in doubt whether the whole story is fictional, or in some disguised and elusive way referential, 'true', and problematising in the process those terms themselves. But though it withholds the name of the loved one, it substitutes a pronoun, 'you': a shifter, certainly, but no less differential for that. The amorous project is to locate the living object of desire beyond the inherited, dead signifier, to invest it with a transcendent existence outside mortality. At the same time, of course, *The Post Card* recognises this impulse as imaginary, 'metaphysical', and perhaps in the process offers another clue – or possibly a red herring – which might lead us to identify the object itself:

> You have always been 'my' metaphysics, the metaphysics of my life, the 'verso' of everything I write (my desire, speech, presence, proximity, law, my heart and soul, everything that I love and that you know before me).
>
> (p. 197)

The beloved is not named, but is not nameless either, for the lover or the world:

> I have not named you while showing you to others, I have never shown you to others with the name they know you by and that I consider only the homonym of the one that I give you, no, I have called you, yourself.
>
> (p. 219)

'Yourself' is not an unmediated self. It is not a name, but at the same time it is not independent of the signifier. And as a shifter, it patently does not belong to the unnamed object of desire.

Romeo and Juliet are not reducible to their proper names, but they are not beyond them either, though in their idealising, transfiguring imagery they repeatedly locate each other outside mortality, in the heavens, among the inauspicious stars, not at their mercy (II.ii.2; 15–22; III.ii.22–5). And their names are not their property: they do not belong to them in the same way as hand or foot, or any other part. As subjects, the lovers aspire both to love and to immortality only by virtue of the differentiating, inherited signifier, which subjects them, in the event, to death itself.

V

What is at issue in the *aubade* is the name of the lark.

> Wilt thou be gone? it is not yet near day.
> It was the nightingale, and not the lark,
> That pierc'd the fearful hollow of thine ear.
>
> (III.v.I)

The referential truth is available here, but it is not what matters. The debate is about the significance of the birdsong that the lovers hear, its meaning: not ornithology, but the time of day. The same bird known by any other name would make the same sound, but it would be of no interest unless a culture had already invested the song with the meaning of dawn. It is the lark: Romeo proves it on the evidence of other signifiers:

> Look, love, what envious streaks
> Do lace the severing clouds in yonder east.
> Night's candles are burnt out
>
> (III.v.7)

The lark is already inscribed as 'the herald of the morn' (l.6), and while the time of day is also referential, a matter of fact, it too is in question here in its meaning, as the signifier of the moment when Romeo's banishment takes effect, separating, because of their names, the desiring bodies of the lovers. The world of nature, of birdsong and morning, is already invaded by culture, even though it also exceeds it, and the knowledge that it purveys is necessarily at the level of signification.

Juliet's epithalamion is uttered, ironically, in the direct shadow of the Prince's sentence, immediately after it is pronounced (III.i. 186–97), but thanks to the Postal Principle she does not yet know it. When the message that Romeo is banished is finally delivered by the Nurse, her account initially obscures the truth, and Juliet believes that Romeo is dead (III.ii.36–70). Juliet's premature lament for Romeo here finds a parallel in the family's lamentations for her apparent death (IV.v). Both are displaced, inappropriate, and yet not wholly irrelevant, since they anticipate the events of the play, as if the signifier lived a life of its own, partly but not entirely independent of the referent. Meanwhile, Friar Lawrence's letter fails to reach its destination and Romeo, in possession of another narrative, the public account relayed by Balthasar, tragically returns to act on Juliet's supposed death.

The Prince speaks the sentence of banishment, but it is to be carried out on Romeo's body, causing either his absence or his death. Romeo's absence is a kind of death for Juliet too, she affirms:

> Some word there was, worser than Tybalt's death,
> That murder'd me; I would forget it fain,

But O, it presses to my memory
Like damned guilty deeds to sinners' minds:
'Tybalt is dead, and Romeo banished.'
                                    (III.ii.108)

The insistent signifier is determining for the bodies of the lovers, and yet at the same time it is not definitive, in the sense that its implications are not contained by its meaning. ' "Romeo is banished": to speak that word, / Is father, mother, Tybalt, Romeo, Juliet, / All slain, all dead' (ll.122–4). The signifier, which differentiates, specifies limits and imposes boundaries, also evokes an unspeakable residue, boundless and unlimited: 'There is no end, no limit, measure, bound, / In that word's death, no words can that woe sound' (ll.125–6). The woe exceeds the word because no word can make it present. Supplanted by the signifier, it exists as an absence hollowed out within the utterance – just as it does within the corresponding signifying practice of the body, the weeping which is to follow (ll.130–1).

In the same way, the signifier cannot exhaust desire, since desire inhabits the residue that exceeds what can be said. Challenged to 'unfold' in speech the happiness of her marriage, Juliet replies:

Conceit, more rich in matter than in words,
Brags of his substance, not of ornament;
They are but beggars that can count their worth,
But my true love is grown to such excess
I cannot sum up sum of half my wealth.
                                    (II.vi.30)

Love, Juliet claims, like the unnamed rose or the untalked of act, is more substantial than mere words. For this reason, she continues, its substance cannot be counted, cannot be summed up in words. And she makes the affirmation in an ornamental metaphor, an analogy between love and wealth familiar to us from the *Sonnets* and from Theseus's opening speech in *A Midsummer Night's Dream*. The comparison, which brings the intensity of the love before us, simultaneously has the effect of supplanting it, replacing it by the signifier, so that the speech demonstrates precisely the impossibility it affirms of putting love into words. This excess of love over the signifier is what invests desire with metaphysics, and at the same time, if Derrida is to be believed, the metaphysical with desire. As speaking subjects, we long for the unattainable verso of signifying practice – proximity, certainty, presence, the thing itself. Lovers long to make present the unspeakable residue which constitutes desire.

VI

Shakespeare's play ends with death, the golden statues – and names again. At the beginning of the final scene Paris decorously strews Juliet's tomb with flowers and sweet water, in a gesture appropriate to a man who would have been her bridegroom. He is interrupted by her actual bridegroom, whose intentions, in contrast, are excessive, in every sense of the word: 'savage-wild, / More fierce and more inexorable far /Than empty tigers or the roaring sea' (V.iii.37–9). Alan Dessen makes the point that modern productions commonly include a structure which represents the tomb. This, he argues persuasively, is not necessarily how the scene would have been staged in the 1590s. On the contrary, the tomb might well have been no more than a stage door or a trap door in the stage, and Juliet's body might have been thrust out on a bier at the point when the scene shifts to the inside of the tomb. Including the tomb, as they do, Dessen says, modern productions often leave out Romeo's mattock and crowbar. In consequence, they fail to do full justice to the emblematic contrast the scene sets up between Romeo and Paris, the one sprinkling scented water on the grave, and the other violating the tomb with an iron bar, forcing open what he himself calls this 'womb of death' (l.45).[17] When Romeo, who is beside himself with passion, offers to *strew* the churchyard with the interloper's limbs, the contrast is surely complete.

Explaining his purpose, Romeo 'lies' to Balthasar:

> Why I descend into this bed of death
> Is partly to behold my lady's face,
> But chiefly to take thence from her dead finger
> A precious ring . . .
>
> (V.iii.28)

The lie is also intelligible as a coded truth, a cryptic declaration of a real purpose, not intended to be legible to Balthasar, of re-enacting his clandestine marriage by a second exchange of rings. In the grotesque parody of the wedding night that follows, Romeo seeks a repetition in the tomb of the original darkness, silence and secrecy invoked so eloquently in Juliet's epithalamion, though once again these amorous rites are to be lit by beauty, as Juliet, who once taught the torches to burn bright (I.v.44), now 'makes / This vault a feasting presence full of light' (V.iii.85–6).

This time, too, the body signifies. There is blood in Juliet's face once more, to the point where Romeo seems almost to read the message it puts out:

> O my love, my wife,
> Death, that hath suck'd the honey of thy breath,
> Hath had no power yet upon thy beauty:
> Thou art not conquer'd, beauty's ensign yet
> Is crimson in thy lips and in thy cheeks,
> And death's pale flag is not advanced there.
> (V.iii.91)

But because his understanding at this moment is constructed in accordance with another narrative, he cannot read the story of Juliet's living body. Again he turns to her, this time with a question: 'Ah, dear Juliet, / Why art thou yet so fair?' (ll. 101–2). The audience could have told him the answer (and perhaps did in early productions?). But Romeo, in the light of what he thinks he knows, produces another hypothesis:

> Shall I believe
> That unsubstantial Death is amorous,
> And that the lean abhorred monster keeps
> Thee here in dark to be his paramour?
> (V.iii.102)

(It is tempting, especially in the context of Georges Bataille's current popularity, to find an erotics of death in this conceit, but it is worth bearing in mind that from the point of view of the audience, the account is ironic, since it represents precisely the wrong answers.)[18] The re-enacting of the wedding night remains in consequence imaginary. They die, as Juliet performed their epithalamion, separately. 'These lovers of the night remain', as Kristeva puts it, 'solitary beings.'[19]

Their grave is not, however, a private place. On the contrary, it is the family vault of the Capulets, a memorial, precisely, to the name, which is all that remains of their ancestors, but which lives on to shadow the present so tragically. Moreover, no sooner has he established the close-curtained secrecy of this second wedding night, than

Romeo interrupts his address to Juliet to recognise the dead body of Tybalt in its bloody sheet (l.97). Once again Tybalt, who insisted on the importance of Romeo's name and the 'stock and honor' of his own kin (I.v.54, 58, 61), and who for that reason fatally sustained the feud, intervenes between the lovers, as an emblematic third party, representative of the inherited symbolic order in all its dead – and deadly – otherness. Finally, the whole community crowds in, the community which is ultimately responsible for the arbitrary and pointless ancestral quarrel, and which is powerless to reverse the effects of a violence carried on in the names of Montague and Capulet, and enacted on the bodies of the new generation.

VII

Romeo and Juliet are immortalised as signifiers. The promised golden statues are, of course, a metamorphosis, effigies of their bodies, beautiful, precious, and lifeless. Metamorphosis enacts something of the project of desire, arresting, and stabilising the object, fixing it as possession – and supplanting it in the process. Like metaphor, metamorphosis offers an image in place of the thing itself, but the image is precisely *not the same*. Venus is able to hold the flower that Adonis becomes, but the flower is no longer Adonis. The reconciling golden statues appear too late to interrupt the fatal invasion of the signifier into the living organism. Verona will recognise the effigies of Romeo and Juliet, but the effigies will signify concord, not desire.

And yet finally, as is to be expected of signifiers, the lovers are incorporated into a love story, foretold by the Prince, dramatised by Shakespeare. The play closes, appropriately, with their names, which are not synonymous with the lovers themselves, but which are not independent of them either. The play, and the legend of love that the play has become, have been astonishingly popular from the Restoration period on. The text has been performed, adapted, cut, reinterpreted, rewritten as a musical, filmed,[20] and now produced as a movie starring cats. Even in death, therefore, the record of the lovers' desiring, inscribed bodies is preserved in the archive, filed, appropriately enough, under their names:

> For never was a story of more woe
> Than this of Juliet and her Romeo.
> (V.iii.309)

Evidently it was possible, before the dualism of the Enlightenment separated us all neatly into minds and bodies, to identify another relationship between the organism and the culture in which it becomes a human being. *Romeo and Juliet* dramatises the sexual desire which is produced at the level of the signifier and inscribes the body of the lover. The play also acknowledges the slippage between the signifier and the world it defines and differentiates. But above all, it puts on display the hopeless longing to escape the confines of the signifier, to encounter directly, immediately, the rose that exists beyond its name. And to this extent *Romeo and Juliet* suggests the degree to which the named, differentiated lover is always only a stand-in for something which cannot be embraced, a reminder, as Plato proposes, of 'an ideal that is out of sight, but present in the memory'.[21]

Does the continued popularity of the play, even in a predominantly Enlightenment culture, perhaps suggest a dissatisfaction with the neat Cartesian categories by which we have so diligently struggled to live?

From Catherine Belsey, 'The Name of the Rose in *Romeo and Juliet*', *Yearbook of English Studies*, 23 (1993), 126–42.

NOTES

[In the Renaissance sexual desire is attributed equally to men and women. Desire deconstructs the opposition between mind and body familiar in western culture since Descartes famously identified human beings with their consciousness. This pre-Cartesian play is about the tragic implications of the interaction of names and organisms for a desire that longs to exist beyond cultural difference. At the same time, the critic is writing from a post-Cartesian point of view. Catherine Belsey draws on some ideas of Jacques Derrida, the contemporary French philosopher whose name is associated with deconstruction theory. He rejects claims that language holds stable or absolute meanings, or that words can be 'transcendental signifiers'. Meaning always depends on the relationship to surrounding systems, and is derived by its 'difference' from all other possible meanings. Belsey argues that in *Romeo and Juliet* desire is always understood to exceed the language used to express it. Desire constantly deconstructs not only the distinction between mind and body but also language itself, which is shown to be radically indeterminate, 'the rose that exists beyond its name'. The edition of Shakespeare used is *The Riverside Shakespeare*, ed. G. Blakemore Evans et al. (Boston, 1974). Ed.]

I am grateful to Alan Dessen and Cynthia Dessen for their incisive comments on an earlier version of this essay.

1. The dualism of the Enlightenment differs from Plato's and Augustine's. Both Platonic and medieval souls are immortal and their affiliations are divine. But the Cartesian mind is predominantly secular and human. Nor is its relation to the body always one of superiority. Enlightenment science, paradoxically, had the eventual effect of reversing Descartes' hierarchy.

2. Charles Shepherdson, 'Biology and History: Some Psychoanalytic Aspects of the Writing of Luce Irigaray', *Textual Practice*, 6 (1992), 47–86. I owe to the clarity of that essay the theoretical framework of my argument here.

3. *The Merchant of Venice*, III.ii.108–14. Shakespeare references are to *The Riverside Shakespeare*, ed. G. Blakemore Evans et al. (Boston, 1974).

4. Thomas Laqueur, *Making Sex: The Body and Gender from the Greeks to Freud* (Cambridge, MA, 1990), p. 43.

5. Jacques Ferrand, *Erotomania*, trans. Edmund Chilmead (Oxford, 1640), p. 214. Female desire was widely taken for granted in the Middle Ages, and natural philosophy commonly presented women as more libidinous than men (Mary Frances Wack, *Lovesickness in the Middle Ages: The 'Viaticum' and its Commentaries* [Philadelphia, 1990], pp. 110–25).

6. The New Historicism sets out to break with this version of the Elizabethan world picture by insisting on the single anecdote which is not offered as 'representative'. But though it produces acute insights, the New Historicist juxtaposition of fiction with quite different knowledges, as if it could be taken for granted that they illuminate each other, risks repeating Tillyard's unifying and simplifying gesture. In 'Fiction and Friction', for example, after a number of disclaimers Stephen Greenblatt goes on to identify Renaissance England as 'a culture that knows, as a widely accepted physical truth, that women have occulted, inward penises' (*Shakespearean Negotiations: The Circulation of Social Energy in Renaissance England* [Oxford, 1988], pp. 66–93, p. 87). He then uses this medical knowledge to explain the transvestite theatre, female cross-dressing in Shakespeare's comedies, and homoerotic desire in the period. All this is suggestive, inventive, and challenging, but it fails to take account of the counter-knowledge, evident in the bawdy jokes of the theatrical tradition itself, that women lacked what men possessed. Greenblatt himself cites Viola's 'a little thing would make me tell them how much I lack of a man' (*Twelfth Night*, III.iv.302–3). Gratiano's 'would he were gelt that had it' is comic if Nerissa is understood to be 'gelded' (*The Merchant of*

Venice, V.i.144). See also: ' "That's a fair thought to lie between a maid's legs." "What is?" "Nothing".' (*Hamlet*, III.i.118–21), and David Wilbern, 'Shakespeare's Nothing', in *Representing Shakespeare: New Psychoanalytic Essays*, ed. Murray Schwartz and Coppélia Kahn (Baltimore, 1980), pp. 244–63.

7. Julia Kristeva, *Tales of Love*, trans. Leon S. Roudiez (New York, 1987), p. 211.

8. Gary M. McCown, ' "Runnawayes Eyes" and Juliet's Epithalamium', *Shakespeare Quarterly*, 27 (1976), 150–70, pp. 156–65.

9. McCown, ' "Runnawayes Eyes" ', p. 165.

10. Rosalie Colie, *Shakespeare's 'Living Art'* (Princeton, NJ, 1974), pp. 135–67, p. 145.

11. Gayle Whittier, 'The Sonnet's Body and the Body Sonnetized in *Romeo and Juliet*', *Shakespeare Quarterly*, 40 (1989), 27–41, p. 27.

12. Jacques Derrida, 'Aphorism Countertime', in *Acts of Literature*, ed. Derek Attridge (New York, 1992), pp. 414–33.

13. Jacques Derrida, *The Post Card: From Socrates to Freud and Beyond*, trans. Alan Bass (Chicago 1987), p. 39.

14. Derrida, *The Post Card*, p. 130. Compare: 'But it is you I still love, the living one. Beyond everything, beyond your name, your name beyond your name' (p. 144).

15. See J. R. Searle, 'Proper Names and Descriptions', *The Encyclopaedia of Philosophy*, ed. Paul Edwards, 8 vols (London, 1967), VI, 487–91.

16. I am grateful to Andrew Belsey for a discussion of the problem of proper names.

17. Alan C. Dessen, 'Much Virtue in "As" ' in *Shakespeare and the Sense of Performance: Essays in the Tradition of Performance Criticism in Honor of Bernard Beckerman*, ed. Marvin and Ruth Thompson (Newark, NJ, 1989), pp. 132–8.

18. See Georges Bataille, *Erotism: Death and Sensuality*, trans. Mary Dalwood (San Francisco, 1986); and *The Tears of Eros*, trans. Peter Connor (San Francisco, 1989).

19. Kristeva, *Tales of Love*, p. 216.

20. See Jill L. Levenson, *Romeo and Juliet*, Shakespeare in Performance (Manchester, 1987).

21. Kristeva, *Tales of Love*, p. 269.

3

Romeo and Juliet: Love-Hatred in the Couple [Le couple amour-haine selon *Roméo et Juliette*]

JULIA KRISTEVA

OUTSIDE THE LAW

Transgression love, outlaw love, these are the notions that prevail in ordinary consciousness and literary texts as well; Denis de Rougemont in his *Love in the Western World* largely contributed toward imposing the concept in its strongest form: love is adulterous (cf. *Tristram and Isolde*).

Such a patently obvious statement rests upon the incompatibility between idealisation and the law, to the extent that compliance with the latter depends on the superego. It is a fact that the lover (especially the woman lover) desires his or her passion to be legal. The reason may be that the law, which is external to the subject, is an area of power and attraction that can merge with the Ego Ideal. Nevertheless, once instituted for the subject, the law reveals its no longer ideal but tyrannical facet, woven with daily constraints and consonant hence repressive stereotypes. Out of this amatory 'we' in a delightful state of destabilisation, the law then produces a coherent set, a mainstay of reproduction, of production, or simply of the social contract. Because it has merged with the superegotic practice of law, marriage – a historically and socially determined institution – is antinomic to love. There is, however, no reason not to think of other settings of legality in the matrimonial relationship in which the law would preserve its ideal facet and thus shelter the idealisation that is so favourable to our loves and at the same time trim its superegotic features. Marriage turned into the social mirror that acknowledges our loves, without for that matter setting itself up as an authority checking our desires? Is it a perversion in marriage that one thus imagines to be possible? And what if, as literature testifies more openly than the discourse of analysands, the very essence of the amatory relationship lay in preserving the necessity of the Ideal and its detachment from the Superego? And what if the economic evolution of technical societies allowed one more and more to relegate outside the family those constraints upon which the life of the species depends? It is not that the family might become a place unencumbered by authority. But is [it] not an authority that one might idealise rather than fear, for it is first an ideal and secondarily a constraint, an authority to be loved? Perversely? In utopian fashion?

ON SECRET AND THE FIGURE 3

The loving couple is outside the law, the law is deadly for it – that, too, is what the story of Romeo and Juliet proclaims, as immortalised in Shakespeare's play. And young people throughout the entire world, whatever their race, religion, or social status, identify with the adolescents of Verona who mistook love for death. No other text affirms as passionately that, in aspiring to sexual union as well as to the legalisation of their passion, lovers enjoy only ephemeral happiness. The story of the famous couple is in fact a story of the impossible couple: they spend less time loving each other than getting ready to die. That accursed love, however, has nothing in common with the impossible meeting of lovers in the Song of Songs; where the Bible posited an erotic and metaphysical distance that actually guaranteed the durability of the Jewish couple, here the Renaissance, humanistic, and total merging leads straight to death through the device of an antiquated, tribal law that, from the very beginning, rejects the jouissance of bodies and decrees social incompatibilities. But before turning to this morbid feature, apparently more unusual as one considers the tale of the young lovers, let me first emphasise their happiness. For if the couple is destined for death, Shakespeare seems to tell us, clandestine loves are the paradise of amorous passion.

Breaking the law is the initial condition of amatory exhaltation: even though the Capulets and the Montagues hate one another, we are going to love each other. This *challenge* (for Romeo knows perfectly well that both Rosaline and Juliet belong to the enemy family) is protected by *secrecy*.

In Verona and universally. Ardent glances exchanged on the sly, go-betweens one hopes will never be caught. Words that are whispered or disguised within the banality of trivial conversation, unperceived by others. Slight touches under the watchful eyes of those who suspect nothing, which arouse the senses more than the most obscene embrace might do. There is, in the happiness of secret lovers – as in that unique, elusive scene of the play set in the Capulets' orchard, with Juliet on her balcony, against a backdrop of moon and stars (II.iii) – the intense feeling of being within a hairsbreadth of punishment. Do they joy in the fullness of being together or in the fear of being reproved? The shadow of a third party – relatives, father, husband or wife in the case of adultery – is doubtless more present to the mind during carnal excitement than the innocent seekers of happiness together are willing to admit. Take away the third party and the whole construct often crumbles, lacking a cause for desire, after having lost some of its passional tinge. In fact, without this third party, this commandant of the secret, the man loses his amatory submission to the threatening father. While in her avenging ardour against her own father or husband, the woman recaptures with her secret lover the unsuspected jouissances of maternal fusion. Let us not forget the case of the unfaithful husband who, in his wife, flees what he imagines to be a possessive mother, in order to find in the series of his conquests the assurance of an unfailing autoeroticism ... Through such challenge to law, secret lovers come close to madness, they are ready for crime.

It would be inaccurate to call their fire perversion. Unless one uses that word in a very broad sense, suggesting that we are all perverts because we are neoteinic, incapable of subsisting solely within the symbolic order, constantly driven to seek the animal sources of a passion that defies the Name to the advantage of loss of self in the flood of pleasure. ''Tis but thy name that is my enemy; thou art thyself, though not a Montague. What's Montague? It is nor hand nor foot, nor arm, nor face, nor any other part belonging to a man …' Juliet complains, burning with the desire to possess a 'part belonging to a man'. 'O be some other name! … Romeo, doff thy name, and for thy name, which is no part of thee, take all myself' (II.ii.38–49). Lose your symbolic entity to enable me, on the basis of your loved, fragmented body, to become entire, whole, one: out of myself and myself alone there becomes a couple! In other respects, as we shall see when taking up the couple from the viewpoint of hatred, Juliet is mistaken and the name of her lover is not irrelevant to the triggering of their passion; quite the contrary, it determines it.[1] But let us remain within the romance.

THE LOVING DEATH

'The Most Excellent and Lamentable Tragedie of Romeo and *Iuliet*' is, as the second quarto edition title page suggests, a deeply ambivalent text, 'excellent and lamentable' since the amatory situation of which it sings is lamentable and excellent. For we are indeed dealing with a *song*, and the lyrical qualities of the play have often been pointed out (the rhymed prologue is followed by blank verse; Benvolio and Romeo speak in rhymed couplets when they speak of love; Capulet switches to rhyme when speaking of Juliet's early childhood; Benvolio uses the sonnet form to propose that he seek a new mistress for Romeo in place of Rosaline, etc.). The sonnet is clearly in evidence at the time of the ecstatic encounter between the two lovers and one can imagine how novel the absorption of the sonnet form by the action of the play appeared to an audience captivated by the playwright's art.[2] Probably influenced by Sidney's *Astrophil and Stella*, which depended on a melancholy lover's code with a slightly literary sensitivity (it will be noted that Shakespeare emphasised this tendency by having the play and its developments rely on the sending of messages and their erroneous interpretations),[3] the play nevertheless remains wholly Shakespearean on account of death's immanent presence within love. All this leads him to accentuate the *present moment* and, where expression is concerned, an abrupt, resolute, imperative discourse, which shows up as soon as Romeo falls in love with Juliet, in contrast with his previous speech. That is because the time of his love is 'wild': 'The time and my intents are savage-wild, more fierce and more inexorable by far than empty tigers or the roaring sea' (V.iii.37–9). Filtered by loving, idealising passion, the presence of death endows death symbolism with a fully gothic character: 'Shall I believe that unsubstantial death is amorous, and that the lean abhorred monster keeps thee here in dark to be his paramour?' (V.iii.102–5).

SOLAR OR BLIND LOVE

Only the very first meeting of the lovers seems to be free of the ambiguous compression of time caused by the immanence of death.[4] Their first glances nevertheless infer a mutual dazzlement and produce, in their loving discourse, the metaphor of metaphors, that is, the Sun – clue to the metaphoricalness of the loving discourse, to its non-representability. 'It is the east, and Juliet is the sun! Arise, fair sun, and kill the envious moon ...'

Out of time, out of space, this solar disposition, dazzling with love, as Brian Gibbons points out, impugns even the proper name and identification itself (Romeo says that he 'never will be Romeo'). The time of love would be that of the present moment (no sorrow can 'countervail the exchange of joy that one short minute gives me in her sight' – II.vi.4–5), and marriage, as continuity, is its opposite. The rhythm of meetings, developments, and mischances is not only the result of that incompatibility between the amorous instant and temporal succession; it also displays how demiurgic passion truly, and thus in fact magically, modifies temporal succession for its subjects. At this point of its trajectory, certain of its solar power, love selects as its target the opposite of the solar metaphor – the nocturnal metaphor. When idealising, love is solar. Condemned in time, squeezed into the present moment, but just as magnificently trusting of its power, it takes refuge in blindness, in darkness.

> Or, if love be blind, it best agrees with night. Come, civil night, thou sober-suited matron, all in black ... Come, gentle night, come, loving, black-brow'd night, give me my Romeo; and when he shall die, take him and cut him out in little stars, and he will make the face of heaven so fine, that all the world will be in love with night, and pay no worship to the garish sun.
>
> (III.ii.9–25)

Let me make it clear once again: the shattered, murdered solar metaphor displays Juliet's unconscious desire to break up Romeo's body. Within the sombre blindness of such a passion, there never-theless arises the meaning of another metaphor – the metaphor of Night. As if love drew from two sources, light and darkness, and could maintain its insolent self-confidence only from their alterna-tion – day and night. What is Night? – Woman Night, and it is indeed Juliet who speaks of it; or death Night ... Night, however, is, like its opposite the sun, not only half of real time-space but an essential part of metaphorical meaning germane to love. It is not nothingness, lack of meaning, absurdity. In the polite display of its black tenderness there is an intense longing that is positive with respect to meaning ... Let me emphasise the nocturnal motion of metaphor and *amor mortis*: it bears on the irrational aspect of signs and loving subjects, on the non-representable feature on which the renewal of representation depends. Because it is Juliet who reveals that infernal quickening leading to the night of death, a quickening peculiar to amorous feeling, this does not only signify that a woman is, as they say, in direct contact with rhythm. More imaginatively, feminine desire is perhaps more closely umbilicated with death; it may be that the matrical source of life knows how much it is in her power to destroy life (see Lady Macbeth), and moreover it is through the symbolic murder of her own mother that a woman turns herself into a mother. Cradled on the spate of such an uncon-scious stream, the woman-subject does not control it, but who can? The poet's dramatic assertion involves a 'we', all of us: 'It lies not in our power to love, or hate, for will in us is over-rul'd by fate.'[5] Finally, a certain intrinsic melancholy with Juliet contrasts sharply with Romeo's solar eagerness when she expresses her own luminos-ity not by means of the sun but by the stars and meteors: 'Yond light is not day-light, I know it, I: it is some meteor that the sun exhales, to be to thee a torch-bearer, and light thee on thy way to Mantua' (III.v.12–15).

There is nevertheless a comic vein in this tragedy, as if Shakespeare wanted to maintain a belief in vitality beyond the dis-astrous passion. But what comic strain there is is displayed by the Nurse and Mercutio, for instance (I.ii.12–57, and I.iv.53–103), outside the passion of the two lovers properly speaking. Now, even the friendly, reassuring figure presented by the Nurse during the early portion of the play seems to betray the vital current of the work and act, after Romeo's banishment, like an opportunist matron, insensitive to Juliet's feelings, and advises her to marry Count Paris. Moreover, are not all comic scenes dominated by fury rather than joyous laughter (thus, Mercutio speaking of Queen Mab, in Act I, scene iv, and also his remarks in Act II, scene iv)?

Death, like a final orgasm, like a full night, waits for the end of the play. When death appears in the text as such and not simply as insinuation or foreboding, it is a death that mistakes its object. It is the wrong, ironic if you will, death of a rival who did not deserve that much. Neither Tybalt nor Paris, killed by Romeo, can reduce the passion mixed with violence that impels amorous feelings. They leave us dissatisfied, as they leave Romeo himself dissatisfied and disturbed – not guilty but nonplussed because he did not strike the right object. As a consequence of having thrust his sword into two rivals Romeo released the fury that underlies his love, and it will never leave him. 'Away to heaven, respective lenity, and fire-eyed fury be my conduct now! ... O, I am fortune's fool!' (III.i.124–5, 138). Juliet, too, feels panic-stricken as death is set loose, and the mini-glossolalia of her speech should be noted: 'I am not I, if there be such an I, or those eyes shut, that make the answer "I" ' (III.ii.48–9), she tells the Nurse who gives a confused account of Tybalt's murder at Romeo's hands. But it is in truth the young lover of Verona who speaks of her loss of identity in the face of death's incoming tide that henceforth threatens the lover's universe.

A last sign of the passion carried along by its opposite may doubtless be found in the paradoxical imbroglio of the protagonists' death. What artful devices, what misunderstandings indeed are needed in order to produce a Juliet who is rigid but not dead, put to sleep by the potion, and more beautiful than ever in her rigidity. What is this body, erroneously dead and beautiful, if not the image of a contained, padlocked, one could say frigid passion because it was not able to give its violence free rein? She goes back into the night, at the end of the play, joying to penetrate herself with Romeo's dagger. All by herself. Romeo, after he has possessed his rivals, Tybalt and Paris, by means of death, meets his own death, by his own hand, without ever embracing Juliet.

There is something autarkic about night-jouissance for each of the two partners of the amorous couple. The dark cave is their only common space, their sole true community. These lovers of the night remain solitary beings. There you have the most beautiful love dream in the Western world. Love, a solar dream, a thwarted idea? And a nocturnal, solitary reality, a frigid death together. Whose fault is it? The parents? Feudal society? The Church, for it is true that Friar Laurence departs in shame? Or love itself, two-faced, sun and night, delightful, tragic tenseness between two sexes?

SALVATION THROUGH THE COUPLE: SHAKESPEARE AND HAMNET

If there is a romance, and it is there indeed, it is guaranteed by secrecy and sanctioned by brevity. Let us imagine Romeo and Juliet liberated, living according to different customs, little concerned over the animosity between their kin – and surviving. Or what if, within the same Shakespearean framework, a mediocre dramatist made them survive; Friar John, for instance, might have been able to warn Romeo in time about that most peculiar sleep Friar Laurence induced in Juliet, and the beautiful bride might have awakened in Romeo's arms? What if they had escaped their persecutors, and once the clans' hatred had been appeased they experienced the normal existence of married couples? There would then only be two borderline situations, with obvious combinations and variations possible between the two. Either time's alchemy transforms the criminal, secret passion of the outlaw lovers into the banal, humdrum, lacklustre lassitude of a tired and cynical collusion: that is the normal marriage. Or else the married couple continues to be a passionate couple, but covering the entire gamut of sadomasochism that the two partners already heralded in the yet relatively quiet version of the Shakespearean text. Each acting out both sexes in turn they thus create a foursome that feeds on itself through repeated aggression and merging, castration and gratification, resurrection and death. And who, at passionate moments, have recourse to stimulants – temporary partners, sincerely loved but victims still, whom the monstrous couple grinds in its passion of faithfulness to itself, supporting itself by means of its unfaithfulness to others.

Let us imagine the two lecherous lovers of Verona, possible survivors of their dramatic story, as they chose the second path. One might find arguments for such a scenario even in their own lines. But as far as Shakespeare is concerned, he seems to have wished to conform to proprieties, for once; by having them die, he saved the pure couple. He safeguarded the innocence of marriage under the shroud of death; in this text, he did not want to go to the end of the passionate night that belongs to the durable couple. Why not?

Shakespeare preserving the idea of marriage that perishes only through the fault of others? Whereas if marriage is wedded to passion, how could it last without some rehabilitation of perversion? Oh Lady Macbeth, oh the foul couples that surround Hamlet … But in that case, does it not mean the end of the beautiful dream, henceforth called 'Oedipal', that all children have: 'Your relatives perhaps, but not mine …' If everything is thus malevolent, perverse, foul, does it not mean the end of the immaculate home, of aseptic marriage – the pillar of the State? Is that not outrageous?

In 1596 Shakespeare had no need for such a subversion. Published in 1597, probably written in 1595 or 1596 when Shakespeare was about thirty, *Romeo and Juliet*, his ninth play, belongs to what has been called his second period, that of his lyrical plays and masterpieces (such as *A Midsummer Night's Dream*), and proved his first great success. Some critics, basing their argument on a reference to an earthquake in the text, date it back to 1591, and this would make it his first play. If one adopts the first hypothesis, which is generally accepted today, it would seem that Shakespeare composed this drama of lovehate exactly when he was 31–32. Young, without doubt. But a major fact of his biography appears to be more important: his son Hamnet (born in 1585) died in 1596 at age eleven. Already eleven years earlier, after the birth of the twins, Hamnet and Judith, he left his wife Anne Hathaway and settled down in [London]. *Romeo and Juliet* reaches us, against that background, as a kind of nostalgic feeling for marriage, henceforth seen as impossible, but ideally maintained in the face of a guilty sorrow caused by the loss of the son. As a youthful fervour attempting to preserve the image of two lovers whom life undertakes to separate. Such an idyllic colouring of the play doubtless betrays the playwright's youth. I might also advance the hypothesis, with no other evidence than possibly cross-checking the unconscious paths of the reader with those of the writer (text and biography), that Hamnet's death triggered within Shakespeare the nostalgia for a couple that would have been in love. In love as precisely William and Anne were not able to be, with Anne older than her husband and giving him a daughter in 1582, after six months of marriage, and twins three years later.

Against the backdrop of his own marriage made commonplace by births, branded by death, Shakespeare, the dreamer and already a relentless blasphemer of matriarchal-matrimonial power, sets up the dream of lovers scalded by the law of hatred but in themselves immortally sublime. Ideal lovers, impossible couple: promising eros and real hatred weave reality. Shakespeare seems to apologise:

hatred has come from others. Let us then think of *Romeo and Juliet*, in its idyllic tinge, as a dirge for the son's death. The father's guilt confesses in this play, along with hatred for marriage, the desire to preserve the myth of the enamoured lovers. To preserve the idealisation of the couple, ephemeral as it may be, to keep from having to enter into the hatred that dwells in marriage and pro-duces death (of the children: Romeo, Juliet, and perhaps Hamnet?). It may be the father's gift to the son's tomb. A gift from William Shakespeare to Hamnet Shakespeare. The law, full of hatred, is intact. To let the sons sleep in peace and whitewash the fathers, it is henceforth endowed with a luminous reverse – the sublime love of young outlaws.

Later, when Shakespeare's father died in 1601, the law collapsed. There then appeared, with the same similarity that linked *Romeo and Juliet* to Hamnet's death, the play *Hamlet*, related this time to the father's death. In *Hamlet*, as an echo to both the son's and the father's deaths but in antithesis to *Romeo and Juliet*, no couple can withstand the onslaught of the corrosive tongue of Shakespeare, who carried revenge for the paternal ghost against the mother, the criminal wife, to the point of making any couple appear hideous.[6] Then, in 1609, the poet's mother died, and Shakespeare published his Sonnets, which extol homosexual love for [Mr W.] H., the [Dark] Lady, William Hamnet, the son, or the father who discovered himself as son, flesh-man, woman-man, or rather a Christlike passion of the body ...[7]

But in 1596 that point had not been reached. *Romeo and Juliet* exists as a casting out of Hamnet's death, as an antidote for a failed marriage. Hamnet is dead, nevertheless sublime and untouchable lovers are needed. Nostalgia for amorous happiness? Nostalgia: *nostos*-return; *algos*-pain. A painful return to a past that is dead, however, and leads to a dead person? Accept, dear Hamnet, as a funeral wreath, the immortal image of your parents' passionate love, who, ardent lovers, might have saved you from death or, ac-cursed lovers in the manner of Romeo and Juliet, might have spared you existence. For you, Shakespeare immortalises love, but your death is the symptom, the evidence that hatred triumphs ...

'MY ONLY LOVE, MY ONLY HATE'

One often likens Romeo and Juliet as a couple to Tristan and Isolde, producing the evidence of a love thwarted by social rules;

emphasising how the couple is cursed and destroyed by Christianity, which smothers passion at the heart of marriage; seeking a revelation of the death that rules at the core of amatory jouissance. Shakespeare's text includes, with all that, an even more corrosive element, which his skill with ambiguity and the reversal of values handles with insidious magic in the very height of the most intense glorification of love. Under the guise of sex, it is hatred that prevails, and that comes out most obviously in the very first pages of the text. In the first scene, the two servants' remarks, peppered with puns and obscenities, cause the darkness of sex and inversions of all sorts to hang over this presumably pure romance. One is already prepared for Romeo's remark terming love 'a madness most discreet' (I.i.192), even saying that 'it is too rough, too rude, too boisterous, and it pricks like thorn' (I.iv.25–6). A little later it will be described by Mercutio – a baneful character who, along with Benvolio, brings about a chain of violence and whose death in the third act forces Romeo to avenge him by killing Tybalt – by means of the allegory of the fairies' midwife, Queen Mab. A gnomelike ghost, fascinating and hideous, ruler of amorous bodies, the dark, drunken, and murderous other side of loving radiance, it is Queen Mab who calls the tune with 'her whip of cricket's bone; the lash, of film' (I.iv.63).

It is Juliet, however, who finds the most intense expressions to show that this love is supported by hatred. One could possibly see in the words of this noble maiden a simple rhetorical device at once heralding a final death, or an ambiguous language clause, blending opposites, something that is operative at other moments of the play and in Shakespeare's aesthetics in general. But more deeply, what is involved is hatred at the very origin of the amorous surge. A hatred that antedates the veil of amorous idealisation. Let us note that it is a woman, Juliet, who is most immediately unconscious of it, senses it with a sleepwalker's lucidity. Thus, as early as their first meeting – while Romeo suddenly forgets Rosaline, whose love nevertheless tortured him sorely a short time before and only admits 'The more is my unrest' when he is told Juliet is the daughter of the enemy family – it is Juliet herself who states frankly, 'My only love sprung from my only hate!' (I.v.139).

Did not Romeo himself, however, go to the Capulets' feast knowing that he was going to a feast of hatred? Juliet, again: ''Tis but thy name that is my enemy' (II.ii.38). Or else, at the very height of the amatory monologue that sets in place the passion of waiting and extols the lovers' qualities ('Come, night, come, Romeo, thou day in night; ...'), Juliet continues innocently, 'come, gentle night, ... and, when he shall die, take him and cut him out in little stars, and he will make the face of heaven so fine, that all the world will be in love with night ...' (III.ii.19–24). 'When he shall die, take him and cut him out': it is as if one heard a discreet version of the Japanese *Realm of the Senses*. That feeling goes unnoticed because it is swept along by a hatred that one can look in the eye – the familial, social curse is more respectable and bearable than the unconscious hatred of the lovers for each other. The fact remains that Juliet's jouissance is often stated through the anticipation – the desire? – of Romeo's death. This, long before her drugged sleep deceives Romeo and leads him to suicide, long before she turns that death wish back upon herself at the sight of Romeo's corpse, driving herself to suicide, too: 'Methinks I see thee, now thou art below, as one dead in the bottom of a tomb' (III.v.55–6).

Such frequent evocations of death are not simply intended to state that there is no room for passion in the world of old people, and, more generally, in marriage – that love must die on the threshold of its legislation, that eros and the law are incompatible. Friar Laurence says it indeed, and this is a leftover from vulgarised Christian asceticism: 'She's not well married that lives married long, but she's best married that dies married young' (IV.v.77–8).

More deeply, more passionately, we are dealing with the intrinsic presence of hatred in amatory feeling itself. In the object relation, the relation with an other, hatred, as Freud said, is more ancient than love.[8] As soon as an *other* appears different from myself, it becomes alien, repelled, repugnant, abject – hated.[9] Even hallucinating love, as distinct from autoerotic satisfaction, as a precocious feeling of narcissistic fulfilment in which the other is not sharply separated from myself, does not otherwise come up in relation to that other until later, through the capacity for primary idealisation. But as soon as the strength of desire that is joined with love sets the integrity of the self ablaze; as soon as it breaks down its solidity through the drive-impelled torrent of passion, hatred – the primary bench mark of object relation – emerges out of repression. Eroticised according to the variants of sadomasochism, or coldly dominant in more lasting relationships that have already exhausted the delights of infidelity, as delusive as it is seductive, hatred is the keynote in the couple's passionate melody. Whether heterosexual or homosexual, the couple is the utopic wager that paradise lost can be made lasting – but perhaps it is merely desired and truly never known? – the paradise of loving understanding between the child and its parents. The child, male or female, hallucinates its merging with a nourishing-mother-and-ideal-father, in short a conglomeration that already condenses two into one. That child, the loving child, in its couple mania, tries to make two where there were three. Man or woman, when he or she aspires to be a couple, the lover goes through the mirage of being the 'husband' or 'wife' or an ideal father: that is the extent to which the idealised object of love dons the finery of that 'father of individual prehistory' Freud talked about, the one who absorbs those delightful primary identifications.[10] In such a coupling with the ideal, shored up by a happy, domesticated fatherhood, man becomes feminised; is there anything more androgynous, or even feminine, than the adolescent madly in love with an adolescent of the opposite sex? One soon notices, however, in the last instance (that is, if the couple truly becomes one, if it lasts), that each of the protagonists, he and she, has married, through the other, his or her mother.

THE MOTHER – PEDESTAL OF THE COUPLE

The man then finds a harbour of narcissistic satisfaction for the eternal child he has succeeded in remaining: an exquisite normalisation of regression. The woman calms down temporarily within the restoring support furnished by the mother-husband. This brings about, in a first stage, feminine homosexuality, which has thus become preconscious and seeks satisfaction as such; unless it causes depression as a result of finding herself dispossessed, by a penis-bearing being, of the nourishing values yet phantasmatically attributed to an inaccessible mother. Such a wife, happy because she found a mother in her husband, will then require sound phallic satisfactions, through the intermediary of children or of reiterated social rewards, so that the equilibrium of the couple might continue to prevail.

With man as with woman, meeting up with the partner's mother means finding the pedestal of the couple, thereby perpetuating it. But that life-giving figure paradoxically induces death – unavailingly checked by means of phallic reinforcements. Mother, mortal ... Why?

'The earth that's nature's mother is her tomb; what is her burying grave, that is her womb' (II.iii.9–10), Friar Laurence sententiously declares. The jubilatory vanishing of identity at the heart of a nostalgic love for a maternal embrace is nevertheless felt by the adult as a loss, even as a mortal danger. The defence mechanisms then react, kneaded by drives and by egotic and superegotic hatred, in order to give back shape, identity, and existence to the *same* swallowed up in the *other*. The alternating love / hatred braids passion's tangle, and its eternal return never produces a 'better' couple than the sadomasochistic one. Better, because it feeds on its internal possibility for libidinal charging and discharging, and this supposes that each partner assumes sexual ambivalence. Does this mean androgynism? Not exactly. For man's 'feminine' is not woman's 'feminine', and the woman's 'masculine' is not the man's 'masculine'. The asymmetrical bond of the two sexes with the phallus, which determines their sexual character, causes them to be four who want to be two within the couple, and thus set the insoluble harmonisation of the uneven. To make a couple out of the child–father–mother triad where the third party has become subject only because excluded. Love-hatred is the squaring of that imaginary circle that ideal love should be if *I* could be father-mother-and-myself united in a Whole.

Juliet, so cold with her mother, sends back, mirrorlike, to her progenitress the icy distance that Lady Capulet maintains with her daughter. Juliet imagining her lover dead; Juliet rebelling against the Nurse, an apparently good mother, when the latter does an about-face and urges her to forget Romeo; Juliet stabbing herself with Romeo's dagger. One should note that 'the hopeful lady of [her father's] earth' (as Capulet himself says, I.ii.15), who provokes her father to a wrath that is too passionate to be innocent when she refuses the man he has chosen to be her husband (III.v), is possessed by refusal and a presence of mind that must be called phallic, marking a certain violence, a possible aversion. 'My only love sprung from my only hate!'

It is Friar Laurence, moreover, who points to the femininity of Romeo, whose warm masculine friendships, doubtless common at the time, nevertheless reveal that such friendships are built upon the comparison, the commensuration, with the (sexual) power of others, and at best with that of the enemies (privileged objects of passion). For this reason, it is the passional excitement of men belonging to inimical families that leads Romeo to present himself to his first love, Rosaline, to discover the second, Juliet, before penetrating Tybalt and Paris with his sword. It will be noted that Tybalt, the cousin, is the substitute of Capulet, the father, just like

Paris, the husband chosen by the same father. Likewise, the ease
with which Romeo switches from Rosaline to Juliet may be explained because they both proceed from the same source of hatred,
the Capulet family. But the learned priest reveals the other side of
this coin, so aggressive and vengeful in its loving passion – a certain
'femininity' in Romeo. 'Art thou a man? Thy form cries out thou
art; thy tears are womanish; thy wild acts [the murder of Tybalt]
denote the unreasonable fury of a beast ... But, like a misbehaved
and sullen wench, thou pout'st upon thy fortune and thy love: take
heed, take heed' (III.iii.109–11, 143–5).
[...]

THE SLEEP OF LOVERS

Even though the death of the Verona lovers is beyond remedy,
the spectator has the feeling that it is only sleep. In the denial
that makes us dream of the two corpses as being mere sleepers it
is perhaps our thirst for love – magical challenge to death – that
speaks out. The risky game with the sleeping drug in the very
events of the play already suggests such a confusion.
Nevertheless, the final image of the motionless couple perhaps
leads us to the promised land constituted by the sleep of lovers.
Indeed, the erotic satisfaction of desires is not the soothing
primary identification, and in that sense 'love confiscates narcissism'.[11] Sleep is then both a restoration of narcissism, exhausted
through desire, and a protective shield that allows amatory representation to take shape. Without the representation of the lovers'
union, sleeping in each other's arms, erotic expenditure is a race
toward death. The sleep of lovers, moreover, merely refills a stock
of imaginative energy that is ready, at the wakening, for new ex-
penditures, new caresses, under the sway of the senses ... Romeo
and Juliet, in their sleeping death, are, like our sleep together
when we are in love, a stock of fusional images that assuage
erotic frenzy for a while before stimulating it again ...

The transference situation and analytical discourse also provide
us with a certain amorous, imaginary stock for our erotic and social
dramas. But without allowing us to fall asleep, analysis sets out to
be the lucid wakening of lovers ...

From Julia Kristeva, *Tales of Love* (New York, 1987) pp. 209–25,
233.

NOTES

[Julia Kristeva illustrates the psychoanalytical approach described in the Introduction to this collection. The kind of love depicted in the play is 'transgression love, outlaw love' which is necessarily clandestine and oppositional. It depends on, in some sense, breaking laws. One example would be adultery. In the instance of *Romeo and Juliet* the law is represented by families, not simply in terms of the feud between parents but more generally they combine as a patriarchal constraint which operates, according to Freud, like the controlling and repressive Superego in the human mind. The intensity of their love actually depends on 'being within a hairsbreadth of punishment', and requires the opposition of a third party. 'Take away the third party and the whole construct often crumbles, lacking a cause for desire, after having lost some of its passional tinge'. In the compression of time, love becomes inextricably connected with death; 'death is amorous' says Romeo in the crypt. This connection becomes a positive desire to murder the love-object, as Juliet desires to break up Romeo's body, to 'cut him out in little stars' – Kristeva suggests that 'feminine desire is perhaps more closely umbilicated with death … it is through the symbolic murder of her own mother that a woman turns herself into a mother'. In fact, the mother becomes 'pedestal of the couple' in the process of mutual narcissism which expresses the desire of lovers to remain eternal children and return to the womb: 'The earth that's nature's mother is her tomb; what is her burying grave, that is her womb', as Friar Laurence says. In her challenging reading, Kristeva reiterates that these meanings are largely 'unconscious' in their expression and carried through inadvertent imagery, but that they are no less powerfully present in the play's full vision for that. Quotations are from the Arden edition, *Romeo and Juliet* (London, 1979). Ed.]

1. As for Romeo, he suspects that the Name is obscene, like an obscene part of the body, and consequently (we may say it, but he cannot) the name is the source of desire: 'In what vile part of this anatomy / Doth my name lodge? tell me, that I may sack / The hateful mansion' (III.iii.105–7).

2. See the Arden Edition of the Works of Shakespeare, *Romeo and Juliet*, ed. Brian Gibbons (London, 1979).

3. Ibid., p. 41.

4. Perhaps one should also mention the nurse's speech, the good mother, who maintains her trust in time and takes pleasure in evoking Juliet's birth, childhood, and destiny, as well as earthquakes that are casually, innocently suggested …

5. 'It lies not in our power to love or hate, / For will in us is over-rul'd by fate' – Christopher Marlowe, *Hero and Leander*, I, 167–8.

6. See A. Green, *Hamlet et Hamlet* (Paris, 1982) and particularly his thesis, which holds that Polonius' children are the King's illegitimate children; it would have been to avenge that unfaithfulness that the Queen killed the father-King and married his brother. A marriage of betrayal and hatred, that generalised oedipal perspective that Hamlet may have gained over his destiny forces the primal science itself into the heart of his psychic experience. As a super-representable, a primal spectacle, a prime mover of the play that extols the representation of representation.

7. See Philippe Sollers, *Femmes* (Paris, 1983), pp. 467–9, where he suggests that interpretation of Shakespeare's 'homosexuality'.

8. See 'Drives [instincts] and their vicissitudes', in *Papers on Metapsychology* (1915). Quotations from Freud are taken from the *Standard Edition of the Complete Psychological Works of Sigmund Freud*, 24 vols, James Strachey trs and ed. (London, 1953–74).

9. In that connection, see Julia Kristeva, *Powers of Horror* (New York, 1982).

10. *Three Essays on the Theory of Sexuality*.

11. See *Eros et Antéros*, pp. 195ff.

4

The Ideology of Romantic Love: The Case of *Romeo and Juliet*

DYMPNA C. CALLAGHAN

'To this end ... is this tragicall matter written, to describe unto thee a couple of unfortunate lovers, thralling themselves to un-honest desire, neglecting the authority and advice of parents and friends ...'[1] Thus Arthur Brooke defines the ideological project of his poem, *The Tragical History of Romeous and Juliet* (1562), which was to become Shakespeare's primary source for *Romeo and Juliet*. The lovers' 'unhonest desire' was always a compelling feature of the story, but in Shakespeare's version the fate of that desire is presented as profound injustice as much as proper punishment.[2] For Brooke's rendition of the story bears a moral aversion to what Shakespeare's tragedy accomplishes in producing for posterity the lovers' desire as at once transgressive ('unhonest') and as a new orthodoxy (tragically legitimated). It is precisely this ambivalence that is at the heart of the play's appeal as one of the pre-eminent cultural documents of love in the West.

Romeo and Juliet was written at the historical moment when the ideologies and institutions of desire – romantic love and the family, which are now for us completely naturalised – were being negotiated. Indeed, the play consolidates a certain formation of desiring subjectivity attendant upon Protestant and especially Puritan ideologies of marriage and the family required by, or least very conductive to the emergent economic formation of, capitalism.[3]

The goal of this essay is to examine the role of *Romeo and Juliet* in the cultural construction of desire. Desire – variously generated, suppressed, unleashed, and constrained – is particularly significant for feminist cultural studies because in its most common formulation as transhistorical romantic love it is one of the most efficient and irresistible interpellations of the female subject, securing her complicity in apparently unchangeable structures of oppression, particularly compulsory heterosexuality and bourgeois marriage.

It would be wrong to suggest that romantic love is devoid of positive and even liberatory dimensions. As Denis de Rougement has shown in *Love in the Western World*, its advent in the twelfth century represents something of an improvement on earlier organisations of desire. It seems likely, however, that the extra-marital love that flourished among the feudal aristocracy was considerably less restrictive for women (though not actively empowering) than was the marital version that emerged with early capitalism. Feudal romantic love was generally constructed as the unrequited passion of a male subject leading ultimately to his own spiritual self-transcendence, as opposed to the emergent construction of romantic love as mutual heterosexual desire leading to a consummation in marriage, a union of both body and spirit. One of its crucial features, a signal of its effectiveness, is that the ideology of romantic love centres from the Renaissance onward on women's subjective experience. Yet this focus serves to control and delimit intimate experience rather than to allow the fullest possible expression of female desire. It is also true that when we are in its throes, romantic love is a classic instance of false consciousness. Among its oppressive effects, the dominant ideology of (heterosexual, monogamous) romantic love relegates homosexuality to the sphere of deviance, secures women's submission to the asymmetrical distribution of power between men and women, and bolsters individualism by positing sexual love as the expression of authentic identity. Men are not, of course, immune to these effects, but they are more likely than women to derive benefit from them. My analysis of this phenomenon proceeds first by examining the ideological function of *Romeo and Juliet* in the Renaissance and in the present, and then moves on to critique the discourses (those of psychoanalysis and history) which should enable the historicisation of desire in Renaissance studies, but which in certain key respects actually impede it. Here, my approach is necessarily and deliberately synoptic because I endeavour to place desire in terms of the determinate, global conceptual categories of Marxism. The final sections of the essay address the complex operations of desire within the play itself.

REPRODUCING THE IDEOLOGY OF ROMANTIC LOVE

Shakespeare's text has been used to perpetuate the dominant ideology of romantic love, and its initial ideological function has intensified since its first performance. The play enacts an ideological propensity to posit desire as transhistorical. For what is extraordinary about the version of familial and personal relations – of desire and identity and their relation to power – endorsed by *Romeo and Juliet* is that they are in our own time so fully naturalised as to seem universal. Feminist psychoanalytic critic Julia Kristeva writes: 'Young people throughout the entire world, whatever their race, religion, or social status, identify with the adolescents of Verona ...'[4] According to Kristeva and countless Shakespeareans, the play constitutes a universal legend of love representing elemental psychic forces of desire and frustration purportedly characteristic of the human condition in every age and culture.[5]

The iteration of a particular configuration of desire does not end, therefore, in 1595 when the first performance puts it in place, but rather is a phenomenon that has been perpetuated, indeed universalised, by subsequent critical and theatrical reproductions of the play.[6] As Joseph Porter points out, *Romeo and Juliet* 'has become far more canonical a story of heterosexual love than it was when it came to Shakespeare's hand'.[7] Consider, for example, that in its Elizabethan production, Romeo and Juliet were portrayed not by an actor and actress but by a suitably feminine-featured male performer and a slightly more rugged youth, and that the erotic homology produced by this situation was compounded by the presence of the profoundly homoerotic Mercutio. The play's initial ideological project – the valorisation of romantic love between the young couple – thus becomes consolidated and intensified with subsequent re-narrations. Indeed, the affective power of the story and of romantic love itself – its 'dateless passion'[8] – occurs not in spite of its repetition but rather depends precisely on reiteration.

The narrative mechanisms of the text itself tend towards self-replication. Shakespeare's play perpetuates an already well-known tale, and Act V produces 'closure' on desire only by opening up the possibility of endless retellings of the story – displacing the lovers' desire onto a perpetual narrative of love.[9] The lover's story is recapitulated by the prologue, by the lovers, and by the Friar. The Prince offers the concluding incitement to 'more talk': 'never was a story of more woe / Than this of Juliet and her Romeo' (V.iii.307; 309–10). The play's ending thus constitutes a means of monumentalising (quite literally in the golden statues of the lovers) and thereby reproducing *ad infinitum*, 'whiles Verona by that name is known' (V.iii.300), the ideological imperatives of the lovers' most poignant erotic moments. Crucially, then, the social effectivity of the ideology of romantic love is characterised fundamentally by its capacity for self-replication. Thus, the narrative imperative of *Romeo and Juliet* to propagate the desire with which it is inscribed constitutes a resistance to historicisation that has been extended by criticism's production of the play as universal love story. In this respect, the mimetic dynamic curiously mirrors the capitalist mode of production, whose goal is not immediate use but accumulated and multiplied future production.[10] The play's inclination towards replication and multiplication is a manoeuvre that propagates a version of erotic love which is consonant with the needs of an emergent social order.

Romeo and Juliet, then, marks the inauguration of a particular form of sexual desire produced in accordance with the specific historical requirements of patriarchy's shifting modality. As Eli Zaretsky argues in his pathbreaking study *Capitalism, the Family, and Personal Life*, 'courtly love anticipated ideals of love and individualism that the bourgeois located within the family and that were generalised and transformed in the course of capitalist development'.[11] In the early modern teleology of desire, the family, newly emphasised as the focus of political, social, legal, and economic organisation becomes the social destination of desire.[12] Thus, *Romeo and Juliet* both instantiates the ideology of romantic love as universal, timeless and unchanging and yet is marked by its own historical specificity. The degree to which *Romeo and Juliet* appears to constitute the transcription of the universal features of the experience of love indicates its profoundly 'ideological' nature; that is to say, the play's ideological project has become the dominant ideology of desire. In this way, the text both positions itself within and reproduces the hegemonic. *Romeo and Juliet* consolidates the ideology of romantic love and the correlative crystallisation of the modern nuclear family. [...]

DESIRE AND THE POSTMODERN PRESENT

Renaissance literary studies, in contrast to social history, has been less impervious to postmodern interrogations of history as an epistemological configuration – that is, the discursive practices, rhetorical devices, and narrative strategies through which historical knowledge is constituted.[13] Postmodern interrogations of history are diametrically opposed to the verities of traditional historiography, especially the belief that 'historical facts are prior to and independent of interpretation'.[14] This cognitive revolution may be characterised as the recognition that history is an epistemological category, even an anachronism relying upon causality and teleology and the exclusion of 'marginal' populations, and that history no longer functions as a simple container for immutable essences with their superficial temporal and cultural variations.[15] As Alice Jardine has pointed out, 'even history – that most encompassing of master narratives, the one to which we in the West have always been able to turn as a last resort – becomes problematic in and of itself (it becomes historicisable) and turns back upon itself'.[16] Significantly, the postmodern crisis of history can be seen in Renaissance studies in its engagement with psychoanalysis. I will offer two symptomatic and important examples of this phenomenon rather than an exhaustive survey of it.

In *Fashioning Femininity*, Karen Newman argues that the details of English witchcraft practice may be 'mere incidentals' for social historians, but for her they 'adumbrate a peculiar narrative of motherhood and the unconscious'.[17] Further, she defends the use of psychoanalysis, which 'need not inevitably make ahistorical claims about human development that preclude historical analysis' (p. 62), on the Derridean grounds that a text's context is limitless, there is no ground, no centre: 'there are only contexts' (p. 65). Nonetheless, Newman's attempt to make psychoanalysis and history compatible rests on deconstructive undecidability: 'the object of sexuality is socially and ideologically produced in a given culture', the 'unfixed', and 'denaturalised' 'precarious' result of historical evolution (p. 63). While this remains a sophisticated interrogation of the interrelation between the two categories, it does not explain why denaturalising and unfixing in and of themselves help us historicise. For instance the trajectory of women in patriarchal history, although not inevitable, presents a compulsively repetitive narrative rather than an undecidable one. The endless unfixings Newman proposes, while they certainly free her compelling readings from the limitations of traditional historical methods as well as from essentially allegorical, mechanical applications of psychoanalysis to the literary text, obscure the determinate positions of the oppressed. Newman's emphasis is not the material oppression of women, but the profoundly poststructuralist 'threat posed through representation' dangerously unmoored from material conditions (p. 69). Crucial though this strategy is, it remains difficult to see how Newman's use of psychoanalysis, apart from the mere assertion of historicism, differs substantially from those she critiques.

Stephen Greenblatt's brilliant and pathbreaking 1986 essay, 'Psychoanalysis and Renaissance culture', argues for a complex rather than a categorical disjunction between the early modern period and the post-psychoanalytic moment. He suggests we can discern in the early modern era the conditions which gave rise to the development of psychoanalysis.[18] That is, the Renaissance helped 'fashion the historical mode of selfhood that psychoanalysis has tried to universalise into the very form of the human condition' (p. 216). For Greenblatt, '[p]sychoanalysis is ... less the privileged explanatory key than the distant and distorted consequence of this cultural nexus' (p. 216). Renaissance subjectivity, then becomes 'more an historical condition that enables the development of psychoanalysis than a psychic condition that psychoanalysis itself can adequately explain' (p. 221).

What is at stake in Greenblatt's critique, however, is not psychoanalysis itself, which it soon becomes clear he finds wholly inadequate for a truly historical project – 'the universalist claims of psychoanalysis are unruffled by the indifference of the past to its categories' (p. 215) – but rather the postmodern crisis of history in which there is no 'solid and single truth, or (in more subtle versions) interesting variants on the central and irreducible universal narrative, the timeless master myth' (p. 217). There are only *'histories,* – multiple, complex, refractory stories' (p. 217). While this position does threaten the coherence of liberal, empiricist history, and while these multiple histories do not claim to be value-neutral, Greenblatt's invocation of multiplicity is, nonetheless, almost identical with the value-neutral relativism he eschews. His position is a poststructuralist one, of undecidable (undecided) political and logical investment: 'the intimations of an obscure link between ... distant events and the way we are' (p. 217). History again subsumes psychoanalysis, and the account of our desires, 'the way we are', becomes almost mysteriously unknowable.

The demise of history as *grand récit*, replaced by a sophisticated if diffuse understanding of 'a network of lived and narrated stories, practices, strategies, representations, fantasies, negotiations, and exchanges that, along with the surviving aural, tactile, and visual traces, fashion our experience of the past, of others, and of ourselves' (p. 218) may finally share the ideological effects of the liberal model it purports to replace.[19] In its postmodern and new historicist renovation, history has more texture, 'complexity' and aesthetic appeal, but it does not offer a conceptual frame possessed of expanded powers of explanation. Specifically, it evades the motivating dynamic of historical contestation, the operations whereby all representations are not equal; some are repressed and deleted beyond any resuscitation or reinstatement that might be effected by new historicist methods.[20]

In contrast, a materialist history of desire, in this case one which takes *Romeo and Juliet* as its literary object, entails an insistence on the holistic claims of Marxist historical methods, which (very often) collide head on with the micro-analyses of essentialist social historians. Indeed, an insistence on certain global conceptual categories distinguishes materialist analysis from a local, purely textual one. For historical materialism is not about amassing historical detail; it is about history as structured material conflict.

The play produces one version of desire as paramount among the range of those it negotiates, and in doing so participates in the cultural production of desire required by the rise of absolutism, the centralisation of the state, and the advent of capitalism. These developments, while not linear and continuous historical developments, constitute the advent of modernity, and it is surely only the burden of traditional critical practice that has contrived to place them as either remote from or irrelevant to the textual details of Renaissance drama.[21] The hegemonic ideology of romantic love is crucially related to some of the definitive conditions of nascent modernity: the construction within the domestic sphere of the realm of the personal, an increased emphasis on the nucleated unit rather than the extended clan, the reinforcement of patriarchy in the household and in the absolutist state, and the advent of absolute private property in land.[22] The point here is not to concentrate on the conjunctural level (that is, to draw extensive analogies between the text and the broad shift from one form of economic organisation to another) but on the prior conceptual one (antecedent in the mediation between chains of intelligibilities). That is, *Romeo and*

Juliet does not exemplify the actual, empirical, social circumstances of its production, but rather participates and intervenes in the ideological / historical conditions of its own making.

PATRIARCHAL LAW AND THE CENTRALISATION OF THE STATE

The move from the family allegiances associated with feudalism to those identified with centralisation of the state constitutes the overarching narrative of *Romeo and Juliet*. That is, the *shifting configurations* of patriarchal law and the changing formations of desire which attend it comprise the structure and substance of Shakespeare's text.[23] In this sense, the play articulates a crisis in patriarchy itself – specifically the transference of power from the feuding fathers to the Prince so that sexual desire in the form presented here produces the required subjectivities and harnesses them for the state above all other possible levels of allegiance. Desire needs to be refigured in order to manage the contradiction produced by the way the ideology of absolutism employed familial rhetoric in order to maintain feudal domination and exploitation despite the advent of a commodity economy.[24] As a result, the mode of desire disapproved of in the old order becomes valorised in the new one. However, that the ideological project of *Romeo and Juliet* is now completely coincident with the dominant ideology of desire does not mean that the play circulates only one discourse of desire. Rather, multiple and contradictory discourses of the desire are negotiated in the isolation and idealisation of romantic heterosexual love.

That desire seems malleable, something that can be reordered, is apparent, in Mercutio's Queen Mab speech, which charts the various courses a disembodied libido can take, from the sexual desires of women – kisses of ladies to the unseemly lust of maids – to the greed and blood-lust of men:

> And in this state she gallops night by night
> Through lovers' brains, and then they dream of love;
> O'er courtiers' knees that dream on cur'sies straight
> O'er lawyers' fingers, who straight dream on fees;
> O'er ladies' lips, who straight on blisters dream,
> Which oft the angry Mab with kisses plagues,
> Because their breath with sweetmeats tainted are ...
> Sometime she driveth o'er a soldier's neck,

And then dreams he of cutting foreign throats,
Of breaches, ambuscadoes, Spanish blades ...
This is the hag, when maids lie on their backs,
That presses them and makes them first to bear,
Making them women of good carriage
                                                (I.iv.70–94)

Although a force penetrating the unconscious of the dreamer from outside, desire is already socially scripted here (ladies and maids do not dream of cutting soldiers' throats); it is not 'free'. (There is no desire hovering in some metaphysical space prior to its social production.) Desire is simultaneously controlled and aberrant, chaotic – its objective is either death or reproduction: 'For this drivelling love is like a great natural that runs lolling up and down to hide his bauble in a hole' (II.iv.91–3). In Mercutio's comic teleology, desire is directed, driven, and yet indiscriminate about its sexual object – a 'drive' in the psychoanalytic sense.

That it is Mercutio who articulates the plasticity of desire is particularly significant.[25] His cynicism, as well as his sexual predilection for men and his kinship with the Prince rather than the warring feudal houses, enables him to articulate the social construction of desire in which his companions are too fully invested. No maidens weep for Mercutio when he is killed. Rather, Escalus and Romeo are the characters who bear the loss of the master of the phallic pun. When Escalus comments on the lovers' tragedy, he also refers to his private grief for 'a brace of kinsmen', of whom Mercutio is the one we know by name (V.iii.295). As absolutist monarch, Escalus seems to retain homoeroticism among his kin group. If this notion seems implausible to us, it is probably because, as Bruce Smith points out, we think of social sites of sexual experience as exclusively private and of sexuality in terms of 'acts' rather than as relational dynamics:

> For us, the most significant loci of sexuality are private life and the family. It was during the sixteenth and seventeenth centuries that sexuality first came to be seen as a private concern, but sexuality was located even more solidly within social institutions that strike us today as remote or inappropriate.
>
> (p.21)

The male power structure in general was indeed itself a force which generated male homoerotic desire, and with the rise of absolutism 'the explicit disparities in power that animated homosexual desire in early modern England' (Smith, p.23) would have been focused with increasing intensity on the figure of the monarch himself. It is the Prince who monopolises male bonding, aggression, and homo-erotic desire.[26]

Yet Escalus also attempts to direct the multiple possible modes of desire in socially appropriate, explicitly heterosexual ways. Indeed, in a number of important respects it is Prince Escalus who becomes the play's pivotal figure rather than the tragic couple. Shakespeare imposes the ordering principle embodied in Escalus on Brooke's rambling structure at the play's opening, closing, and centre so that the strong literary design is coincident with the authority he wields in turbulent Verona. In addition, in Shakespeare's symbolic redistri-bution of the city's property, Escalus is accorded a castle in Freetown, which belongs to Capulet in Brooke and Painter, and to which he summons Montague and Capulet from their more humble merchants' homes after the first disturbance of the peace.[27]

More importantly, Escalus intervenes in the feud with absolute power of life and death. Even that intervention, however, is not im-mediately effective because he must struggle to become the pre-eminent patriarchal power in Verona. The Law of the Father in the psychoanalytic framework is constituted by precisely the power of intervention – that which disrupts in the dyad of mother and child, as the symbolic representative of culture. Although Escalus is essen-tially intervening between fathers, he nonetheless takes the place of the father in relation to the infantile feuding, feudal fathers who resist the exogamous relationship between their offspring, objecting to their quarrel as profane, bestial, and 'cankered' (I.i.82–95). As Coppélia Kahn points out, Prince Escalus 'embodies the law', and in relation to him it is 'Montague and Capulet who are childishly refractory' (p. 172):

> Rebellious subjects, enemies to peace,
> Profaners of this neighbour-stained steel –
> Will they not hear? What ho! You men, you beasts!
> That quench the fire of your pernicious rage
> With purple fountains issuing from your veins,
> On pain of torture from those bloody hands
> Throw your mistempered weapons to the ground
> And hear the sentence of your moved prince.
> (I.i.81–8)

Escalus strives to control the flow of blood, a metonym of lineage, class, and succession – the very essence of the patriarchal imperative. In so doing, the dangers of consanguinity are displaced onto the feuding feudal family:

> Two households, both alike in dignity,
> In fair Verona, where we lay our scene,
> From ancient grudge break to new mutiny,
> Where civil blood makes civil hands unclean.
> From forth the fatal loins of these two foes
> A pair of star-cross'd lovers take their life.
> (Prologue, 1–6)

In this passage, the symmetry between the houses suggests an ominous familial resemblance. The ancient blood they share is the bloodshed of enmity. They are star-crossed by a common inheritance – the brutal engagement that has in enmity mangled and enmeshed the blood and loins of their houses so that, as Kay Stockholder has argued, their relationship verges precariously on the incestuous:

> The image of 'fatal loins' suggests a kind of copulation in hatred between the feuding families ... It suggests that they die not because they are children of warring families, but rather that their feuding parents are the circumstances of their meeting, their loving, and their death. The same magnetism that brings the two families together in order to fight also brings the two young people together in order to love and die.[28]

Thus for Stockholder the lovers' marriage merely continues the feud. Although this is certainly the case in Bandello's prior version of the story where Romeo and Juliet's love ignited a well-nigh extinct enmity, it is not the case in Shakespeare where the lovers mark the end of incest and the beginning of exogamy, the emergent ideology of the family. We see this, for example, in Juliet's ironic articulation of the transfer of her desire from kin to foe upon Tybalt's death: 'To wreak the love I bore my cousin / Upon his body that hath slaughtered him!' (III.v.101–2). The Prince's prohibition against the feud is, then, synonymous with a prohibition against endogamy – 'the sentence of your moved prince' (I.i.88) – and it is a prohibition with which Romeo and Juliet almost instinctively comply.[29]

In contrast to the civil and civilising intervention of the Prince, the atrophied, macerated power of the belligerent secular fathers is rendered in comic fashion in the brawl scene of Act I, where they appear in ridiculous *déshabillé*:

> (*Enter old Capulet in his gown, and his Wife.*)
> **Capulet**   What noise is this? Give me my long sword ho!
> **Lady Capulet**   A crutch, a crutch! Why call you for a sword?
> **Capulet**   My sword, I say! Old Montague is come,
>   And flourishes his blade in spite of me.
> (*Enter old Montague and his Wife.*)
> **Montague**   Thou villain Capulet! – Hold me not; let me go.
> **Lady Montague**   Thou shalt not stir one foot to seek a foe.
>   (I.i.75–80)

It is the women here who deflate the exaggerated phallic proportions of their husbands, whose long swords refer us back to Sampson and Gregory's 'comic' meditations on erection and rape that began the affray. Lady Montague's command prefaces the Prince's admonition that the battle end on pain of death. In her mouth the injunction is an instance of comic inversion of authority, and it serves both to align her with the will of the Prince, as opposed to the will of her husband, and to show that her husband cannot rule even his own wife.

Old Capulet's power is equally diminished. While well able to rail at his daughter he cannot control the precocious Tybalt, whose libido is violently unleashed upon the world:

> The fiery Tybalt, with his sword prepar'd;
> Which, as he breath'd defiance to my ears,
> He swung about his head cutting the winds,
> Who, nothing hurt withal, hissed him in scorn.
>   (I.i.109–12)

There is a marked contrast here with the manageable masculinity of Romeo, with whom Tybalt seeks mortal engagement at the Capulet festivities, who is 'so secret and so close, / So far from sounding' (I.i.149–50). Unlike Romeo, Tybalt refuses to take his proper place in the hierarchy of male authority:

> **Capulet**   He shall be endured.
>   What, goodman boy? I say he shall. Go to!
>   Am I the master here, or you? Go to!

You'll not endure him! God shall mend my soul,
You'll make a mutiny among my guests!
You will set cock-a-hoop! You'll be the man!
(I.v.76–81)

Capulet derides Tybalt with the diminutives 'saucy boy' and
'princox', which depredate Tybalt's phallic pretensions to 'set cock-
a-hoop' (I.v. 81–6). The inappropriate phallic competition here is
not resolved but, like Freud's account of the child's submission to
the Law of the Father, is deferred with a view to later satisfaction:

Patience perforce with wilful choler meeting
Makes my flesh tremble in their different greeting.
I will withdraw, but this intrusion shall,
Now seeming sweet, convert to bitt'rest gall.
(I.v.89–92)

Tybalt's trembling flesh resembles the agitated state of *coitus inter-
ruptus* in the language of his withdrawal and the visitors' intrusion;
his erotic object is a highly sexualised violence.

Capulet's intervention clearly lacks decisive power. Nonetheless,
no matter how diminished their authority the presence of the
fathers of both Church and household is what threatens the power
of the Prince. The benign and dangerously ineffectual Friar
Lawrence must become abject before Escalus's castrating power,
finally submitting himself 'Unto the rigour of severest law'
(V.iii.269) in order that Prince Escalus appropriate the castrating
capacity which constitutes the Law of the Father.

The consolidation of Escalus's power is evident in the play's conclusion when the warring fathers make a belated public solemnisa-
tion of the marriage contract:

Capulet O brother Montague, give me thy hand.
This is my daughter's jointure, for no more
Can I demand.
(V.iii.296–8)

The end of enmity is contingent upon the feuding fathers' submission to the Prince:

Prince Capulet! Montague!
See what a scourge is laid upon your hate,
That heaven finds means to kill your joys with love.

> And I for winking at your discords too,
> Have lost a brace of kinsmen. All are punish'd.
> (V.iii.291–5)

The result of this shift in power is 'glooming peace' and its price has been the sacrifice of the fathers' children (V.iii.305).

A crucial dimension of Escalus's appropriation of the power of the secular and religious fathers, as we noted at the outset, is the control over the narrative of the love tragedy. It is Romeo's letter to his father that becomes, amid a series of recapitulations of the play's tragic matter, the version of events authorised by the Prince for further dissemination:

> **Balthasar** I brought my master news of Juliet's death;
> And then in post he came from Mantua
> To this same place, to this same monument.
> This letter he early bid me give his father,
> And threat'ned me with death, going in the vault,
> If I departed not and left him there.
> **Prince** Give me the letter. I will look on it ...
> This letter doth make good the friar's words,
> The course of love, the tidings of her death ...
> (V.iii.272–87ff)

This missive, like the Friar's letter to Romeo, does not reach its intended destination, but instead is confiscated by the Prince who symbolically absorbs the power of Romeo's father – 'I will look on it' – even though the mourning Montague, its intended recipient, is himself fully available to peruse it. In taking the role of coordinator and interpreter of the various renditions of the tragic events in the play's coda (the Friar's, Balthasar's), the Prince consolidates his power over the errant feudal forces that have previously sought to dissipate it. This monopoly on interpretation is appropriate given Romeo's earlier alignment with the Prince's peace, under whose auspices he made the fatal intervention that cost Mercutio his life, 'the Prince expressly hath / Forbid this bandying in Verona streets' (III.i.88–9). What the Prince expropriates in taking up Romeo's letter is his legacy to the world. The letter serves as a symbolic substitute for the 'name' he would have passed on to posterity had he survived to produce progeny with Juliet. In this sense, his letter resonates with the play's earlier concern with the politics of naming (II.iv.39–40). The issue of Romeo's name stands in direct relation to his tragic struggle to articulate an identity distinct from the feudal one he wished to revoke. It is this version of identity – defined in terms of interiority and individual autonomy – and desire, disarticulated from the animosities of the feud (Romeo but not a Montague, so to speak), that the play unambiguously validates. For it is the identity required by what the tragic couple represent, namely, the tragic inauguration of a romantic love validated by marriage.

INSTITUTIONALISING 'UNCONSTRAINED' LOVE: THE RISE OF THE NUCLEAR FAMILY

As I have argued, *Romeo and Juliet* makes its cultural intervention at a moment when the ideology of love and marriage and the organisation of desire required to sustain it is undergoing change. In its articulation by Protestant (mainly Puritan) churchmen, the paradigm of marriage was profoundly imbued with idealism, stressing less the evils of voracious female sexuality, as earlier writings had done, and more the benefits of pliant femininity.[30] The production of female desire is the mechanism whereby female subjectivities were recruited to changing understandings of marriage and society. The Puritan doctrine of marriage requires nothing less than that women are endowed with desiring subjectivity, which can then be actively solicited and controlled by the social order. The crude sexual and economic exchange of enforced marriage is displaced by the concept of freely circulating love (especially freedom of choice about one's marriage partner) and wealth. Thus, despite the contradictions entailed in the Protestant articulation of domestic harmony, namely, the superiority of the husband versus the 'equality' of his wife who is both helpmate and subject, and the endeavour to bolster the often competing power of *both* husbands and fathers, romantic marriage is inscribed with a displaced utopianism. At the ideological level at least, buttressed by lyric and aesthetic convention, marriage has not yet disintegrated into the more mundane bourgeois monogamy described by Kristeva as 'the banal, humdrum, lacklustre lassitude of a tired and cynical collusion: that is the normal marriage'.[31]

In *Romeo and Juliet*, we see the idealisation of desire situated within lyrical and tragic aesthetic conventions which distance the play from the practical tone of the marriage treatises whose ideological project it shares. While the lovers are thwarted by external forces, their frustration is of an entirely different order from that of

Romeo's unrequited love for Rosaline. Romeo and Juliet's love at least entails physical consummation after a very brief courtship in which Juliet has been surprisingly forthright about her desires:

> but farewell, compliment!
> Dost thou love me? I know thou wilt say 'Ay',
> And I will take thy word; yet, if thou swear'st,
> Thou mayest prove false: at lovers' perjuries
> They say, Jove laughs. O gentle Romeo,
> If thou dost love, pronounce it faithfully.
> Or, if thou thinkest I am too quickly won,
> I'll frown and be perverse, and say thee nay,
> So thou wilt woo, but else not for the world.
> In truth, fair Montague, I am too fond,
> And therefore thou mayest think my behaviour light,
> But trust me, gentleman, I'll prove more true
> Than those that have [more] coying to be strange.
> (II.ii.89–101)

While there are traces of Catholic reticence about sexual desire in the late sixteenth-century drama,[32] in *Romeo and Juliet*, the symbolic systems of Catholicism – pilgrimage, the palmer's kiss, veneration of saints, and the sacrament of confession – are displaced onto the rites of specifically sexual love. In the above passage, Juliet refuses to engage further in these elaborate, ritualised negotiations and exchanges of erotic power that constitute courtship. This is attributable to the fact that the play is not about power within the couple – this is completely idealised – but about the power relation between the amorous couple and the outside world. The lovers' free choice of each other seems to dissolve the power relation between them and to absolve them of the necessity to defer to any authority other than their own. Indeed, it is the idealisation of the couple's love that aligns *Romeo and Juliet* with comedy and repeatedly suggests, despite forebodings to the contrary, the possibility of a happy conclusion.

In Act I, scene ii, where the initial desires of both lovers are presented, the perimeters of his daughter's desire are laid out by Capulet:

> But woo her, gentle Paris, get her heart,
> My will to her consent is but a part;
> And she agreed, within her scope of choice
> Lies my consent and fair according voice.
> (I.ii.16–19)

Capulet is woefully unaware of what is required to get his daughter's heart, or of the power differential that constitutes the distance between his will and the troublesome issue of female consent. The passion of romantic love requires an inexplicable and mutual abandonment of 'mastery'. It is mutuality, of course, that signals the crucial difference between Romeo's infatuation with Rosaline and his love for Juliet: 'Now Romeo is beloved and loves again, / Alike bewitched by the charm of looks' (II, Prologue, 5–6). Critics have remarked upon the occult connotations of 'bewitched', but bewitched also implies enchantment as a psychological state, an erotically charged ideological interpellation. Juliet has no choice about the depth to which she will 'endart' her gaze on Romeo, because the condition of love she experiences is far in excess of either her own will or that of her father. The mutuality of mirrored passion fosters the notion that one's authentic identity is revealed in romantic love.

It is important to emphasise the degree to which this freedom of choice in marriage is linked to economic considerations, especially the oxymoronic notion of 'free exchange'. Unconstrained choice about one's marriage partner relies to some degree on the ideological separation of psychic and monetary economies. Ideally, both parents and child will agree on a match, but what is at stake here is not so much the right of liberty in love, as an endeavour to prevent parents marrying off their children for financial gain, a phenomenon which became more marked with the bourgeoisification of the aristocracy. George Whetstone writes:

> I cry out upon forcement in Marriage, as the extremest bondage that is ... the father thinks he hath a happy purchase, if he get a rich young ward to match with his daughter: but God he knows, and the unfortunate couple often feel that he buyeth sorrow to his child, slander to himself and perchance the ruin of an ancient gentleman's house by the riot of the son in law not loving his wife.[33]

The situation here is addressed in explicitly economic terms. Similarly, the *Tell-Trothes New-Yeares Gift* (1595) complained, 'when as parents do by compulsion couple two bodies, neither respecting the joining of their hearts, nor having any care of the continuance of their welfare, but more regarding the linking of wealth and money together, than love with honesty'.[34] While this concern may not be unique to this period, it is newly emphasised. Indeed, Peter Laslett has argued that it is precisely as a result of 'choice and deliberation' in marriage – evident in the large gap between repro-

ductive age and age of marriage and a high rate of non-marriage –
that permits the development of capitalism in the West.[35]

Lady Capulet's statement that 'Thou hast a careful father, child'
– suggests that he is not only solicitous but perhaps penurious, and
in the scene where he tries to coerce Juliet's consent to the match
with Paris, he does it by negating female power – silencing all the
women around him, 'Speak not, reply not, do not answer me!'
(III.v.106,163). The Nurse rebels, 'May not one speak', 'I speak no
treason', while Lady Capulet, the obedient wife, vows 'I'll not speak
a word' (III.v,173, 172, 202). Only after such pressure upon her at-
tempted intervention, in a gesture more pragmatic than immoral,
does the Nurse advise her charge to comply with the paternal order.
Despite his initial uncertainty – 'too soon marr'd are those so early
made?' (I.ii.13) – Capulet's concern with financial gain and social
status is thoroughly apparent; it is even more so in Quarto 1 where
the line about the statues at the end of the play reads 'no figure
shall at such price be set'. As Michael Mooney has observed, the
sense is then one of cost rather than value.[36] The warring feudal
families here become an amalgam of warring nobility and rising
bourgeois merchants engaged in economic competition, both of
which offered some threat to absolutism.[37] Military antagonism in
which fixed quantities of ground are won or lost is replaced by a
more benign economic engagement (though of course, historically,
it proved the downfall of absolutism) wherein rival parties may
both expand and prosper 'because the production of manufactured
commodities is inherently unlimited'.[38]

In contrast to the formal settlement arrived at in Capulet's negotiations with Paris, in the dealings of the lovers, the Nurse is the
unruly woman, the comic agent of their *ad hoc* marriage arrangements. Her disorderly transactions are reminiscent of the illicit exchanges of the brothel. Hence, Mercutio calls out, 'A bawd! A
bawd! A bawd!' (II.iv.130):

> Romeo   Here's for thy pains.
> Nurse   No truly, sir; not a penny.
> Romeo   Go to, I say you shall.
> (II.iv.182–4)

Significantly, the financial power here is in the hands of Romeo, not
the bride's father, as Romeo recognised at the moment he discovered Juliet's identity: 'O dear account! My life is my foe's debt'

(I.v.118); 'As that vast shore [wash'd] with the farthest sea, / I should adventure for such merchandise' (II.ii.83–4). That is, his 'free' choice is bolstered by economic independence. Just before their marriage, Juliet too refers to her dowry:

> They are but beggars that can count their worth,
> But my true love is grown to such excess
> I cannot sum up sum of half my wealth.
>   (II.v.32–4)

That her 'wealth' consists of love rather than property exemplifies the shift here, and again it is she not her father who controls it. Financial metaphors reconfigure patriarchal economic transactions. Thus, the reordering of desire is attendant on the economic transformations sketched above – though of course in the play these transformations are metaphoric rather than literal – and the ideology of romantic love works to obscure them. We know, for instance, that there was considerable struggle over financial matters between husbands and wives. William Gouge's *Of Domesticall Duties* (1622) defensively seeks to placate those women whose remonstrance he endured after preaching at St Paul's that women should defer to their husbands in the matter of the wives' personal property: 'This just apologie I have been forced to make, that I might not ever be judged (as some have censured me) an hater of women' (pp. 3–4).

WAYWARD FEMALE DESIRE

There is, then, in *Romeo and Juliet*, a production of a specific form of female desire, benign and unthreatening, easily recruited to emergent absolutism and nascent capitalism. Whereas in the figure of Mercutio there is an alternative to the kind of heterosexual masculine desire that Romeo comes to represent by the end of the play, there appears to be no radically alternative regime of female sexuality to that represented by Juliet. However, this is not quite the case. For in Act I, scene iii there is a production of a highly sexualised, ribald female desire that parallels the 'rough love' of male homoeroticism that immediately follows in the next scene in the exchanges of the 'lusty gentlemen' Benvolio, Romeo, and Mercutio (I.iv.25, 112). The purpose of this scene is to inform Juliet of the marriage negotiations between Capulet and the County Paris, but what emerges is a women's scene, which disrupts the patriarchal project by presenting maternal eroticism, child sexuality, and female bawdy. The scene is freighted with multiple erotic possibilities, and in particular it is the displaced nature of maternality that produces a form of eroticism neither generated nor contained by the patriarchal order, feudal or otherwise.

In the very opening lines of the scene, Lady Capulet makes formal demand to the Nurse for 'my daughter' (I.iii.i). The Nurse's summons in itself produces a range of female erotic possibilities:

> Now, by my maidenhead at twelve year old,
> I bade her come. What, lamb! What, lady-bird!
> God forbid! Where's this girl? What Juliet!
> (I.iii.3–5)

The Nurse's comic invocation of her long-departed maidenhead suggests a connection between her own 'grotesque' body, with its four teeth and over-sucked dugs (grotesque insofar as it insists on its excess of the contained limits of the 'classical' body) and the maidenhead of 'this girl', Juliet, who is the object of affections which exceed the class-demarcated bounds of maternal propriety: 'lamb!'; 'lady-bird!' (I.iii.3–4). The point here, of course, is not to suggest that Juliet is the victim of the Nurse's improper sexual conduct, but rather that the business of nursing is itself sexual in ways that are difficult to grasp because nursing is now almost completely desexualised. It is interesting to compare the mutual pleasure of 'giving suck', where the woman actively provides oral gratification to the infant she nurtures with the pleasures of fellatio. Almost all the sexual dimensions of sucking have now been transferred to the latter practice and therefore onto the male organ.

The Nurse offers a sensual recollection of Juliet's weaning:

> And she was wean'd – I never shall forget it –
> Of all the days of the year upon that day;
> For I had then laid wormwood to my dug,
> Sitting in the sun under the dove house wall.
> My lord and you were then at Mantua –
> Nay, I do bear a brain – but, as I said,
> When it did it taste the wormwood on the nipple
> Of my dug, and felt it bitter, pretty fool,
> To see it teachy, and fall out wi' th' dug!
> (I.iii.24–32)

The fact that the Nurse is a comic figure has all too often obscured the fact that she bears events as indelible maternal memory: 'I never shall forget'; 'I do bear a brain'. Juliet is weaned by the Nurse while her parents are away, a process which seems to mark her as an initiate of sexual knowledge:

> For then she could stand high-lone; nay, by th' rood,
> She could have run and waddled all about;
> For even the day before, she broke her brow,
> And then my husband – God be with his soul!
> 'A was a merry man – took up the child.
> 'Yea,' quoth he, 'dost thou fall upon thy face?
> Thou wilt fall backward when thou hast more wit,
> Wilt thou not, Jule?' and, by my holidam,
> The pretty wretch left crying and said 'Ay'.
>
> (I.iii.36–44)

The Nurse extends the sexualisation of this recollection by adding to the description of Juliet a phallic 'bump as big as a young cockerel's stone', that recalls the violence of heterosexual relations, and is reminiscent of her later remark that 'bigger; women grow by men' (I.iii.53,95). In contrast, it is Lady Capulet who invokes the romantic imagery of 'This precious book of love' (I.iii.87), which dominates the rest of the play.

This scene, then, represents in palimpsest, female sensuality, maternity, and eroticism which, while they are clearly subordinated to patriarchal rule in the feudal order have become virtually unintelligible, undiscernible, in our own.

GENRE AND IDEOLOGY IN THE TRAGIC ENDING

The post-coital satisfaction of Romeo and Juliet as autonomous conjugal unit is short-lived and remarkably clandestine. Tragic events never allow time to fulfil the Friar's hopes of making the marriage public: 'To blaze your marriage, reconcile your friends' (III.iii.151–4). Bruce Smith argues 'Mercutio may die, but only bad timing keeps *Romeo and Juliet* from reaching the comic conclusion of married love'.[39] In this he points to the crucial distinction between the demise of the erotic mode represented by Mercutio and that represented by the lovers.

Had it not been aimed at sexual access rather than escape with Juliet, Romeo's rope-ladder scheme might have avoided the tragic conclusion.[40] In fact, the legitimate secrecy, so to speak, of 'privacy' is the order in which such a love as that of Romeo and Juliet would thrive.[41] The marriage of Romeo and Juliet could, after all, have provided the diplomatic solution to the feud; this pragmatic solution is opposed by the fathers so that the apparently antithetical ideal of romantic love as autonomous and inherently resistant to all social constraints can be incorporated into the diplomatic solution.[42] In fact, Romeo and Juliet's love, while it offers resistance to their feudal households is perfectly compatible with the interests of society as a whole. Thus, the utopian, dangerous, and paradoxical notion of a law that ratifies (inherently transgressive) passion, becomes the desideratum of early modern marriage.[43]

The lovers' desire as both transgressive and a new orthodoxy indicates the dislocation and relocation of authority that I have argued occurs by the end of the play. Yet, very clearly, the play is not didactic. As Frank Kermode puts it, albeit in the rhetoric of authorial intent,

> [W]e should beware of supposing that Shakespeare's sympathies lay strongly in this or that direction; that he was on the Friar's side when he uttered the conventional condemnation of the lovers in a story which must always have thrived on their attractiveness; or, on the other hand, that he was committed to this surreptitious but virtuous passion as in itself of the highest value.[44]

What is at stake is not simply an endorsement of the desire of the lovers or the control of the fathers; it is whether the play is an argument for absolutism, whether it approves the government of the crown above all others. This does not, however, mean that fathers are now without authority.[45] Rather, *Romeo and Juliet* addresses some of the contradictions in post-Reformation patriarchy where there is an endeavour to produce the authority of husbands, fathers, and thence the state as mutually reinforcing and simultaneously an effort to appropriate the transgressive aspects of desire.[46] Lawrence Stone points out:

> The enhancement of the importance of the conjugal family and the household relative to the kinship and clientage at the upper levels of society was accompanied by a positive reinforcement of the despotic authority of husband and father – that is to say, of patriarchy. Both

Church and state provided powerful new theoretical and practical support, while two external checks on patriarchal power declined as kinship ties and clientage weakened.[47]

While the 'raw power' of fathers does not necessarily increase, the recognition that such power is legitimate is fully and unequivocally established. Paternal power has now superseded 'raw power' as such (p. 151). 'Authoritarian monarchy and domestic patriarchy form a congruent and mutually supportive complex of ideas and social systems' (p. 152). As marriage was increasingly sanctified, so too was the authoritarian role of husband and father, guardian of the sacred state (p. 654). Thus, Stone argues that after 1640, the 'restricted patriarchal nuclear family' becomes the 'closed domesticated nuclear family' (p. 655).

Romeo and Juliet are simultaneously sacrificed to the old feudal order of Montague and Capulet and to patriarchy's new order of the unified power of the state represented by Escalus.[48] The play's contradictions, its combination of residual and emergent elements are subordinated by the strictures of the genre's conclusion to a single ideological effect. This does not, however, sweep away all earlier contradictions; it has taken 400 years and many times that number of pages of literary criticism to accomplish that. *Romeo and Juliet* stands as an apparently benign, lyrical document of universal love. What I have argued here is that it does not stand above history, but rather within it, doing the work of culture, instigating and perpetuating the production of socially necessary formations of desire.

When this play was written, Shakespeare was just about to begin writing the high comedies, and it fits in very well with the celebration of romantic love in those texts while it is something of an anomaly in the tragic canon. For while *Romeo and Juliet* consolidates the power of the absolutist prince as he who can take marriage alliances out of the hands of kin and promote what is to become a bourgeois family form, the tragic genre in general is unable to sustain such an ambitious and contradictory agenda. Indeed, after 1600 the increasingly retrograde cast of the tragedies is connected to their failure to imagine a synthesis of absolutism and the emerging family form. Paradoxically, however, the failure of the genre to promote the ideology of romantic love merely added cultural weight to *Romeo and Juliet*, so that it remains across the centuries the iconic text of romantic love.

From Dympna C. Callaghan, Lorraine Helms and Jyotsna Singh, *The Wayward Sisters: Shakespeare and Feminist Politics* (Oxford, 1994), pp. 59–62, 71–88.

NOTES

[Dympna Callaghan writes as a feminist new historicist in this essay. She argues that, however 'natural' it may seem to us, romantic love is an ideology formed from protestant ideologies of marriage and the family, which were being negotiated at the historical moment when Shakespeare wrote *Romeo and Juliet*. The play drew from and powerfully consolidated the ideology and made it seem transhistorical and universal. The values of 'compulsory heterosexuality and bourgeois marriage' which the play endorses are, in fact, patriarchal in origin and serve to delimit female desire and experience. For reasons of space, the middle sections of the essay are not reproduced here, but they are interesting and significant and can be consulted in Callaghan's book. One section critiques the way in which psychoanalysis, by ignoring history and universalising issues, has colluded in naturalising tendentious ideologies of desire, and the other section amplifies the historical study of the formation of modern ideas about love and the family. Alert readers will notice throughout this collection many debates and disagreements between the critics. One interesting disagreement occurs as a sort of 'battle of the footnotes'. Callaghan (note 41 below) dismisses a central point made by Ryan in the first published essay which appears in revised form here as essay 5. In his revision, Ryan answers Callaghan's criticism. Other critical intertextualities occur. Callaghan opposes the psychoanalytical approach of Kristeva (essay 3), but implicitly supports her anti-patriarchal feminist stance; Goldberg (essay 10) allies himself with the general enterprise of feminism but challenges readings of *Romeo and Juliet* along the lines of Callaghan's, because they maintain rigid gender boundaries. These kinds of debate should be noticed and explored since they empower individual readers to define their own positions with freedom. All quotations from the play are from *The Riverside Shakespeare*, ed. G. Blakemore Evans et al. (Boston, 1974). Ed.]

1. Evans et al., Riverside edition, p. 1057.

2. There is in Shakespeare's play only a dim residue of this earlier moralism in the Friar's caveat that 'these violent delights have violent ends' (II.vi.9).

3. For a useful guide to the literature on the debate about the transition from feudalism to capitalism, see Barry Taylor, *Society and Economy in Early Modern Europe: A Bibliography of Post-War Research* (New York, 1989). See also: Perry Anderson, *Lineages of the Absolutist State* (London, 1979) and *In the Tracks of Historical Materialism* (London, 1983); Jean Baechler, *The Origins of Capitalism*, trans.

Barry Cooper (Oxford, 1975); Jean Baechler, John Hall and Michael Mann, *Europe and the Rise of Capitalism* (Oxford, 1988); Robert Brenner, 'The origins of capitalist development: a critique of neoSmithian Marxism', *New Left Review*, 104 (1977), 25–92; Paul Q. Hirst, *Marxism and Historical Writing* (London, 1985); Claudio J. Katz, *From Feudalism to Capitalism: Marxian Theories of Class Struggle and Social Change* (New York, 1989); Eugene Kamenka and R. S. Neale, *Feudalism, Capitalism and Beyond* (London, 1975); Hans Medick, 'The transition from feudalism to capitalism: renewal of the debate', in Samuel Raphael (ed.), *People's History and Socialist Theory* (London, 1981); Colin Mooers, *The Making of Bourgeois Europe: Absolutism, Revolution and the Rise of Capitalism in England, France, and Germany* (New York, 1991); Immanuel Wallerstein, *Historical Capitalism* (London, 1983).

4. Julia Kristeva, *Tales of Love*, trans Leon S. Roudiez (New York, 1987), p. 210.

5. For example, Arthur Kirsch who uses a Christian / Freudian approach comments: 'Central to my understanding of the treatment of love in Shakespeare has been the assumption that the plays represent elemental truths of our emotional and spiritual life, that these truths help account for Shakespeare's enduring vitality ...' (p. ix). In such criticism, Freud merely discovered a different way of expressing what Shakespeare had already said. History becomes the changing stage scenery of a continuum – the costumes may change, but the essence remains unchanged. Arthur Kirsch, *Shakespeare and the Experience of Love* (New York, 1981), p. 6.

6. Even when the text was staged in a version thought more suited to the times, the result was the enhancement of its message for a post-Puritan world wherein the ideals it presented required a certain modification. The Restoration saw the popularity of a happy ending (Riverside edn, p. 1802).

7. Joseph Porter, 'Marlowe, Shakespeare, and the canonization of heterosexuality', *South Atlantic Quarterly*, 88 (1989), 127–47, p. 141

8. Evans, Riverside edition, p. 1057.

9. See Gayle Whittier, 'The sonnet's body and the body sonnetized in *Romeo and Juliet*', *Shakespeare Quarterly*, 40 (1989), 27–41, p. 41 and Barry Jones, '*Romeo and Juliet*: the genesis of a classic', in Eric Haywood and Cormac O Cuilleanain (eds), *Italian Storytellers: Essays on Italian Narrative Literature* (Dublin, 1989), pp. 150–81.

   For Kristeva, however, such repetition is born not of ideological necessity but of a psycho-linguistic one. Commenting on the centrality of night imagery in the play, she argues: 'it is not nothingness, lack of meaning, absurdity. In the polite display of its black tenderness there is an intense longing that is positive with respect to meaning ... Let me emphasise the nocturnal motion of metaphor and amor mortis: it bears on the irrational aspect of signs and loving subjects, on the non-representable feature on which the renewal of representation depends.' (*Tales of Love*, p. 214 [ellipsis in the original].)

10. See Eugene Kamenka and R. S. Neale, *Feudalism, Capitalism and Beyond* (London, 1975), p. 18.

11. Eli Zaretsky, *Capitalism, the Family and Personal Life* (London, 1976), p. 38.

12. As Susan Amussen puts it, in nascent modernity '[b]oth economic realities and political and social thought, then, draw us to the family as a central institution': *An Ordered Society: Gender and Class in Early Modern England* (Oxford, 1988), p. 2. Further, J. A. Sharpe points to the irrefutable arrival of one new family type: 'the legitimate family of clergymen': *Early Modern England: A Social History 1550–1760* (London, 1987), p. 61. For debates on the family see also: Miranda Chaytor, 'Household and kinship: Ryton in the late sixteenth and early seventeenth centuries', *History Workshop Journal*, 10 (1980), 25–6; Ralph A. Houlbrooke, *The English Family, 1450–1700* (New York, 1988); R. B. Outhwaite (ed.), *Marriage and Society: Studies in the Social History of Marriage* (New York, 1981); Lawrence Stone, *The Family, Sex and Marriage in England 1500–1800* (New York, 1977).

13. See Peter Novick, *That Noble Dream: The 'Objectivity Question' and the American Historical Profession* (Cambridge, 1988), pp. 545–618. For a related account of resistance to Continental thought and to African-American and feminist historiography, see Novick, especially chs 14 and 15.

14. Ibid., p. 2.

15. Alice Jardine notes: 'In contemporary French thought, it is not the "event" that assumes importance as a historical mark, but the epistemological configurations surrounding that event, especially with regard to language' (*Gynesis: Configurations of Woman and Modernity* [Ithaca, NY, 1985], pp. 82–3). Also, it is worth pointing out that the problem of legitimation addressed by Lyotard and the problem of knowledge articulated by Foucault are, then, 'historical' problems with the very idea of history itself.

16. *Gynesis*, p. 81.

17. Karen Newman, *Fashioning Feminity and English Renaissance Drama* (Chicago, 1991), p. 58. [Further references are given in parentheses – Ed.]

18. Stephen Greenblatt, 'Psychoanalysis and Renaissance culture', in Patricia Parker and David Quint (eds), *Literary Theory / Renaissance Texts* (Baltimore, MD, 1986), pp. 210–24. [Further references are given in parentheses – Ed.] Psychoanalysis, at least in Greenblatt's rendition of it, threatens to ground history in identity:

If psychoanalysis was, in effect, made possible by (among other things) the legal and literary proceedings of the sixteenth and seventeenth centuries, then its interpretive practice is not irrelevant to those proceedings, nor is it exactly an anachronism. But psychoanalysis is causally belated, even as it is causally linked: hence the curious effect of a discourse that functions as if the psychological categories it invokes were not only simultaneous with but even prior to and themselves causes of the very phenomena of which in actual fact they were the results. (p. 221)

Of course, Greenblatt has himself very effectively deployed psychoanalysis in his treatment of desire in Othello in *Renaissance Self-Fashioning from More to Shakespeare* (Chicago, 1980). He writes:

Shakespeare's military hero, it may be objected, is particularly far removed from this introspective project, a project that would seem, in any case, to have little bearing upon any Renaissance text. Yet I think it is no accident that nearly every phase of Lacan's critique of psychoanalysis seems a brilliant reading of Othello, for I would propose that there is a deep resemblance between the construction of the self in analysis – at least as Lacan conceives it – and Othello's self-fashioning. The resemblance is grounded in the dependence of even the innermost self upon a language that is always necessarily given from without and upon representation before an audience. I do not know if such are the conditions of human identity, apart from its expression in psychoanalysis, but they are unmistakably the conditions of theatrical identity, where existence is conferred upon a character by the playwright's language and the actor's performance. (pp. 244–5)

19. It is not of course that undecidability can never be intellectually productive, whatever its political limitations. For example, Greenblatt comments ' "psyche" is neither a mere mystification for "property" nor a radical alternative to it' ('Psychoanalysis and Renaissance culture', p. 224; see also pp. 220–1).

20. Because of his immensely influential pioneering work in the field, there is something of a danger of equating new historicism with Greenblatt alone. Other new historicists such as Louis Montrose and Don Wayne are rather more concerned with class and gender struggles as motivating historical contestation. Undoubtedly, also, Geenblatt has exerted a powerful (and for that matter positive) effect on scholarship which is explicitly Marxist and feminist. See Jean Howard, 'The New Historicism in Renaissance studies', *English Literary Renaissance*, 16 (1986), 13–43; Louis Montrose, 'Renaissance literary studies and the subject of history', *English Literary Renaissance*, 16 (1986), 5–12; Aram H. Veeser (ed.), *The New Historicism* (New York, 1989); Don E. Wayne, 'New historicism', in Martin Coyle, Peter Garside, Malcolm Kelsall, and John Peck (eds), *Encyclopaedia of Literature and Criticism* (London, 1990).

21. See Perry Anderson, *Lineages of the Absolutist State* (London, 1979), pp. 8–10.

22. See ibid., pp. 25–6. While it would be naïve to claim a straightforward functional relation between the nuclear family and the capitalist mode of production, it would fly in the face of historical fact to ignore the changes in familial structure and function that the changing organisation effected. The degree of debate about this shift cannot be overemphasised. It is difficult to offer empirical evidence for changing family forms. However, Stone notes the fact that in the fourteenth century only a small proportion of homicides were committed within the family, in comparison with the majority today: 'What is so striking, however, is that the family was more a unit for the perpetuation of crime – a third of all group crimes were by family members – than a focus of crime. It is tempting to argue that the family that slayed together stayed together' (*The Family, Sex and Marriage*, p. 95). Even on a less lethal level, community interactions seem to have revolved around identification with a larger unit than the one we think of as the nuclear family: 'Everything we know about the pre-modern community, such as the village, indicates that it was riddled with competitive feuds and factions, usually organised around kinship groups' (p. 660).

23. In contrast, psychoanalytic readings of the play, even as they demonstrate the way feudal patriarchy naturalises itself, themselves succumb to that naturalisation, accepting its self-representation as static and monolithic. For example, Coppélia Kahn argues that *Romeo and Juliet* demonstrates a certain inevitability or fate as intrinsic to the feudal patriarchal scheme which produces such strain on the young people who must come of age in Verona (*Man's Estate: Masculine Identity in Shakespeare* [Berkeley, CA, 1981], p. 186). [Further references are given in parentheses – Ed.]

24. See Anderson, *Lineages*, p. 19. For the family was the central unit of most production as much as it was an institution of ideological importance for social and political theory and 'the domestic relations of the household were an explicit part of the production relations of early capitalism' (Zaretsky, *Capitalism*, p. 38). '[P]roperty was a central factor in family relations, from decisions to get married to the distribution of property at the time of death' (Amussen, *An Ordered Society*, p. 94).

    In a similar vein, Immanuel Wallerstein argues

    ... the image of historical capitalism having arisen via the overthrow of a backward aristocracy by a progressive bourgeoisie is wrong. Instead, the correct basic image is that historical capitalism was brought into existence by a landed aristocracy which transformed itself into a bourgeoisie because the old system was disintegrating. Rather than let the disintegration continue to uncertain ends, they engaged in radical structural surgery themselves in order to maintain and significantly expand their ability to exploit the direct producers. (*Historical Capitalism*, p. 105–6)

25. 'When verbal sparring about phalluses turns into physical sparring with swords, Mercutio is killed. An exemplar of male violence and misogyny? A martyr to male friendship? A victim of sexual desire that he cannot, will not, or must not acknowledge directly? Mercutio is all three'; Bruce R. Smith, *Homosexual Desire in Shakespeare's England: A Cultural Poetic* (Chicago, 1991), p. 64 [Further references are given in parentheses – Ed.]

26. On the violence of male bonding, see Kahn, *Man's Estate*, pp. 82–118; Marianne Novy, *Love's Argument: Gender Relations in Shakespeare* (Chapel Hill, NC, 1984), pp. 99–142; Smith, *Homosexual Desire*, ch. 2.

27. See Brian Gibbons (ed.), *Romeo and Juliet*, The Arden Shakespeare (London, 1980), pp. 39, 87.

28. Notably, the fathers loom so large in the play in Stockholder's psycho-analytic interpretation that she views Capulet as the protagonist (Kay Stockholder, *Dreamworks: Lovers and Families in Shakespeare's Plays* [Toronto, 1987], p. 31).

29. In fact the incest taboo is more vulnerable when it operates in the tense nuclear arrangement where any affective relations outside the nuclear unit are discouraged and deemed inappropriate; see Juliet Mitchell, *Psychoanalysis and Feminism: Freud, Reich, Laing and Women* (New York, 1975). Yet in this play, it is the feudal that is presented as an aberrant way of organisation desire, as perverted and death-marked.

30. See Newman, *Fashioning Femininity*, p. 27.

31. Kristeva, *Tales of Love*, p. 217.

32. 'Nevertheless, the dramatic representation of that [neo-Catholic] sensibility is at its most commanding and pristine in Elizabethan, rather than in Jacobean, tragedy' (Mary Beth Rose, *The Expense of Spirit: Love and Sexuality in English Renaissance Drama* [Ithaca, NY, 1988], p. 105).

33. Cited in Alan MacFarlane, *Marriage and Love in England: Modes of Reproduction 1300–1840* (Oxford, 1986), p. 134.

34. Ibid., pp. 134–5.

35. Peter Laslett, 'The European family and early industrialization', in Jean Baechler et al. (eds), *Europe and the Rise of Capitalism*, pp. 234–41, 236.

36. Michael Mooney, 'Text and performance: *Romeo and Juliet*, Quartos 1 and 2', *Colby Quarterly*, 26:2 (June 1990), 122–32, p. 131

37. Anderson, *Lineages*, pp. 19–22.

38. Ibid., p. 31.

39. Bruce Smith, *Homosexual Desire*, p. 64.

40. See Gibbons, *Romeo and Juliet*, p. 92.

41. For Kay Stockholder the threat to the couple is externalised: 'The freer the lovers are from violent emotions, the more violent is the world they encounter': Stockholder, *Dreamworks*, p. 30. And for Kiernan Ryan the play represents a subversive utopian vision, born of an initial freedom from social identity (a namelessness), cruelly dashed: Kiernan Ryan, '*Romeo and Juliet*: the language of tragedy', in Willie van Peer (ed.), *Taming the Text* (New York, 1988), pp. 106–21. Ryan suggests that the play is revolutionary and argues for a love untrammelled by the social order. Such a suggestion seems beside the point – love is always, first and foremost, social. [Callaghan is referring to an earlier text of Ryan's essay. In the present volume, Ryan (essay 5) responds to Callaghan's point – Ed.]

Kristeva (*Tales of Love*), considers the couple a 'utopic wager that paradise lost can be made lasting' (p. 222), but this is exactly the dominant ideology of love in modernity, and it is for Kristeva a utopian option she rejects out of hand where authority constitutes itself as that which is to be loved (p. 210).

42. Stone argues that there is a 'clear conflict: between romantic love and the notion that it is an impractical basis for marriage' (*The Family, Sex and Marriage*, p. 181). I disagree because it seems to me that 'romantic love', the ideal of a love between equals (that is, people of the same class status), is one of the most successful ways of internalising the social order – that is, producing it in socially appropriate ways.

43. See Kristeva, *Tales of Love*, p. 210.

44. Riverside edition, p. 1057.

45. See Stone, *The Family, Sex and Marriage*, ch. 5.

46. Alan Sinfield remarks: 'The ... disjunction in Reformation doctrine of marriage occurred because theorists wanted to maintain, as well as the husband's authority, the father's. They did not mean to let their young folk get out of hand, or to let human feeling supplant the other important things in life. The ideal of affectionate marriage was held alongside a continuing belief in parental control, mainly in the interests of social standing and financial security': *Literature in Protestant England, 1560–1660* (Towota, NJ, 1983), p. 7.

47. Stone, *The Family, Sex and Marriage*, p. 151. [Further references are given in parentheses – Ed.]

48. John Donne, in one of his typically perverse wedding sermons, proclaims that proper godliness should obviate desire and obliterate lack:

'And what can that soul lack that hath all God?' (Rose, *Expense of Spirit*, p. 104). The state of fulfilment, a state beyond desire, is envisaged here. A perfect Christianity, it would seem, obliterates lack, that precondition of desire produced by an initial failure of satisfaction and as the effect of a primordial absence. Donne reduces sexual desire back to the order of a need; something that could be satisfied: see J. Rose, 'Introduction II', Juliet Mitchell and Jacqueline Rose, *Feminine Sexuality: Feminine Sexuality and the école freudienne*, trans. Jacqueline Rose (London, 1982), p. 32.

5

'The Murdering Word'

KIERNAN RYAN

The present value of Shakespeare's tragedies stems from their refusal to resolve the contradiction between justified desires and their unjustifiable suppression: the heartbreaking contradiction between what men and women could be, and what time and place condemn them to become, in spite of the superior selves and fuller lives struggling within them for realisation. Shakespearean tragedy is organised by its awareness of alternative potential; it demonstrates that what happens in these plays results from a specific constellation of conditions and pressures, and thus that human lives could take quite different paths under other conceivable circumstances. It is the conditional, contestable nature of the plight that grinds down the protagonists, regardless of merit or their capacity to live otherwise, that defines the tragic quality of the drama.

Shakespeare's tragedies oblige us to confront without illusions the appalling cost of beliefs whose absorption dooms people to destroy not only others, but also themselves, making a cruel farce of their conscious intentions. Shakespeare's great tragic protagonists are indeed 'fools of Time' (Sonnet 124),[1] but in the sense that they are hoodwinked by history. They are overpowered by the prevailing tides of their moment, which sweep them unawares out of their depth, rather than by some metaphysical misfortune or by some flaw, whether culpable, haphazard or innate, in the composition of their characters. Romeo and Juliet, Hamlet, Othello and Desdemona, King Lear, Macbeth, Antony and Cleopatra: all of them resonate in retrospect as figures born before their time, citizens of an anticipated age, whose transfigured values their suffering discloses, pointing us towards more desirable destinies yet to be scripted by history. Their tragedy is to find themselves stranded back in time, far from that foreshadowed future; marooned in a hostile, alien reality, which has already contaminated their hearts and minds, and eventually crushes them completely.

Conventional criticism has mustered all the standard ruses to prevent *Romeo and Juliet* from being read in this way. The lovers' fate is most commonly ascribed to the rigidities of natural or super-natural law. J. W. Draper goes so far as to suggest that they are the literally 'star-cross'd' victims of astral determinism, 'the puppets of the stars and planets and of the days and times of day'.[2] A more typical tack, however, is pursued by John Lawlor, who believes that what conquer Romeo and Juliet are the 'unchanging limits' of life and love, the inflexible imperatives of human existence.[3] As Frank Kermode puts it: 'just as [love] is in its very nature the business of the young, with passions hardly controlled, so it is in its very nature associated with disaster and death'.[4] Norman Rabkin, too, regards the lovers as inherently doomed by 'the self-destructive yearning for annihilation that we recognise as the death-wish'.[5]

Another school of critics spotlights the failure of Friar Lawrence's message to reach Romeo in Mantua and the calamitous timing of events at the tomb. From these facts it concludes that the play's emphasis 'seems to be, rather more than we should like, on chance', and that perhaps 'we understand the play better if we think of it as a tragedy of "bad luck" '.[6] To such critics, as Franklin Dickey observes, the tragedy seems deeply flawed, because the catastrophe is 'embarrassingly fortuitous ... the accident of chance to which all human life is subject'.[7] For yet another group, however, there is little doubt that 'the causes of the tragedy lie in the sufferers themselves', whose 'dangerous fault ... is their extreme rashness'.[8] Virgil Whitaker locates the chief authority for this judgement in the Friar, who underscores 'the irrational violence, and therefore the culpability, of the haste with which Romeo acts'.[9] In this kind of account, *Romeo and Juliet* depicts the penalty paid by those who demand too much too soon, who refuse to let their desires be bridled by the reasonable rules of their society.

By explaining the torments and suicide of Romeo and Juliet as a perennial tragedy of 'the human condition',[10] as the random result of misfortune, or as the protagonists' just deserts, these critics have obscured the true significance of their love and the play's disclosure of the forces that destroy it. Appeals can, of course, be made to the evidence of the text. The moralistic interpreter can invoke Friar Lawrence's warning that 'these violent delights have violent ends' (II.vi.9). Romeo himself can be subpoenaed to confirm that he is the victim of 'some consequence ... hanging in the stars' (I.iv.107). Nor could anyone dispute that accidental factors play a crucial role in sealing the lovers' final doom. But it is a mistake to equate one character's viewpoint with the perspective formed by the play, or to construct from isolated incidents an explanation of the entire pattern of events. For *Romeo and Juliet* creates a concerted vision more searching than such methods are equipped to discern.

Not that recent feminist and psychoanalytic approaches have proved less problematic. The deep-seated urge to distil from the play an enduring human plight seems determined to survive the transformation of Shakespeare studies ushered in by the advent of theory. In *Tales of Love*, Julia Kristeva reads the tragedy as Shakespeare's displaced lament for the death of his son Hamnet, as a chapter in the Bard's psychobiography, which betrays 'the intrinsic presence of hatred in amatory feeling itself'.[11] Irene Dash drops de Beauvoir for Dr Johnson to prop up her view that Juliet's adolescent bind 'has a universality not limited to a particular place' or period.[12] Edward Snow's suggestive essay on the tragedy cannot resist freezing male and female mentalities into primal states of being, purged of circumstance and historicity.[13] Coppélia Kahn detects in the cultural conflict between two styles of manhood 'the all-embracing opposition of Eros and Thanatos',[14] whose rapprochement the lovers' death alone can effect. And Dympna Callaghan offers a bleak critique of the play's supposedly innate 'ideological propensity to posit desire as transhistorical', and thus lock women into 'apparently unchangeable structures of oppression, particularly compulsory heterosexuality and bourgeois marriage'.[15]

What all these interpretations screen off are precisely the qualities which account for *Romeo and Juliet*'s profound hold on the hearts of generations of spectators and readers down through the centuries. The source of the play's abiding power lies in the way it foreshadows a more satisfying kind of love, freed from the coercion that continues to drive men and women apart and prevents their meeting each other's emotional needs. Not the least remarkable feature of the text, moreover, is its revelation that the crippling constraints on the lovers are largely enforced through the language that binds them to a world with which they cannot compromise, and which they would therefore rather relinquish.

Throughout Act I, while he is still fixated on Rosaline and before he has met Juliet, Romeo is trapped inside the hackneyed role and ossified verse of the Petrarchan lover. His rhyming speech is paralysed by the dead weight of clichéd paradoxes and inert metaphors, exiled from actual experience and emotions:

> She is too fair, too wise, wisely too fair,
> To merit bliss by making me despair.
> She hath forsworn to love, and in that vow
> Do I live dead that live to tell it now.
>   (I.i.221–4)

Romeo speaks more truly than he knows when he describes himself as 'Shut up in prison, kept without my food, / Whipt and tormented' (I.ii.55–6). For he is indeed the prisoner of an abject attitude, which turns the woman into a sadistic goddess and the man into a tortured slave, condemning both sexes to a degrading charade of domination and subjection. Even here, however, Romeo seems aware that his true identity exists beyond the confines of his masochistic role: 'I have lost myself, I am not here: / This is not Romeo, he's some other where' (I.i.197–8).

Mercutio's cynical mockery travesties Romeo's posturing and punctures his inflated speech:

> Romeo! humours! madman! passion! lover!
> Appear thou in the likeness of a sigh!
> Speak but one rhyme, and I am satisfied;
>   (II.i.7–9)

But it is soon clear that Mercutio's disillusionment offers no valid alternative. On the contrary, he shares with the belligerent servants in the opening scene a reductive, aggressive conception of sex, which is the inverted mirror-image of what he satirises in Romeo: 'If love be rough with you, be rough with love; / Prick love for pricking, and you beat love down' (I.iv.27–8). From Mercutio's equally stale standpoint, love means nothing more than male penetrating female in a stark gratification of animal appetite: 'O, Romeo, that she were, O that she were / An open-arse, thou a pop'rin pear!' (II.i.37–8). Romeo and Mercutio are steered by the same ubiquitous disposition, which denies men and women the option of love unfettered by subjugation.

Juliet's domestic subjection to this mentality is more blatant. The first we hear of her is in Act I, scene ii, where her father is wondering whether to give her in marriage to Paris: even before she enters, she is defined as an object of male choice and negotiation. The following scene shows Juliet being pressed by her mother to accept Paris's suit and persuade herself to love him. The terms in which Lady Capulet strives to secure her daughter's compliance are revealing:

> Read o'er the volume of young Paris' face,
> And find delight writ there with beauty's pen;
> Examine every married lineament,
> And see how one another lends content;
> And what obscur'd in this fair volume lies
> Find written in the margent of his eyes.
> This precious book of love, this unbound lover,
> To beautify him, only lacks a cover ...
> That book in many's eyes doth share the glory,
> That in gold clasps locks in the golden story;
>   (I.iii.81–8, 91–2)

The elaborate book metaphor points to the correspondence between Juliet's situation and Romeo's. Romeo's Petrarchan bondage to his mistress is matched by the projected binding of Juliet to 'the golden story' of her husband's destiny. The husband is assumed to be the author and the subject of the 'precious book of love', whose 'content' the wife is expected to digest and merely embellish with a glamorous 'cover'. The prospective marriage submits Juliet, like Romeo, to a set text dictated by the sexual conventions of their society, which forbids them to invent their own script, create their own roles or speak lines of their own devising.

Because words are the chains that bind the lovers to the sexual norms and social imperatives of Verona, their struggle for fulfilment expresses itself as a struggle to free themselves from the way Verona has taught them to speak. It is no accident that Romeo and Juliet meet and fall in love (I.v.) while Romeo is masked and before they learn each other's name. For while they are nameless they are untrammelled by their given identities, which would prevent their meeting purely as a man and a woman. For a moment the festive licence of the masquerade relieves them of their obligations and inhibitions as Montague and Capulet, waiving the strict codes of courtship, which would normally make such a direct and intimate first encounter between any man and woman of their class unthinkable. Before long, the outraged Tybalt will identify Romeo's voice, triggering again the mindless machinery of the feud, which drives its lethal wedge between the lovers in Act III. But this privileged interlude allows them to touch and kiss with frank immediacy, and their fragile love unfolds.

Their entire exchange (I.v.93–110), initiated by Romeo, is enclosed in the contrived form and idiom of the love-sonnet, whose artifice still constricts Romeo's emotions and imagination. They complete their first sonnet together with a kiss (I.v.93–106), and at once begin a second (I.v.107–10). But, having played his language-game so far, Juliet sabotages this sonnet in the fourth line begun by Romeo, turning its second half back against the speaker in playful mockery of his textbook courtship:

> Romeo   Thus from my lips, by thine, my sin is purg'd.
>   [*Kissing her.*]
> Juliet Then have my lips the sin that they have took.
> Romeo   Sin from my lips? O trespass sweetly urg'd!
>   Give me my sin again.   [*Kissing her again.*]
> Juliet   You kiss by th' book.

Juliet's teasing quip reflects the gap already divorcing undefined feelings from this formal literary discourse, which distorts and stuns those feelings in the act of voicing them. Seconds after their exchange, however, each discovers the name of the other, and instantly, with the pronouncing of the words 'Capulet' and 'Montague', the licence of the moment is cancelled and the tragic conflict between the lovers and their world begins. From now on they are forced, as the Chorus foretells, 'to steal love's sweet bait from fearful hooks' (II.Chorus.8).

The linguistic dimension of the tragedy becomes explicit in the balcony scene of Act II. Believing herself to be alone, and thus relieved of the burden of self-censorship that a public statement would impose, Juliet soliloquises on the problem at the heart of the play:

> O Romeo, Romeo, wherefore art thou Romeo?
> Deny thy father and refuse thy name;
> Or, if thou wilt not, be but sworn my love,
> And I'll no longer be a Capulet ...
> 'Tis but thy name that is my enemy;
> Thou art thyself, though not a Montague.
> What's Montague? It is nor hand nor foot,
> Nor arm nor face, nor any other part

Belonging to a man. O, be some other name!
What's in a name? That which we call a rose
By any other word would smell as sweet;
So Romeo would, were he not Romeo call'd,
Retain that dear perfection which he owes
Without that title.

And Romeo replies:

                    ... By a name
I know not how to tell thee who I am.
My name, dear saint, is hateful to myself,
Because it is an enemy to thee;
Had I it written, I would tear the word.
              (II.ii.33–6, 38–47, 53–7)

These passages spell out the stifling contradiction between being a
man and being a Montague, between a potentially unshackled self
and the disabling controls and commitments inscribed in such a
family name. The designations 'Capulet' and 'Montague' fix Romeo
and Juliet within a patriarchal power-structure, whose demands
frustrate their self-sanctioned needs as human beings. 'The tradition of the dead generations', as Marx memorably observed,
'weighs like a nightmare on the minds of the living.'[16] *Romeo and
Juliet* makes plain the extent to which that tradition is felt as the
weight of words, the discursive gravity that pins individuals to in-
voluntary lives.

It is not only their names from which the lovers are straining to
cut themselves loose. As the balcony scene attests, Romeo's love for
Juliet has begun to transmute his language into a mode of expression which is much more direct, personal and resolute. The transmutation is far from sustained, and traces of the old Petrarchan
diction, with all that it implies, cling to his phrasing and Juliet's to
the end. A complete break with the accepted idioms of their world
is impossible. But they have already leaped far enough beyond them
to define the gulf that yawns between their dawning identities and
their former selves.[17]

Thus Juliet rejects the impulse to bury the intensity of her desire
beneath the decorum of polite public speech: 'Fain would I dwell on
form, fain, fain deny / What I have spoke, but farewell compliment!'
(II.ii.88–9). She turns down the part of the devious courtly mistress,
with its obligation to be reserved and 'strange' (II.ii.101–2), 'to
frown and be perverse, and say thee nay' (II.ii.96). And she forbids

Romeo to cast himself in the corresponding role of devoted wor-
shipper at her shrine. When he threatens to slip back into the
routine pose of submissive suitor by swearing an elaborate oath to
his lady, she cuts him off with 'Do not swear at all' (II.ii.112). To
succumb to these stances and the locutions that confirm them
would be to linger in a realm of assumptions which Romeo and
Juliet have abandoned. 'Love goes toward love,' remarks Romeo,
'as schoolboys from their books' (II.ii.156). The new kind of union
developing between them means tossing aside the obsolete texts of
the school of love in which they have been educated and finding
fresh answers elsewhere.

What they fleetingly discover is a form of love which propels
them not only beyond the divisive social formation epitomised by
the feud, but also beyond the established sexual order, and thus
beyond the scope of the discourse that helps perpetuate that order.
The verbal horizon that once circumscribed them cannot contain
what they are now experiencing and their revised sense of themselves. A way of life which had seemed unquestionable is exposed
as a prison-house, whose walls are built of words. For Romeo and
Juliet, those walls prove in the end too strong, but their struggle to
demolish them affords the audience a prospect of release, by
confirming that what Verona enforces as normal is neither pervasive nor impregnable.

The innovative character of their love is stressed from the
opening of Act II. Its utopian impact is produced by the fact that it
is founded on reciprocity rather than subservience. As the Chorus
puts it: 'Now Romeo is belov'd and loves again, /Alike bewitched
by the charm of looks ... /And she as much in love' (II. Chorus.
5–6, 11). Romeo himself employs symmetrically balanced syntax
and diction to express the perfect equivalence of attraction and
power that distinguishes their relationship: 'one hath wounded me /
That's by me wounded' (II.iii.50–1); 'As mine on hers, so hers is set
on mine' (II.iii.59); 'Her I love now / Doth grace for grace and love
for love allow; / The other did not so' (II.iii.85–7).[18] It is, moreover,
a mutually enhancing, limitless love, whose value defies selfish
quantification. In Juliet's wonderful words:

> My bounty is as boundless as the sea,
> My love as deep; the more I give to thee,
> The more I have, for both are infinite.
> (II.ii.133–5)

> They are but beggars that can count their worth,
> But my true love is grown to such excess
> I cannot sum up sum of half my wealth.
>
> (II.vi.32–4)

Romeo and Juliet's 'true-love passion' (II.ii.104) goes much further than dramatising the pernicious effects of the family feud. That the play vindicates the emergent right to love whoever one chooses, regardless of arbitrary prohibitions or prejudice, has long been recognised. What has not been appreciated is its still vital quest to envision beyond that a bond uncontaminated by the urge to use and dominate, which perverts love into an instrument of pain. Romeo and Juliet's real tragedy is that they are caged in a culture which precludes the survival of such emancipated love. This is 'the true ground of all these piteous woes' (V.iii.179), not some flaw in the fabric of young love, and not some preternatural fiat, whatever the Friar may say or Romeo believe. Moreover, the accidental confusions which result in the double suicide spring from the institutional pressures that split and isolate the lovers, leaving them prey to such chance adversities. The question is not whether their fate might have been averted if only their luck had held, but why they should have been driven to the point where their lives are at the mercy of mere luck at all.

A long stride towards disaster is taken when Mercutio's death compels Romeo to shoulder again the name he had shed for Juliet, re-enter the arena of the family feud and kill Tybalt in revenge (III.i.). As a consequence, the lovers must undergo the agonies of separation, inflicted once again by a single word:

> **Juliet**   Some word there was, worser than Tybalt's death,
> That murd'red me ...
> ... 'Romeo is banished'!
> There is no end, no limit, measure, bound,
> In that word's death,
>
> (III.ii.108–9, 124–6)
>
> **Romeo**   'Banished'?
> O Friar, the damned use that word in hell;
> Howling attends it. How hast thou the heart ...
> To mangle me with that word 'banished'?
> (III.iii.46–8, 51)

A word can maim or kill as surely as poison or a bullet. But, even as they writhe under this realisation, Romeo and Juliet insist on the rift between their secretly evolving selves and the intolerable identities that the language of their world weaves round them:

> Juliet   Hath Romeo slain himself? Say thou but ay,
> And that bare vowel *I* shall poison more
> Than the death-darting eye of cockatrice.
> I am not I, if there be such an ay,
> Or those eyes shut, that makes thee answer ay.
>
> (III.ii.45–9)

> Romeo   As if that name,
> Shot from the deadly level of a gun,
> Did murther her, as that name's cursed hand
> Murder'd her kinsman. O, tell me, friar, tell me,
> In what vile part of this anatomy
> Doth my name lodge?
>
> (III.iii.102–7)

The tragic sense of being turned into a character in a script beyond one's control suffuses Juliet's poignant line, 'My dismal scene I needs must act alone' (IV.iii.19). It also informs Romeo's compassion for his dead rival, Paris, in whom he perceives a fellow victim of the same remorseless narrative: 'O, give me thy hand, / One writ with me in sour misfortune's book!' (V.iii.81–2). The final chapter of that text is penned by Capulet's demand that Juliet obey the word of her father and marry the husband he has chosen. The drug plot is a last vain attempt to convert their tale into a truly 'precious book of love'. Its denouement is aptly staged in the Capulet crypt, repository of the dead generations and symbol of the patriarchal family, whose legacy of repression has gripped Romeo and Juliet from the start. In this sense both of them have been all along a 'Poor living corse, clos'd in a dead man's tomb' (V.ii.30), and their self-inflicted deaths transform that virtual entombment into a fearful reality.

Romeo's total dislocation from the matrix of their doom emerges in his bitter words to the impoverished apothecary, from whom he seeks the means of death in the closing act:

> The world is not thy friend, nor the world's law,
> The world affords no law to make thee rich ...
> There is thy gold, worse poison to men's souls,
> Doing more murther in this loathsome world,
> Than these poor compounds that thou mayest not sell.
> I sell thee poison, thou hast sold me none.
>
> (V.ii.72–3, 80–3)

Romeo and Juliet lays siege to the legitimacy of a world which deprives men and women of boundless love as surely as it deprives the poor of their share in the world's wealth. The reconciliation of the families and the promise of golden memorials cannot redeem the brute fact that Romeo and Juliet were trapped in their fatal impasse by the injustice of 'the world's law', by the tyranny of its customs and prescriptions. But, by sundering the lovers from the discourse that defines them, Shakespeare shows their plight to be man-made and mutable, the local imposition of a transient culture. The crude radical critic indicts the play for colluding in 'the cultural production of desire required by the rise of absolutism, the centralisation of the state, and the advent of capitalism'.[19] But *Romeo and Juliet* in fact foretells the demise of the dispensation that produced it. In the estranged idiom of the lovers can be read the tragedy's estrangement from its era, the imprint of its commerce with futurity.

From Kiernan Ryan, *Shakespeare*, 2nd edn (Hemel Hempstead, 1995), pp. 74–86.

NOTES

[Kiernan Ryan's essay challenges both traditional and more recent radical readings of *Romeo and Juliet* and Shakespearean tragedy. Ryan finds the notion that the play reflects the timeless tragedy of human love as unsatisfactory as the idea that its vision is restricted to the views of gender and desire that prevailed in Shakespeare's day. In Ryan's view, what distinguishes Shakespearean tragedy is its capacity not only to contest the destructive divisions and inequities of his world, but also to reveal the human potential to live and love according to values that remain tragically beyond the reach of our own world. In the case of *Romeo and Juliet*, he argues, the lovers fleetingly discover a form of love that is founded on equality and mutuality rather than domination and subjection, and their tragedy is to find themselves trapped in a culture that finds love on such terms intolerable, and consequently drives them to the point where death is the only option. The most striking feature of this tragedy, however, is that the conflict between the lovers and their world is dramatised as a conflict within the realm of language, as a fatal war of words. For it is by this means, Ryan contends, that the tragedy is revealed as the result of circumstances that are neither fixed nor universal, but open to question and open to be changed. Quotations are from *The Riverside Shakespeare*, ed. G. Blakemore Evans et al. (Boston, MA, 1974). Ed.]

1. The phrase adopted by Northrop Frye for the title of his *Fools of Time: Studies in Shakespearean Tragedy* (Oxford, 1967).

2. J. W. Draper, *Stratford to Dogberry* (Pittsburgh, PA, 1961), p. 88.

3. John Lawlor, '*Romeo and Juliet*', in *Early Shakespeare*, ed. John Russell Brown and Bernard Harris (London, 1961), p. 132.

4. Frank Kermode, 'Romeo and Juliet', in *The Riverside Shakespeare*, ed. G. Blakemore Evans et al. (Boston, MA, 1974), p. 1057.

5. Norman Rabkin, *Shakespeare and the Common Understanding* (New York, 1967), p. 151.

6. T. J. B. Spencer (ed.), *Romeo and Juliet* (Harmondsworth, 1967), pp. 21, 22.

7. Franklin M. Dickey, *Not Wisely But Too Well: Shakespeare's Love Tragedies* (San Marino, CA, 1957), p. 63.

8. D. A. Stauffer, 'The School of Love: *Romeo and Juliet*', in Alfred Harbage (ed.), *Shakespeare: The Tragedies* (Englewood Cliffs, NJ, 1964), p. 30.

9. Virgil K. Whitaker, *The Mirror Up To Nature* (San Marino, CA, 1965), p. 115.

10. Larry S. Champion, *Shakespeare's Tragic Perspective* (Athens, GA, 1976), p. 84.

11. Julia Kristeva, 'Romeo and Juliet: Love-hatred in the Couple', in *Tales of Love*, trans. Leon S. Roudiez (New York, 1987), p. 222.

12. Irene G. Dash, *Wooing, Wedding and Power: Women in Shakespeare's Plays* (New York, 1981), p. 71.

13. Edward Snow, 'Language and Sexual Difference in *Romeo and Juliet*', in Peter Erickson and Coppélia Kahn (eds), *Shakespeare's 'Rough Magic': Renaissance Essays in Honor of C. L. Barber* (Newark, DE, 1985), pp. 168–92.

14. Coppélia Kahn, 'Coming of Age in Verona', in Carolyn Ruth Swift Lenz, Gayle Greene and Carol Thomas Neely (eds), *The Woman's Part: Feminist Criticism of Shakespeare* (Urbana, IL, and London, 1980), p. 185.

15. Dympna Callaghan, 'The Ideology of Romantic Love: The Case of *Romeo and Juliet*', in Dympna Callaghan, Lorraine Helms and Jyotsna Singh, *The Weyward Sisters: Shakespeare and Feminist Politics* (Oxford, 1994), pp. 61, 59–60. [Reprinted in this volume, essay 4 – Ed.]

16. *Marx: Surveys from Exile*, ed. David Fernbach (Harmondsworth, 1973), p. 146.

17. Further reflections on the mutations of the lovers' language can be found in Harry Levin, 'Form and Formality in *Romeo and Juliet*', in Douglas Cole (ed.), *Twentieth Century Interpretations of Romeo and Juliet* (Englewood Cliffs, NJ, 1970), pp. 85–95.

18. See too the striking instances Snow cites of verbal echoes whose 'effect is of two imaginations working in the same idiom', and which 'imply the existence of a single world of desire encompassing the two lovers' separate longings' ('Language and Sexual Difference in *Romeo and Juliet*', p. 169).

19. Callaghan, 'The Ideology of Romantic Love', p. 71.

6

Baz Luhrmann's *William Shakespeare's Romeo + Juliet*

BARBARA HODGDON

I want to begin with an anecdote. When I proposed writing about Leonardo DiCaprio – and titling my essay, 'Was This the Face that Launched a Thousand Clips' – one colleague, taking me somewhat seriously, mentioned the best-selling Leo books, and another sent me a Hong Kong action comic in which 'Leon' single-handedly foils an evil gang and gets the girl. A third, addressing my penchant for reading Shakespearian and popular bodies, glanced at how the Shakespeare myth insists on the physical spectre of the Bard with the Forehead and at the delicious possibility that someone like DiCaprio might have played Cleopatra. A fourth was decidedly visceral: 'The most watery Romeo in film history? His acting is appalling, his affect minimal, and his intelligence – well, why go on? I can understand why teenage girls fall all over themselves for him. But you? Tell me it isn't so!'[1] Such concerns about my 'low' taste and possible adolescent regression point to the lack of critical distance and loss of rational control associated with an intense engagement with the popular; but then, such over-involvement and over-identification, traits traditionally ascribed to women, do mark the popular (and especially its emphasis on the body) as a feminine realm.[2]

These fraught notions trope what I take to be the competing, contradictory horizons of reception surrounding Baz Luhrmann's

1996 *William Shakespeare's Romeo + Juliet*. How, I want to ask, does that film resonate within both 'Shakespeare-culture' and global popular culture? And how are those echoes linked to DiCaprio, the film's 'beautiful boy' star and 'modern-day Romeo', for whom Prince William has recently emerged as a royal twin?[3] Although I am especially interested in looking at how diverse audiences refunction Luhrmann's film and DiCaprio's presence to serve their own uses and pleasures,[4] I also want to look at the relations among text, image and music in the film itself and at how citations from those economies escape and are caught up in a cultural narrative that offers to renegotiate the fictions of and frictions between the academic study of filmed Shakespeare and the 'popular' – what Internet discourse calls DiCaprio ideology or, alternatively, DiCapriorgasm.

Among recent Shakespeare films, Luhrmann's not only most stridently advertises itself as a product of global capitalism but also knowingly flaunts how that culture consumes 'Shakespeare'. In an America where Wendy's Dave, wearing a silly floppy hat, holds up a burger and intones 'To be or not to be'; where 'Something wicked this way comes' promotes the newest black Lexus; and where a clip of Kenneth Branagh's St Crispin's Day speech, equated with a football coach's locker-room pep talk, climaxes a (1997) Superbowl pre-game show, seeing Shakespeare's words appear on billboards for loans or massage parlours – The Merchant of Verona Beach, Mistress Quickly's – as product slogans for Phoenix gasoline or ammunition – 'Add more fuel to your fire', 'Shoot forth thunder' – and brand names – Romeo drives a silver Eclipse – comes as no surprise. The logical Madison Avenue descendants of Matthew Arnold's touchstones and of New Criticism's emphasis on language as glowing artifact, these sound bites sign Shakespeare in and on the film's surface in flashes, confirming that he is indeed the universal brand name and, as Bill Worthen writes, extending beyond *Romeo + Juliet* to embrace Shakespeare the Author and cultural icon, marking how the film traces and re-places signs of its origins.[5]

The film's opening, where a grainy image of an African-American TV anchorwoman speaking the prologue grounds Shakespeare's language in the familiar discourse of popular news-speak, stages that replacement: nearly half the speech turns into print headlines or graphic poster art, further fragmented through flash edits and slammed at viewers. Elsewhere, especially but not exclusively in the ball sequence, the film restyles textual culture as fashion or fetish and writes it onto actors' bodies or their props, as with Montague's

'Longsword' rifle, Tybalt's Madonna-engraved pistol, or Mantua's 'Post-post haste' dispatch van. At times, this traffic between verbal and visual imagery reads as hyped-up anti-Shakespeare-culture panache; at others, it appears curiously literal. Although *Romeo + Juliet* is clearly a film with an attitude, its tone ricochets between Wall-and-Moonshine tongue-in-cheekiness and playing it straight, between selling Shakespeare as one-off visual in-jokes and tying its scenography, almost over-explicitly, to the word. Voguing in a white Afro, silver bra and garter belt that evoke Mab's 'moonshine's wat'ry beams', Mercutio not only punningly embodies the fairy Queen but outmasquerades Lady Capulet's Cleopatra, marking the power of his own extravagant artifice in terms of her even more parodic bodily display. Juliet's white dress and wings literalise her as Romeo's 'bright angel'; he becomes her 'true knight', a Boy King Arthur in shining armour – guises that situate the lovers within medieval Christian romance even as it sends up that myth. Although Dave Paris's astronaut get-up connects him metonymically to the heavenly Juliet, it just as clearly spaces him out to the story's margins, together with those like Capulet's gold-bespangled, purple toga-ed Nero / Antony, the Tramalchian host of this feast of poses and corruptions.[6] Equally saturated with signs, Tybalt's pointed face, neat moustache and black disco outfit, complemented by red-sequinned devil's horns and vest, code him as a macho Prince of Cats whose two cronies dressed as white-faced skeletons foreshadow his violent end. And when, after the balcony-pool sequence, Romeo meets Mercutio, his shirt blazons a heart circled by a wreath of roses, capped with a 'very flame of love', and emanating rays of golden light – the Dante-esque symbol that, glossed by 'My only love sprung from my only hate', serves as the signature logo for the film, the CDs and the official web site.[7]

Sensing an obligation to speak for Shakespeare (especially given his perceived demotion within the American academy), most mainstream critics balked at such over-determined commodifications of his text. Mourning the cuts, they produced resistant readings tied to notions about verse-speaking protocols (singling out Pete Postlewaite's properly British Friar and Miriam Margolyes's Latina Nurse for praise) and focused on those aspects of the film – notably, how the storm sequence following Mercutio's death mirrors 'the characters' ageless passions'[8] – which fit within traditional knowledge-making frames. This is hardly an unfamiliar story: critics once attacked Zeffirelli's *cinéma vérité* documentary of Renaissance

Verona, now ensconced in the educational pantheon, on precisely these grounds. But rehearsing it seems curious, given *West Side Story* and, more recently, the Bologna–Taylor film, *Love Is All There Is*, and the Oscar-winning *Titanic*, or *Romeo and Juliet* with three hours of water (and a remodelled close). Certainly the slasher-porn *Tromeo and Juliet*, an evil twin poised between nineteenth-century burlesques and Luhrmann's film, where 'She hangs upon the cheek of night / Like some barbell in a thrasher's ear' describes a Shirley Temple-curled Juliet whose sleeping potion transforms her into a pig, offers a stronger case for devalued Shakespeare.[9] Still, even those who, like the *New Yorker*'s Anthony Lane, preferred 'John Gielgud filling the aisles with noises',[10] acknowledged the appeal of Luhrmann's bizarre parallel universe comprised of twentieth-century icons and inventive raids on the cinematic canon, from *Rebel Without a Cause* to Busby Berkeley musicals, Clint Eastwood–Sergio Leone spaghetti Westerns, and Ken Russell's or Fellini's surreal spectaculars. Freeze-frames identifying characters recall *Trainspotting*; in the high-voltage Capulet–Montague shoot-out, Shakespeare meets cultist John Woo; John Leguizamo's Tybalt sailing through a frame and then appearing in slow motion quotes a device characteristic of contem-porary action-spectacles introduced in *Bonnie and Clyde*; and when, backed by chorus boys in purple sequins, Mercutio performs before a triptych of Madonnas, Shakespeare moves into music video by way of *To Wong Foo, With Love* and *Priscilla, Queen of the Desert*.[11]

If this be postmodernism, give me excess of it: that impulse seems to propel what might be dubbed a semiotician's dream or, as Peter Matthews writes, 'the most radical reinvention of a classic text since [Kurosawa's] *Throne of Blood*'.[12] To say that subscribes to a particular take on postmodernism as well as on viewing pleasure, one that derives a sense of identification from dissonance and dis-juncture: from hearing early modern language through the flat affect of American speech (which at best works productively to remind spectators of the play's provenance at the same time they see it made contemporary); and from seeing the story set in a decay-ing and decadent city over which, à *La Dolce Vita*, a colossal statue of Christ looms, separating the skyscrapers erected by warring cor-porate owners – a world that comments on our own and renders understandable the importance of 'filial duty, religious devotion, family honour, and the institution of marriage [and] emphasises the ritual performance of ancient hates'.[13] That angle of vision aligns

more with the film's target market, youth, than with the adult critical community, who constructed that audience as 'other' – attuned
to a culture of cars, guns, fashion and music but not to Shakespeare
– and, with few exceptions, either disassociated from or conde-
scended to it. 'So enslaved by its worship of Energy that you want
to slip it a Valium', wrote *Newsweek*; 'Watching it simulates having
a teenager in the house', said the *Los Angeles Times*.[14] Teenagers,
however, embraced Luhrmann's move to drag High-Culture Will
over to the neighbourhood: mounting a still-active Internet discourse (in January 1998 alone, some two years after the film's
release, hits on the official web site reached 8 million),[15] they made
Romeo + Juliet their cultural property and took into their own
hands knowledge-making and its attendant power.

Michel de Certeau's distinction between *strategies* – interpretive
modes performed from positions of strength and tradition and em-
ploying property and authority belonging to literary 'landowners' –
and *tactics* – moves belonging to relatively dispossessed and powerless reader-spectators – offers a useful framework for placing the
claims of both communities.[16] Whereas those who seek to monitor
and manage youth culture and uphold the Shakespeare industry
have access to an existing public forum, the young speak freely only
in the marginal spaces they themselves create, absent of parental
control and of educational protocols – circumstances which trope
the power relations of the play.[17] Yet however socially peripheral,
this conversation the young hold with themselves remains symbolically central to a wider conversation that implicates *Romeo + Juliet*
within a network of cultural meanings by which and through which
we – as agents in that culture – live.

Simultaneously commercial teaser and memory archive, the film's
official web site invites viewers to look at image files and video clips
from late-night star interviews, listen to sound bites, meet 'Bill'
Shakespeare, download a *Romeo + Juliet* screensaver, play a 'Do
You Bite Your Thumb at Me' game, and explore a Verona Beach
Visitors' Guide: What to Wear, Getting There (glossed by 'Go forth
with swift wheels'), Night Life (clubs called Midnite Hags, Pound
of Flesh, and Shining Nights) and a list of Sponsors. The site's epi-
graph image – Romeo and Juliet kissing, framed by boys with guns,
all pointing at the couple – perfectly condenses one of the film's
central tropes: the desire for a private, utopian space within a
threatening social world. The film also rehearses other aspects of
this subcultural imaginary: a sense of adult indifference and be-

trayal, of loss, fragmentation, and despair. As one fan writer put it, 'Complete with death, hate, love, feuds and the hopelessness of the inner city, *William Shakespeare's Romeo + Juliet* is a true look at how we live and think today.'[18] In such a world, these viewers perceive Romeo and Juliet's love as an anchor – an 'image of something better' that teaches what utopia would *feel* like; writes one, 'I'm in love with a fictional tragic romance because I don't like tragic reality'.[19] Such longings find their fullest expression on 'Totally Decapitated: World Headquarters of the DiCaprio Cult', a web fanzine (similar to Shaksper) whose contributors 'share Leonardo DiCaprio as a common source of inspiration'; using film and star as experiential resources, they integrate the meanings attached to both into their lives.[20]

Unlike those devoted to 'flaming' or 'foaming' – 'the closest I've ever come to understanding the play ... the only thing missing is SUBTITLES'! or 'I'd die for Leo ... he is such a hot babe'! – this site offers a space for activity and agency where participants can immerse themselves in the film's world, scribble in its margins and create their own texts. A Palace Chat Room, for instance, 'takes you right inside the vibrant and dramatic world of *Romeo + Juliet*, where you can see yourself and others as graphical "heads" ', handle and even create props, move from room to room, and talk with other fans. Each issue prints poetry (in French as well as English): inspired by the film's images, some incorporate Shakespeare's lines; others, such as 'Révicide' and 'Génération virtuelle', link the play's themes to contemporary anomie; still others (future Oxfordians?) play out anagrams of Leonardo. Reproducing Shakespeare's balcony scene, one issue invites readers to compare text to film; in another, one can listen to a piano rendition of Tchaikowsky's ballet music. All suggest fans who have moved beyond their pre-assigned roles as cult consumers to collaborate with Shakespeare, using his texts (much as scholar-critics do) to stage their own performances.

Yet if the 'zine forges an alternative community through Shakespeare, it concentrates primarily on his surrogate, DiCaprio's Romeo – the 'boy-poet [who] embodies the perfect lover'.[21] As Dennis Kennedy writes, the actor's body is not only the object of the most intense and profound gaze in the culture but, at times when notions of the body undergo change, it becomes a site where that cultural crisis is represented.[22] Appealing to the precarious liminality of early to late adolescents, DiCaprio functions as a tabula rasa on which fans project the romance of identity and, using tactics of personalisation and emotional intensification, voice their desire for 'truth' instead of lies, for transparency instead of manipulation, for a 'real' hero in a world without them. As fanwriter Sonia Belasco says: 'When our president is cheating on his wife, when the mayor of the city I live in gets caught doing crack, when everything is about money and hate and violence ... [Leo] mirrors us ... what we want to be, what we are, what we'll never be'.[23] Taking on idealised – and ideological – contours on and off the web, DiCaprio's body morphs into other texts, especially *Titanic* – and especially for girls. My fifteen-year-old niece, who disavows 'loving Leo', nonetheless has seen most of his films, including *Titanic*, three times – but only once with her boyfriend. What threatens him with loss tells her a different story, a 'romantic feminism' found only at the movies.[24]

In a culture fascinated by youth and in a subculture where one is most interesting if one's sexuality cannot be defined, DiCaprio's pale androgynous beauty – sharp Aryan looks and hint of exotic heritage, a quintessential Greek boy god – makes him a polysexual figure, equally attractive to young women and to gay and straight men. Just as *Romeo + Juliet* is not precisely a chick flick – one where more tears than blood are shed – but, given its coterie of boys who crash cars and carry big guns, can be 're-branded' within a masculine discursive space, DiCaprio's Romeo straddles several cultural masculinities. On the one hand, he figures the vulnerable 'new man' (romancing Juliet and spending the last half of the film in tears); on the other, by gunning down Tybalt, he conforms to contemporary fictions of violent masculinity and subscribes to its homosocial honour codes. Moreover, because he is embedded in a fiction that fetishises his body as well as those of other men, one premised on a forbidden, secret love in which Juliet can substitute for Mercutio, his presence yields to a queer reading.[25] As Joshua Runner, author of regularly featured web diaries, puts it, 'Romeo, Romeo whyfore art thou Romeo? Tending to girls' fantasies, leaving nothing for the boys who exist. Juliet, divine perfection, you may be his sun, but the pale moon needs love too.'[26] Indeed, it is precisely because Leo disrupts dominant fictions of masculinity that his transitional, differently eroticised body can be read as exemplary, as providing a safe harbour for sexual awakening; and by offering fan writers opportunities to externalise and work through their anxieties about sexuality, the site serves a therapeutic function.[27]

Although mainstream critics read his body from a greater distance, even the most conservative found DiCaprio riveting; comparing him to James Dean, the cult figure of their generation, many
decoded his affect in terms of intensity and authenticity, citing his
'passionate conviction', 'an ardour you can't buy in acting class', a
performance that is 'all raw emotion'.[28] Favouring him with 'brood-
ing rock-star close-ups',[29] the film urges a near-oneiric encounter
with Leo's face. Writes José Arroyo, 'He ... bears the brunt of the
feeling ... It's his face in close-up ... indicating how he wants, longs,
feels, and suffers. [But] it's [also] the way he *moves* in the Mantuan
desert when he hears of Juliet's death, not just that the camera lifts
up suddenly to crush him that expresses his grief but the way he
falls on his pigeon-toed heels. It's a superb performance.'[30] Or,
more specifically, a superb *physical* performance, for even the
friendly *Rolling Stone* was hearing echoes of another Romeo: '[Leo]
doesn't round out vowels or enunciate in dulcet tones, but when he
speaks, you believe him'.[31] In short, the idea that both DiCaprio
and Claire Danes are 'doing Shakespeare' lends a kind of pseudo-
Brechtian distantiation to their performances, marking off Danes's
Valley-speak – 'I was about to do the famous balcony scene, and I
was thinking, like, this is a joke, right? How am I going to do this
in a fresh way?' – from iambic pentameter.[32] Yet because she
handles the unfamiliar verse better than the more awkward
DiCaprio, it feels culturally 'authentic' – at least in relation to gendered adolescent stereotypes about linguistic facility – especially
when, in the balcony scene, as the pair seem to discover words and
ways of thinking, viewers can *see* that happening: he learns from
her how to talk the talk, she from him how to act like a natural
born lover.[33]

A witty send-up of the play's hallmark scene, Luhrmann's
balcony–pool sequence underscores the film's distinctions between
the carnivalesque, associated with Verona Beach, where prostitutes
solicit older men beneath a billboard advertising 'Shoot forth
thunder', or with the Capulets' masquerade ball, and the natural
world inhabited by the lovers. First seen silhouetted in pale orange
light, Romeo gazes out to sea in a deliberately painterly 'still' that
not only sets him apart from the frenzied pyrotechnics of the
opening gang war but links him metonymically to Juliet, introduced
as she surfaces, like a mermaid rising from the sea, from her bath.
At the ball, when Romeo douses his face in water to clear his head,
a cut from his face beneath the water to his mirrored reflection sug-

gests a return to self and keys his glance at Juliet through a fishtank, as, in slow motion, to the opening strains of Des'ree's 'Kissing You', exotic tropical fish glide over their faces, already side by side even though separated. These images culminate in the pool where the pair appear first as bodiless heads floating on its surface, their desire condensed into an exchange of looks.[3] But once they take the plunge, the water joins them as one body, out of their depth in love and immersed in a private space, simultaneously enclosed within the social and remote from it. On the one hand, representing the lovers as at one with life-giving nature – and naturalised within it – situates their rebellion within heterosexual norms; on the other, it plays into a conventional opposition between *eros* and *thanatos* which confuses those assumptions. For another image chain – Romeo submerging in the pool to avoid the guard; Mercutio dying in the same space where Romeo was introduced; Tybalt falling backward into a fountain, a shot reprised as nightmare when Romeo wakes from his tryst with Juliet; and her last sight of Romeo, an extreme close-up of his face under the water – not only places both lovers in jeopardy but catches them up within a widening circle of homoerotic and homosocial relations.

Those relations are most clearly marked when an extended close-up of Romeo embracing the dead Mercutio, framed by the crumbling seaside proscenium arch, dissolves to a shot of Juliet on her bed, reframing her briefly with the fading image to link Mercutio's death and the possibility of her fulfilled desire. Yet meditating on gender is not the only way Luhrmann's film hits the hotspots of current conversations, both within Shakespeare studies and in the culture as a whole. Because it takes place, not in Eurocentric culture, but in a multicultural borderland – a mythic geographical space open to variant readings (Miami, California, Mexico) – the film not only accentuates the performative possibilities for 'othering' but ties its representation of gender to somewhat slippery markers of ethnicity and class. Capulet figures the Mediterranean Old World and a nouveau-riche status which set him apart from the white Montague's tacit, if not precisely represented, affiliation with old money; though inflected with old-world codes, Tybalt and the Capulet boys inhabit a new-generation, New World Latino culture. In this multiethnic mix, Mercutio and Juliet are the two most liminal, most transgressive figures. As the white Romeo's 'double', Mercutio shares his gender-bent androgyny but is marked off from him by a flagrant racial 'exoticism'. From the outset, but especially during the Tybalt–Romeo fight, a series of triangulated shots consistently places Mercutio in the middle, a position he shares with the Chief of Police-Prince figure, also a black actor. Apart from the Friar (differently marked by his RSC-trained voice), coding blackness as the sign of mediation works, somewhat uncomfortably, to attribute the failures of mediation as much to skin colour as to the law's – or religion's – impotence and delay.

Yet by insisting on the significance of black voices – especially those of women (the African-American news anchor, Des'ree's ballad, 'Kissing You' [the film's 'love theme'] and Leontyne Price's rendition of Wagner's *liebestod*) but also that of the choirboy who sings Prince's 'When Doves Cry' – to frame *Romeo + Juliet* and to articulate two crucial events in the lovers' story (their meeting and their death), the film not only gestures toward embracing African-American experience but also acknowledges the contributions of that culture to both popular- and high-culture art forms. Moreover, although the film's overall narrating position differs substantively from that of the TV anchorwoman, that position can be read as a figure for Luhrmann's own marginal status as an Australian national who observes and anatomises a 'foreign' American culture. Simultaneously, however, *Romeo + Juliet* seems unable to register most 'other' identities except in terms of stereotypes – Margolyes's highly exaggerated vocal performance – or drag – Diane Venora's non-Latina Lady Capulet staggering like an Egyptian; Harold Perrineau's Mercutio queening his role. That inability becomes especially slippery in terms of Claire Danes's Juliet, who, much like *West Side Story*'s Maria, does not need to pass to become a Montague: in spite of being a young Hispanic woman whose father is depicted as a 'minority', her white skin already 'places' her. Because of this, her ethnicity appears as a kind of drag impersonation which, in equating her with Mercutio, not only adds an erotic frisson to her attraction for Romeo but also makes his love a promise of integration into some idealised realm of 'whiteness' associated with purity, virginity, and perfection.[36]

Even if these dislocations and slippages of ethnicity operate merely as another instance of the film's postmodern aesthetic, they nonetheless produce potential socio-political resonances. Yet *Romeo + Juliet* makes no overtly tactical alignment with melting-pot ideologies. In decoding it, however, mainstream critics called its ethnic politics into question and gestured toward restoring classical paradigms and privileging 'whiteness'. How, they wondered, could Governor Paris permit his son to woo a Mafia Don's daughter? How could the police chief banish a killer instead of locking him up? And how was it possible that 'the milky-skinned Juliet [could be] daughter to the thuggish Capulet, or that prep-school handsome Romeo's best friend was the black disco-diva Mercutio [and that he hung out] with a crew of boys from the hood via Mad Max'?[37] Coming from the right (*Commonweal*) as well as the left (*Village Voice*), such queries suggest critics who imagine they reside somewhere other than an America where such blurrings and crossings of ethnic, ethical, gender and class boundaries occur daily. Yet even more troubling is how they attest to an ideological failure, offering evidence that the promise of an integrated social fabric ordained by public discourse about constructing nationality is just that – a conversation, not a cultural reality.

As the film negotiates its closing moves, these tropes of failed mediation and integration are remapped in terms of voices and bodies and pushed into a contemporary performative space ideally attuned to the play's imaginative repertoire, music video.[38] For just as the set speech and the soliloquy functioned as verbal icons of inferiority for the early modern drama, music video, which expresses emotions and interior states of mind through lyrics and collaged images, represents a late twentieth-century equivalent. After all, it shares characteristic modes – stylistic jumbling, dependence on fragmentation and pastiche, rapid accumulation of images, blurring of internal and external realities – with Shakespeare's early verse, especially that of this play, which, as Anthony Lane notes, exhibits the ' "just-you-look-at-this" quality of a young playwright' who, like the film's young director, is simply showing off.[39] Heightening the film's strategy of putting text-as-image on commercial display and cutting it to the beat of a non-Shakespearian sound, several mini-music-video inserts refunction the play's ending, unmooring its traditional narrative designs and simultaneously preserving, though reinflecting, its meanings.

Two of these – one keyed by Romeo, the other by Juliet – map their desires onto the Friar, who envisions a happy ending. Interweaving his words with Prince's 'When Doves Cry', the first reprises the opening headline, 'Ancient Grudge', but adds a news photo of Montague and Capulet shaking hands; linked by flash cuts of flames, these yield to a grainy image of Juliet and Romeo kissing, across which a dove flies in slow motion, and then to the radiant heart. Yet, although this vision confirms the Friar's decision to marry the lovers, a cut to Mercutio's and Benvolio's parodic gun-play picks up a billboard ad for recliners – 'Such stuff as dreams are made on' – undermining his hopes of peace and union. Later, when Juliet seeks his advice, the Friar appears in left screen as a talking head, his narrative of the effects and consequences of the sleeping potion glossing an image chain that concludes with an extreme close-up of Juliet's eyes, keying shots of Romeo exchanging smiles with her across a cut and of the fatally mis-sent letter. On the videocassette, this segment is letter-boxed, not scanned, deliberately calling attention to its special status and to what its X-ray vision diagnoses: the most improbable gimmicks that mark the play's early modern heritage – the potion and the letter. Framed up within the Friar's imaginary, made hyper-real and morphed into MTV's contemporary gimmickry, those devices appear indeed the very stuff of dreams. Nonetheless, his visions construct two spaces of ending: one recirculates the religious iconography of divine union, the other anticipates a resolution for the lovers' dilemma. Cutting off the latter's more fully 'real-ised' space, the film draws on the former to generate another, even more breathtakingly surreal, dream space of ending.

That space condenses and intensifies the lovers' desire for a private universe, a utopian room of their own. Visually as well as metaphorically interior, it takes place inside the church but travels beyond Shakespeare's implied setting and his text into a knowing, aesthetically satisfying, cinematic plenitude addressed to and complicit with a spectatorial imaginary that idealises and mystifies the lovers' experience as their own. After Romeo dies, an extreme close-up of the gun pointed at Juliet's temple articulates her own death; as the gun's report bleeds over the cut, a high-angle long shot reveals her body falling beside Romeo's onto the bier, flanked by hundreds of candles that illuminate the church aisle lined with banked flowers and blue neon crosses. The shot holds in silence until Leontyne Price's voice, singing the *liebestod* from *Tristan and Isolde*, keys a cut that shifts the perspective, so that the lovers float above the candles, transforming bier to altar.[40] Images reprising their shared moments – catching sight of one another through the fish tank; laughing together at the ball; the ring, inscribed 'I love thee' – link bier with wedding bed where, beneath a fluttering white sheet, they again exchange smiles across a cut. When the image of the bier returns, the camera angle further inverts and disorients point of view, so that instead of looking down at them, we seem to be looking up at a Tiepolo-like ceiling fresco, and the candle-flames have become radiant catherine-wheels that evoke the exploding fireworks at the ball, as if to visualise Juliet's fantasy of 'cut[ting Romeo] out in little stars'. At the centre of their own jewelled orrery, they appear as a treasured artifact, a pair of saintly pilgrims joined in eternal embrace. Exalting their love-death, the sequence offers a sensual experience in which subject identity is lost in the image: read by the body and through the body, its affect is further enhanced by a visual and aural saturation that makes it appear, not as a sign of absence but of an intensely pleasurable present.[41]

In locating the lovers' mythic union inside rather than outside the narrative design, the film offers to rewrite the traditional reading formations associated with the play, those which, as Jonathan Goldberg notes, not only privilege heterosexual love but, by giving value to the lovers' private experience, disconnect the personal from the political.[42] Although the thousand-candle tableau may suggest that love is all there is, its garish MTV excess also clearly marks it as an imported fantasy, something cooked up when an old play confronts a new medium. And that is precisely the point: highlighting the tension between the two, Luhrmann's film juxtaposes medium and message, has it both ways. As the candle-flames dissolve into bubbles to freeze frame the lovers' underwater kiss, a long fade to white, accompanied by the *liebestod*'s final strains, dissolves in turn to the 'social real' – a white-sheeted body on a gurney. Chastising Montague and Capulet – 'All are punished' – the Police Chief passes their silent figures, looking at the second white-sheeted body being loaded into an ambulance.[43] Glossed by the voice of the newswoman who spoke the opening prologue, these images then turn to grainy video; reframed within a TV monitor, that image fades, finally, to video snow.

Michael Bogdanov's 1986 RSC production, of course, anticipated this ending: there, the unveiling of the golden statues became a photo op that enhanced the Prince's public image, and it was Benvolio who, after all had left, rose from a nearby café table to mourn his friend's death.[44] Ten years later, Luhrmann's film denies, or suspends, any promise of securing the social through either the heterosexual or the homosocial. That points, all too knowingly, to how, in our present cultural moment – at least in America – there seem to be no answers, fictional or real, religious or legal, to gender, ethnic and class differences and conflicts, to generational strife, or boys with guns. If, as the web discourse on Leo tells us, chick flicks do matter, then *William Shakespeare's Romeo + Juliet* matters even more: it bears watching precisely because it has been watching us.

From *Shakespeare Survey*, 52 (1999).

NOTES

[In this essay, Barbara Hodgdon explores the competing, contradictory horizons of reception surrounding Baz Luhrmann's *William Shakespeare's Romeo + Juliet* (1996), focusing especially on how that film and its beautiful boy star, Leonardo DiCaprio, resonate within both Shakespeare-culture, and global popular culture. Framing her analysis with Michel de Certeau's distinction between strategies (interpretive modes used by mainstream critics who speak in a sanctioned public forum) and tactics (modes used by those who speak from the margins on Internet web sites), Hodgdon argues that the claims made by these viewing communities trope the generational inflections as well as the power relations of the play, implicating *Romeo + Juliet* within a network of cultural meanings by which and through which we, as agents in that culture, live. Mapping the relations between text, image, and music in the film not only reveals how it incorporates a range of contemporary media from cult films to music video but also how such citations mark a complex interplay of ethnicity, gender, and class. In detailing how spectators refunction both the film and DiCaprio's androgynous presence to serve their own uses and pleasures, Hodgdon suggests that Luhrmann's film 'bears watching precisely because it has been watching us'. Ed.]

1. In order, these colleagues are Bill Worthen, Joseph Schneider, Peter Donaldson and Jim Bulman, whose e-mail communication I cite. The mass market DiCaprio books are Grace Catalano, *Leonardo: A Scrapbook in Words and Pictures* (New York, 1998); Catalano, *Leonardo DiCaprio: Modern-Day Romeo* (New York, 1997); and Brian J. Robb, *The Leonardo DiCaprio Album* (London, 1997). For the filmscript, see *William Shakespeare's Romeo & Juliet: The Contemporary Film. The Classic Play* (New York, 1996).

2. See, for instance, Mary Ann Doane, *The Desire to Desire: The Woman's Film of the 1940s* (Bloomington, 1987), pp. 2–16.

3. See *Life*, 'Special Royals Issue: A Guide to the 28 Monarchies of the World' (Summer 1998). The cover features 'The Boy who WILL be King'. Remarks Prince William: 'I think [DiCaprio will] find it easier being king of Hollywood than I shall being king of England', pp. 58–9.

4. My framework derives from Paul Smith, *Clint Eastwood: A Cultural Production* (Minneapolis, 1993). As I turn to reception, I am indebted to Janet Staiger, *Interpreting Films: Studies in the Historical Reception of American Cinema* (Princeton, NJ, 1992).

5. W. B. Worthen, 'Drama, Performativity, and Performance', *PMLA*, 113:5 (October 1998) 1103. My thanks to Worthen for providing me with a copy of his essay before publication and for comments on an earlier version of this essay entitled 'Totally DiCaptivated: Shakespeare's Boys Meet the Chick Flick'.

6. As in Luhrmann's debut film, *Strictly Ballroom* (1992), it is parents, not children, who are the 'unnatural' – or parodically perverse – gender performers.

7. As for Zeffirelli's film, two CDs were released, one with and one without dialogue. For the official web site, see http://geocities.com/MotorCity/4147/romeo.html.

8. Janet Maslin, 'Soft! What light? It's flash, Romeo', *New York Times*, 1 November 1996.

9. See *Tromeo and Juliet*, dir. Lloyd Kaufman; Troma Video Entertainment, 1997; 107 minutes.

10. Anthony Lane, 'Tights! Camera! Action!' *New Yorker*, 25 November 1996, p. 66.

11. Most mainstream reviews cite several of these 'classic' filmtexts. I am indebted to seminar students for some of the references to cult films.

12. Peter Matthews, review of *William Shakespeare's Romeo + Juliet*, *Sight and Sound* (April 1997), 55.

13. Speaking of the team's search for a location, Catherine Martin, the film's designer, remarks on how Mexico had many of the elements necessary to make a contemporary version work. 'Religion still has a very strong presence there, culturally and visually; marriage is still big, and sex before marriage is frowned on. There are whole streets in Mexico City which are only bridal shops. And the social structure is closer to that of Elizabethan times than anywhere else in the modern world: a few very rich people with guns, and the vast majority poor.' See Jo Litson, '*Romeo and Juliet*', *TCI: The Business of Entertainment Technology and Design*, 30 (November 1996), 46.

14. See David Ansen, 'It's the '90s, so the Bard is Back', *Newsweek*, 4 November 1996, 73; Kenneth Turan, 'A Full-Tilt Romeo', *Los Angeles Times*, 1 November 1996, F1.

15. Overall, 40 web sites are devoted to the film; 500 to Leonardo DiCaprio. I am indebted to Erik Steven Fisk, 'Professor Shakespeare,

Director Shakespeare: Examining the Role of the Bard on the Way into 2000 à la *Romeo + Juliet'*, unpublished seminar paper.

16. Michel de Certeau, *The Practice of Everyday Life* (Berkeley, CA, 1984; cited in Henry Jenkins, *Textual Poachers: Television Fans and Participatory Culture* (New York and London, 1992), pp. 44–5. These distinctions point to the boundaries separating elitist and popular texts, marking cultural space as a contested territory. The reviewers' comments also point to what Jenkins identifies as a frequent mistake: treating popular culture productions as though they were the materials of elite culture. See Jenkins, *Textual Poachers*, p. 60.

17. Zeffirelli's *Romeo and Juliet* had a similarly divided reception history. See, for example, Jill L. Levenson, *Shakespeare in Performance: 'Romeo and Juliet'* (Manchester, 1987), p. 123; and my 'Absent Bodies, Present Voices: Performance Work and the Close of *Romeo and Juliet*'s Golden Story', *Theatre Journal* (October 1989), 341–59.

18. Comment from fan writer on http//www.Asu.edu.

19. From 'The Diaries of Joshua Runner', a regular feature of 'Totally Decapitated'; the cite is from Issue Four and is dated 25 November 1996. The web site address is http://www.com/leo/issuefour/html. For the idea of using stars as resources, see Richard Dyer, *Stars* (London, 1979), pp. 59–60.

20. Jenkins argues that, by blurring the boundaries between producers and consumers, spectators and participants, both web discourses and fanzines constitute a cultural and social network that spans the globe. See *Textual Poachers*, esp. pp. 45, 279.

21. Quote from 'The Diaries of Joshua Runner', 10 November 1996.

22. See Dennis Kennedy, 'Shakespeare Played Small: Three Speculations About the Body', *Shakespeare Survey*, 47 (1994), 10.

23. Sonia Belasco, 'Totally Decapitated', Issue Ten: prose.

24. See Katha Pollitt, 'Women and Children First', *The Nation*, 30 March 1998, p. 9.

25. See, for instance, Jonathan Goldberg, '*Romeo and Juliet*'s Open Rs', in *Queering the Renaissance*, ed. Jonathan Goldberg (Durham and London, 1994), pp. 218–35 [reprinted in this volume – Ed.]. See also Robert Appelbaum, ' "Standing to the Wall": The Pressures of Masculinity in *Romeo and Juliet*', *Shakespeare Quarterly*, 48: 3 (1997), 251–72; and Paul Smith's notions of hysterical or wounded masculinity in Smith, *Clint Eastwood*. See also Ellen Goodman, 'Romancing a New Generation of Women', *Des Moines Register*, 12 May 1998, 7A; and Pollitt, 'Women and Children First'.

26. 'The Diaries of Joshua Runner', 8 November 1996. Wolf, another frequent contributor, writes, 'He is the embodyment [sic] of what we
need, someone like us to hide with … someplace far away'; responding
to a fan calling himself 'Like Minded' who had rented the film and
found himself desiring Leo, Wolf urges him to read Shakespeare's
sonnets addressed to the young man, saying that he himself had found
comfort in them. 'Totally Decapitated', Issue Five: prose.

27. On fan writers, see Jenkins, *Textual Poachers*, pp. 152–84. On
Internet discourse and therapy, see Sherry Turkle, *Life on the Screen:
Identity in the Age of the Internet* (New York, 1995). See also Janet H.
Murray, *Hamlet on the Holodeck: The Future of Narrative in
Cyberspace* (New York, 1997). Significantly, the fan writers I cite do
not represent all cultures: Joseph Schneider's students (women as well
as men) at the University of Hong Kong, for instance, prefer the Jet Lis
of their world or the Bruce Willises of ours to Leo, who is 'too boyish'
for their tastes – 'not a real man'. Harold Bloom puts such opportunities for meaning-making into a wider context. Shakespeare, he writes,
'teach[es] us how to overhear ourselves when we talk to ourselves';
the true use of Shakespeare, he goes on to say, is 'to augment one's
own growing inner self', a process that will bring about 'the proper
use of one's own solitude, that solitude whose final form is one's con-
frontation with one's own mortality'. See Harold Bloom, *The Western
Canon* (New York and London, 1994), pp. 30–1.

28. In order, quotations are from David Horspool, 'Tabs and Traffic Jams',
Times Literary Supplement, 11 April 1997, p. 19; Peter Travers, 'Just
Two Kids in Love', *Rolling Stone*, 14 November 1996, p. 124; José
Arroyo, 'Kiss Kiss Bang Bang', *Sight and Sound* (March 1997), p. 9.

29. Kuran, 'It's the '90s', F1.

30. Arroyo, 'Kiss Kiss', p. 9.

31. Travers, 'Just Two Kids', p. 124.

32. Claire Danes quoted in Christine Spines, 'I Would Die 4U', *Premiere*,
v. 10 (October 1996), 137.

33. I appropriate 'natural born lovers' from Joe Morgenstern, 'Mod Bard;
Muted Vonnegut', *Wall Street Journal*, 1 November 1996, A11.
Morgenstern, however, in alluding to Quentin Tarantino's *Natural
Born Killers*, gives the phrase a different sense than mine.

34. Just before they fall into the pool together, they are posed on either
side of a statue of Pan, another marker of this 'natural' though man-
made setting.

35. My thanks to Margo Hendricks for pointing out how the film works
to situate black women's voices at its centre.

36. See Arroyo, 'Kiss Kiss', p. 8; and Richard Dyer, *White* (London and New York, 1997), esp. pp. 70–2.

37. These objections, as well as the cites, are from Richard Alleva, 'The Bard in America', *Commonweal*, 6 December 1996, p. 19; and Amy Taubin, 'Live Fast, Die Young', *Village Voice*, 12 November 1996, p. 80. The problematics of reading the film's multiculturalism also embraces how casting invites blending actors' performances in *Romeo + Juliet* with their most recent roles: for instance, American viewers might well connect Brian Dennehy (Montague) to his most recent appearances as a hawker of antacids on TV rather than to his film roles or to stage performances at New York's Public Theater.

38. *Romeo and Juliet*'s focus on adolescent rebellion and narcissistic love and its obsession with sexuality and violence pre-tailors it for MTV, which addresses the desires, fantasies and anxieties of the young. See E. Ann Kaplan, *Rocking Around the Clock: Music Television, Postmodernism, and Consumer Culture* (New York and London, 1987), esp. pp. 5–7, 31. On MTV, see also Jenkins, *Textual Poachers*, pp. 233–40; Richard Dyer, 'Entertainment and Utopia', in *Movies and Methods, Volume II*, ed. Bill Nichols (Berkeley CA, 1985); and John Fiske, 'MTV: Post-Structural Post-Modern', *Journal of Communication Inquiry*, 10: 1 (Winter 1986), 74–9.

39. Lane, 'Tights!', p. 75.

40. Sung by a black contralto, this aria not only connects the lovers to the most famous of all love-deaths but also represents an instance of how the film's soundtrack, much like its casting (which blends stage and film traditions) mixes opera, classical music (phrases from Mozart's Symphony 25 introduce Romeo) and pop culture, especially music from groups that mix white, black and latino/latina or hispanic voices.

41. I adapt these terms from Fiske, 'MTV', pp. 74–9.

42. See Goldberg, '*Romeo and Juliet*'s Open Rs', esp. pp. 219–20.

43. Peter Holland suggests a pertinent analogue: the moment in Bob Fosse's 1979 film, *All That Jazz*, where a cut from Ben Vereen's final production number (celebrating the Fosse-character's death) yields to an image of a body bag being zipped shut.

44. See my 'Absent Bodies, Present Voices', *Theatre Journal*, 41:3 (October 1989), 341–59, especially p. 358, n. 47.

7

The Servants

*BERTOLT BRECHT (*translated by *RALPH MANNHEIN)*

Practice Piece for Actors: (To be played between Scenes i and ii, Act II of Shakespeare's *Romeo and Juliet.)*

1

Romeo and one of his tenants.

Romeo   I've already told you, old fellow, that I need the money and for no unworthy purpose.

Tenant   But where are we to go if your lordship sells the land from one minute to the next? There are five of us.

Romeo   Can't you hire out somewhere? You're a good worker, I'll give you an excellent reference. I must have the money, I have obligations, you don't understand these things, or do I have to explain that when a lady has given me her all I can't put her out in the street without so much as a present? Just bye-bye, my love, and that's all? Would you want me to do anything so contemptible? Then you're a worthless blackguard, a selfish dog. Farewell presents cost money. And you'll have to admit they're unselfish, one gets nothing in return. Am I right, old friend? Don't be a spoilsport. Who rocked me on his knees and carved my first bow, remember? Shall I say to myself: even Gobbo doesn't understand me any more, lets me down, wants me to play the cad? My friend, I'm in love! There's nothing I wouldn't sacrifice. I'd even commit a crime for the girl I love, a murder. And I'd be proud of it, but you don't understand. You're too old, old Gobbo, dried out. Don't you see, I have to get rid of the other one. Now I've taken you into my confidence, and I ask you: are you still the old Gobbo you used to be, or not? Answer me.

Tenant   I'm no good at making speeches, sire. But where will I take my family if you drive me off your land?

Romeo   Poor old Gobbo. He's too old to understand. I tell him I'm dying of love and he mumbles something about land. Do I own a piece of land? I've forgotten. No, I own no land, or rather, my land must go. What's land to me? I'm burning.

Tenant   And we're starving, sire.

Romeo   Dolt. Is it impossible to talk sense to you? Have you animals no feelings? In that case, away with you, the sooner the better.

Tenant   Yes, away with us. Here, do you want my coat too? (*He takes it off*) My hat? My boots? Animals you say? Even animals have to eat.

Romeo   Ah, so that's the tune you sing? So that's your true face? That you've hidden for twenty-five years like a leprous spot? So that's my reward for speaking to you like a human being? Get out of my sight, or I'll thrash you, you animal. (*He chases him away, but during the love scene the tenant lurks in the background*)

Romeo   He jests at scars that never felt a wound.

2

Juliet and her lady's maid.

Juliet   And you love your Thurio? How do you love him?

Maid   At night when I've said my 'Our Father' and the nurse has begun to snore, begging your pardon, I get up again and go to the window in my bare feet, mistress.

Juliet   Just because he might be standing outside?

Maid   No, because he was standing there before.

Juliet   Oh, how well I understand that. I like to look at the moon because we've looked at it together. But tell me some more about how you love him. If he were in danger, for instance …

Maid   You mean if he were dismissed for instance? I'd run straight to the master.

Juliet   No, if his life were in danger …

Maid   Oh, if there were a war? Then I'd keep at him until he pretended to be sick and took to his bed and stayed there.

Juliet   But that would be cowardly.

Maid I'd make a coward of him all right. If I lay down with him, he'd stay in bed all right.

Juliet No, I mean if he were in danger and you could save him by sacrificing your life.

Maid You mean if he got the plague? I'd put a rag soaked in vinegar in my mouth and I'd care for him, of course.

Juliet But would you remember the rag?

Maid What do you mean by that?

Juliet Since it won't help, anyway.

Maid Not much, but it does help some.

Juliet Anyway, you'd risk your life for him, and so would I for my Romeo. But one more thing: If for instance he went to war and came back and something was missing ...

Maid What?

Juliet I can't say it.

Maid Oh, that! I'd scratch his eyes out.

Juliet Why?

Maid For going to war.

Juliet And then it would be all over between you?

Maid Well, wouldn't it be all over?

Juliet You don't love him.

Maid What, you don't call it love that I like to be with him so much?

Juliet That's earthly love.

Maid But isn't earthly love nice?

Juliet Oh yes, but I love my Romeo more, I assure you.

Maid You think because I like so much to be with my Thurio I don't really love him? But maybe I'd even forgive him for what you said. I mean, after the first excitement was over. Oh yes. My love is too strong.

Juliet But you hesitated.

Maid That was because of love.

Juliet (*embraces her*) That's true too. You must go to him tonight.

Maid Oh yes, on account of that other girl. I'm so glad you're letting me off. If he meets her, it will be all over.

Juliet You're sure you can catch him at the back door in the wall?

Maid Oh yes, he can't get out any other way. And he wasn't to meet her until eleven.

Juliet If you leave now, you can't miss him. Here, take this kerchief, it's pretty. And which stockings have you got on?

Maid My best. And I'll put on my sweetest smile, and I'll be nicer to him than ever. I love him so.

Juliet   Wasn't that a branch crackling?

Maid   It sounded like someone jumping down from the wall. I'll look.

Juliet   But don't miss your Thurio.

Maid   (*at the window*) Who do you think has jumped down off the wall and there he is in the garden?

Juliet   It's Romeo! Oh, Nerida, I must go out on the balcony and talk to him.

Maid   But the gatekeeper sleeps downstairs, mistress. He'll hear everything. Suddenly there won't be steps in your room, but there will be on the balcony. And voices, too.

Juliet   Then you must walk up and down in here and rattle the basin as if I were washing.

Maid   But then I won't meet my Thurio and it will be all over for me.

Juliet   Maybe they'll keep him in tonight. After all, he's a servant too. Just walk up and down and rattle the basin. Dear, dear Nerida! Don't let me down, I must speak to him.

Maid   Can't you make it quick? Please make it quick!

Juliet   Very quick, Nerida, very quick. Walk up and down here in the room. (*Juliet appears on the balcony. During the love scene the maid walks back and forth rattling the basin now and then. When the clock strikes eleven, she falls in a faint*)

From *Bertolt Brecht: Collected Plays*, volume 6, ed. Ralph Mannheim and John Willett (New York, 1976), pp. 352–5.

NOTES

[Bertolt Brecht, the great twentieth-century dramatist and theorist of theatre, wrote this short 'Intercalary Scene' or 'Practice Piece', not with the serious intention of adding it to *Romeo and Juliet*, but rather to help the actors about to rehearse Shakespeare's play clarify their attitudes to the central characters. In accordance with his theory of *werfremdungseffekte* (alienation, defamiliarisation, distancing) he wanted both actors and audiences to resist the temptation to identify or empathise with characters. Instead, he wished us to stand back from characters so that they can be judged in behavioural terms according to moral and political issues, undistracted by personalities or psychological concerns. As a Marxist, Brecht was very clearly a cultural materialist. At first the Scene seems comic and irrelevant to Shakespeare's tragedies, but on reflection it provides a genuine question about the play: to what extent are these young lovers just privileged aristocrats, who, by playing out their love fantasies, are unknowingly ruining other people's chances for happiness in what the Maid calls 'earthly love'. The reason why they hold this power over lowlier people like servants, is that they have money, and Romeo especially, in Brecht's Scenes, speaks a lot about money. A prompt for Brecht may have been Shakespeare's Nurse, whose language, attitudes and social position are very different from the other characters: she is, in Marx's sense, one of the few 'proletariats' in the play. Brecht was deeply influenced by Shakespeare's plays (he rewrote *Coriolanus* and *Measure for Measure*, for example), and claimed that his own politically and socially informed theories and practice were based on English Elizabethan 'epic theatre'. Ed.]

8

Romeo and Juliet: The Nurse's Story

BARBARA EVERETT

The heroine of *Romeo and Juliet* enters the play late. Not until the third scene of the first Act is she called on-stage by her mother and her Nurse, who are also appearing here for the first time. The latter part of this scene is given to Lady Capulet's brisk and formal announcement of an offer for her daughter, with Juliet's timid and obedient response. All the earlier part of it is dominated by the Nurse, and her reminiscences of the past set the tone for the first appearance of the only three really important women in this romantic and domestic tragedy. Lady Capulet's conventional niceties make their point too, but it is the Nurse who holds the stage. Indeed, her 'moment' seems to have an importance in the play as a whole which has not been recognised. It demands to be looked at in a little detail. At Juliet's entry, mother and Nurse are discussing her age:

> **Lady C.** She's not fourteen.
> **Nurse.** I'll lay fourteen of my teeth–
>   And yet, to my teen be it spoken, I have but four–
>   She's not fourteen. How long is it now
>   To Lammas-tide?
> **Lady C.** A fortnight and odd days.
> **Nurse.** Even or odd, of all days in the year,
>   Come Lammas Eve at night shall she be fourteen.
>   Susan and she – God rest all Christian souls!–
>   Were of an age. Well, Susan is with God;

She was too good for me. But, as I said,
On Lammas Eve at night shall she be fourteen;
That shall she, marry; I remember it well.
'Tis since the earthquake now eleven years;
And she was wean'd – I never shall forget it–
Of all the days of the year, upon that day;
For I had then laid wormwood to my dug,
Sitting in the sun under the dove-house wall;
My lord and you were then at Mantua.
Nay, I do bear a brain. But, as I said,
When it did taste the wormwood on the nipple
Of my dug, and felt it bitter, pretty fool,
To see it tetchy, and fall out with the dug!
Shake, quoth the dove-house. 'T was no need, I trow,
To bid me trudge.
And since that time it is eleven years;
For then she could stand high-lone; nay, by th' rood,
She could have run and waddled all about;
For even the day before, she broke her brow;
And then my husband – God be with his soul!
'A was a merry man – took up the child.
'Yea', quoth he, 'dost thou fall upon thy face?
Thou wilt fall backward when thou has more wit,
Wilt thou not, Jule?' And, by my holidam,
The pretty wretch left crying, and said 'Ay'.
To see, now, how a jest shall come about!
I warrant, an I should live a thousand years,
I never should forget it: 'Wilt thou not, Jule?' quoth he;
And, pretty fool, it stinted, and said 'Ay'.
Lady C.   Enough of this; I pray thee hold thy peace.
Nurse.   Yes, Madam. Yet I cannot choose but laugh
To think it should leave crying and say 'Ay'.
And yet, I warrant, it had upon its brow
A bump as big as a young cock'rel's stone –
A perilous knock; and it cried bitterly.
'Yea', quoth my husband, 'fall'st upon thy face?
Thou wilt fall backward when thou comest to age;
Wilt thou not, Jule?' It stinted, and said 'Ay'.
Juliet.   And stint thou, too, I pray thee, nurse, say I.
Nurse.   Peace, I have done. God mark thee to his grace!
Thou wast the prettiest babe that e'er I nurs'd;
An I might live to see thee married once,
I have my wish.

The one detail in these rich ramblings that has earned examination is the earthquake. There were real earthquakes in England in the 1580s, and one in 1580 big enough to be long memorable; and some have hoped that the Nurse's allusion might date the play. But this is perhaps to fail to grasp the very special milieu set up in these passages. The Nurse's mind has its precision, but not one such as to make her sums trustworthy. There is even a slight oddity about the figures involving the infant Juliet, since to have been only just weaned, and to be only just 'waddling' about, at rising three years, seems backward even for rustic Tudor non-gentry babies. Mathematical computations clearly increase the Nurse's dither.

'Dither' may be said to be the point of this speech. We can look in it, that is to say, for human interests and purposes even if we cannot trust its figures; indeed, the figures may be there simply to divert us from looking for the wrong thing. The Nurse's speech is a highly original piece of writing. It is perhaps Shakespeare's first greatly human verse speech, so supple in its rhythms that its original text – the Good Quarto – prints it as prose. Indeed, this looseness of rhythm, when added to the idiosyncrasies of the thought-processes as far as logic and mathematics are concerned, has increased the suspicions of some scholars about the authenticity of the whole; suspicions which can only be met by setting forth clearly a justification for it.

In part we can explain what the Nurse says here in terms of 'character' interest. In Brooke, the main source, the heroine's old Nurse holds forth to Romeus about Juliet as a small baby, and tells how she 'clapt her on the buttocks soft and kist where I did clappe', in a moment of coarse and genial humour that Shakespeare is perhaps remembering and adapting. And Brooke too has 'beldams' who

> sit at ease upon theyr tayle
> The day and eke the candlelight before theyr talke shall fayle,
> And part they say is true, and part they do devise ...

The Nurse is a product of this comfortable and recognisable world. Shakespeare has taken Brooke's sketch of a conventional character-type and given it a dense human solidity; moreover, later in the play the Nurse will find herself in a further dimension, a moral context that defines and painfully 'places' her. In this, her opening speech, a mere something given by the story-situation is first and most massively 'rounded out', and there are also perhaps hints of that moral context to come. Her role as Nurse, her comfortable humanity, and her limitations of vision are all revealed in the references backward to Juliet's babyhood, and in the profuse mindlessness which is the medium of narration.

On the other hand, such a character need not have been quite as comical as the Nurse: and something important is contributed to *Romeo and Juliet* by the fact that she and her counter-poise Mercutio are both, in their opposed ways, exceptionally funny. She is a 'natural' and he is a 'fool', and this fact makes a good deal of difference to the way we respond to their two 'straight men', the hero and heroine of the play. Romeo and Juliet are two romantic children, but we take them – or should take them – absolutely straight; and we might fail to do so if it were not for the obliquity, or folly, that characterises their constant companions. That is to say, from the beginning what the Nurse has is more than personality: it is function; and by function she is a 'natural'. The presence of Bottom in *A Midsummer Night's Dream*, a companion piece to this play, serves to suggest that the discourse of Shakespeare's fools and especially of his naturals will provide insight even – or most – where it appears to be failing to provide information. There is a kind of insight early achieved in the Shakespearian comic mode which can shift the comic up and away from the limits of the satirised or satirising and into a medium which is a form of truth; or perhaps one ought to say, which is *another* form of truth. If a fat middle-aged woman congenitally disposed to muddle is made, by function, into a fool licensed to speak profound nonsense, then she may undercut the rational and move into an area of more primitive and powerful (though more elusive and dangerous) utterance. The Nurse's speech is followed by Lady Capulet's thin and superficial conventionalities, and these latter help to intensify by retrospective contrast the crude depth achieved by the Nurse.

I would argue that the major function of the Nurse's speech is to provide a *natural* context for the motif of 'death-marked love' which governs the play. Such intimations of mortality as occur here hardly rise to tragic dignity. But it is commonly agreed that *Romeo and Juliet* makes tragedy out of the lyrical and comical. The Nurse's jokes operate well within that region of the 'painfully funny' which comes fully and deeply into being at the death of Mercutio. Indeed, one might call Mercutio's death-scene, with the astonishing death-blow given unheralded to the irresponsibly free and funny young man, a perfect match or counter-poise in a harsh vein to what is set forth here with a rough tenderness. What the Nurse says at this early point acts as a semi-choric commentary, helping to build up the background of suggestions which in the earlier part of the play act as an unconscious persuasion stronger than the explicit feud-motif in accounting for the catastrophe. It might be objected that this would demand an audience impossibly acute, able at once to laugh at the Nurse, relish her 'character', and respond to the more impersonal connotations of what she says. But it must be pointed out that for the original theatre audience this charmingly comical account of a marriageable girl's infancy was narrated on a stage hung everywhere with black. The reference to 'Juliet and her Romeo' at the end of the play certainly makes it sound a story already very familiar, almost fabulous; but even those not familiar with the tale could hardly fail to observe that a death was likely at some point to take place: that they were assisting at a tragedy. They could not be wholly unprepared to hear, at the very least, a touch of painful irony in the lines that close the Nurse's affectionate apostrophe:

> Thou was the prettiest babe that e're I nursed;
> An I might live to see thee married once,
> I have my wish.

'Married once' just about covers Juliet's case. It seems worth while to look at the Nurse's speech in rather closer focus than it has received.

The passage falls into three sections: the first concerned with Juliet's age and birthday ('On Lammas Eve at night shall she be fourteen'), the second with the child's weaning, and the third with the child's fall. First things first: the birthday. Lammas Eve is July 31st, and so an appropriate date (as the New Penguin editor has pointed out) for a heroine named from July. But there may be a particular resonance in the festival date, which is thrice repeated, with an effect as much of ritual as of wandering memory. The Christian feast of Lammas took the place of what was possibly the most important of the four great pagan festival days, the midsummer feast. 'Lammas' itself meant originally 'loaf-mass', the sacrament at which were offered loaves made from the first ripe corn, the first fruits of the harvest. One therefore might expect Lammas Eve to carry, for an Elizabethan consciousness, mixed and fugitive but none the less suggestive associations, both with Midsummer Eve and with harvest festival. Such associations would be appropriate.

For *Romeo and Juliet* is a summer tragedy as its companion-piece, *A Midsummer Night's Dream*, is a summer comedy. *Romeo and Juliet* so consistently evokes different aspects of high summer, both inner and outer weather, that Capulet's 'quench the fire, the room is grown too hot' (at I.v.29: apparently borrowed from the wintry season in which this part of Brooke's poem takes place) is often noted for its discordance with the general 'feel' of the play. We are told that the furious energies of the fighting, fornicating, and witticising young men are in part to be explained by the season of 'dog-days': 'now is the mad blood stirring'. The relation of hero and heroine embodies a different, more tender aspect of summer: the lyrical sense of a time that 'Holds in perfection but a little moment' (Sonnet 15). In the balcony scene,

> This bud of love, by summer's ripening breath
> May prove a beauteous flow'r when next we meet ...

but in the tomb,

> Death ... hath suck'd the honey of thy breath.

Then at the end of the play, these 'midsummer' associations are replaced by an image in which the golden statues are something much more like first fruits:

> As rich shall Romeo's by his lady's lie –
> Poor sacrifices of our enmity!

A reference to Lammas, then, may carry a proleptic suggestion both of the fall that follows the midsummer equinox in the course of nature and of the sacrificial offerings of first-fruits. And there is a further point to be made, concerning Elizabethan idiom. The expression 'latter Lammas' was used to mean 'Never' – a time that will never come. The more sombre, if tender side of these hints is strengthened by the Nurse's references to Juliet's dead foster-sister, Susan.

> Susan is with God;
> She was too good for me.

In Shakespeare's time, so pitifully small a proportion of babies born survived their first six years that this reminder of a massive infant death-rate brings closer to Juliet the whole context of fatality. Not very many years will separate the deaths of the two girls. And the Nurse's 'She was too good for me' is one way of interpreting the meaning of the destruction of Romeo and Juliet themselves, and it is one that is offered as a possibility by the play as a whole.

It would be unwise to argue, from all this, that a perceptive mind ought to take the hint that Juliet is unlikely to reach or much pass the age of fourteen: or to urge that an audience ought somehow to feel *consciously* that the ludicrous argument about the precise extent of Juliet's past holds ironical premonitions of the absence of her future. But the twice-repeated 'Lammas Eve' line holds between its repetitions the dead Susan: and the conjunction of birthday with deathday lingers in the mind. The effect is not irrelevant to a tragedy in which Juliet reaches maturity with a suddenness and brevity both splendid and shocking.

To speak of maturity here is to bring up the whole question of Juliet's age, on which the passage turns in a more than merely nominal sense. The figure 'fourteen' is obtruded upon our attention so as to make it scarcely forgettable. Shakespeare is choosing an age which makes his heroine two years younger than the already very young heroine in Brooke's poem. In both stories the age of the heroine seems to have more to do with romance than with ordinary bourgeois reality.[1] Marriage at sixteen or fourteen, let alone the Nurse's 'Now, by my maidenhead at twelve year old', cannot be taken as a reflection of ordinary Elizabethan facts of life. It may be that Shakespeare was availing himself of the notion of 'hot Italy', where girls matured far earlier than in his own cooler clime, but for that the original sixteen would presumably have served. It seems important that Capulet should give the impression that Juliet is a little young for marriage –

> She hath not seen the change of fourteen years;
> Let two more summers wither in their pride,
> Ere we may think her ripe to be a bride

and that Lady Capulet should apparently contradict this later:

> By my count,
> I was your mother much upon these years
> That you are now a maid.

Considering all this, we may say that Juliet's age is important, and that the question is brought up by Lady Capulet and

elaborated by the Nurse as a way of giving a good deal of information about the play's heroine, though not exactly of a chronological
kind. Shakespeare is utilising a characteristically poetic sense of
time. On the one hand (he seems to insist) there is nothing abnor-
mal about Juliet's marriage at her present age; on the contrary,
given that we are moving in a romantic world, the event is a part of
a great cycle – both natural and ceremonious or customary – that
occurs generation after generation. On the other hand, the choice of
an age slightly young even by romantic standards achieves the sense
of extremity, of a painful too-soonness: Juliet is a 'rathe primrose',
a 'fairest flower no sooner blown than blasted'. Juliet is so young
indeed that the figure of fourteen seems to suggest a coming-to-
maturity that accompanies the simple physical process of puberty
itself: Juliet is at a threshold. (Such hints are paralleled in Romeo's
case by the adolescent fits of passion, and the rapid change of affec-
tion, which characterise him.) That Juliet is said – with some iteration – to be fourteen, is a way of establishing that she is at an *early*
age for a *natural* process of maturity. Or, to put it another way, our
sense of the tragedy entails both a sharp recognition of unripeness,
of a pathos and gravity recognisably childish, and an acknowledgement that the grief experienced is itself 'full, fine, perfect'.

The fact that the tragic process involves a maturation brings us
back to the Nurse's speech. The first of the two incidents she recalls
concerns Juliet's weaning; which we may now call, in view of that
movement to maturity involved with the whole tragic action,
Juliet's *first* weaning. The interesting fact about the earthquake that
ushers in this first movement of the narrative is not (or not only)
that several such actually happened in England in the last decades
of the sixteenth century, but that in this speech one happens at the
same time as the weaning. This particular specimen is a poetic and
not a historical event and it takes place within a context of its own.
On the one hand there is the earthquake, a natural cataclysm of extraordinary magnitude, such as people remember and talk about
and date things by: something quite beyond the personal – really
unstoppable: it shook the dovehouse. On the other hand, there is
the dovehouse, symbol – as Shakespeare's other references to doves
reveal – of mildness and peace and affectionate love; and there is
the Nurse, 'Sitting in the sun under the dove-house wall'; and in the
middle of this sun and shelter, framed as in some piece of very early
genre painting, there is the weaning of the child. The most domestic
and trivial event, personal and simply human as it is, is set beside

the violently alien and impersonal earthquake, the two things relat-
ing only as they co-exist in a natural span (or as recalled by the
wandering mind of a natural); and because they relate, they interpenetrate. The Nurse's 'confused' thought-processes contemplate
the earthquake with that curious upside-downness that is merely
the reflex of those who communicate most with very small children
and who speak as though they saw things as small children see
them. Her 'Shake, quoth the dove-house' has not been quite help-
fully enough glossed, presumably because few Shakespeare editors
are sufficiently acquainted with what might be said to a very small
child about an earthquake. It does not simply mean, as has been
suggested, 'the dovehouse shook'; it allows the unfluttered dovecote
to satirise the earthquake, as in a comical baby mock-heroic – to be
aloof and detached from what is happening to it. Thus, if the dovecote gains a rational upper hand and superior tone over the earthquake, the same kind of reversal occurs in that the weaning
produces an (if anything) even more formidable storm in the small
child, a cataclysmic infant rage satirised by the unfluttered Nurse:

> To see it tetchy, and fall out with the dug!
> Shake, quoth the dove-house. 'Twas no need, I trow,
> To bid me trudge.

In this last phrase a fairly simple dramatic irony and pathos will
be evident. Since Juliet's marriage is the subject of discussion, it is
nearly time for her to 'bid the Nurse trudge' once and for all. The
situation recurs in the later scene in which the young woman shows
that she no longer needs support:

> Go, counsellor!
> Thou and my bosom henceforth shall be twain …

and helps to bring out the different pathos of the unnatural which is
also latent in the situation. And the two kinds of pathos meet and
fuse when Juliet is finally forced to stand free.

> I'll call them back again to comfort me.
> Nurse! – What should she do here?
> My dismal scene I needs must act alone.

But there is faintly but suggestively shadowed under this straightforward dramatic irony a different kind of irony. Throughout this

whole first-act speech Shakespeare creates a poetic medium for which the Nurse's 'muddled old mind' is something of a subterfuge as Clarence's drowning vision in *Richard III* justifies itself by the conventions of dream. Because the Nurse is stupid she stands outside what she sees, endowing it with a curious objectivity. She has no moral opinion or judgement on the events that, as she pensively contemplates them, detach themselves from her and animate themselves into a natural history of human infancy. Confused and unjudged, earthquake and weaning interpenetrate in the past, sudden event with slow process: the earthquake becomes necessary, a mere process of maturing, and the weaning of a child takes on magnitude and *terribilità*, it shakes nature. The Nurse does not know the difference; and this not knowing becomes, in the course of the play, her innocence and her guilt. She has this in common, to Shakespeare's mind, with 'Mother Earth' herself, who is similarly unaware of vital differences:

> The earth that's nature's mother is her tomb;
> What is her burying grave, that is her womb.
> And from her womb children of divers kind
> We sucking on her natural bosom find ...

The account of the weaning is less 'muddled' than so designed as to give the Nurse impressive associations such as recur much later and in the far more famous image, 'the beggar's nurse, and Caesar's'. The Nurse, lively and deathly as she is, with 'wormwood to my dug', is Juliet's natural context, the place she starts from (and Capulet's pun is relevant here: 'Earth hath swallowed all my hopes but she; She is the hopeful lady of my earth'). Bidding the Nurse 'trudge' is the effort, one might say, of the horizontal man to be a vertical one – the human move to surpass the mere milieu of things.

The Nurse's second anecdote adds a brief, ludicrous, but none the less shrewd comment on that hunger for verticality, the perils of standing 'high-lone'. The ironic and pathetic notes of the earlier part of the speech modulate here into something brisk and broadly comic; hence the introduction of the 'merry man', the Nurse's husband, as chief actor – a replacement of surrogate mother by surrogate father, which explains the slight fore-echoes of the relationship of Yorick and the Gravedigger with Hamlet. Yet even here there is more than the merely anecdotal. The iterations, like those in the first part of the speech, are not circumscribed by the effect of the tedium of folly; there are echoes of the wisdom of folly too.

'Thou wilt fall backward when thou has more wit,
Wilt thou not, Jule?' And, by my holidam,
The pretty wretch left crying, and said 'Ay'.

'Wilt thou not, Jule?' quoth he;
And, pretty fool, it stinted, and said 'Ay'.

'Wilt thou not, Jule?' It stinted, and said 'Ay'.

Such iterations are as close to the rhythm of ritual as they are to tedium. And they are a reminder of the presence in this play of what Yeats called 'custom and ceremony', of the ordered repetitions that frame the life of generations:

Now, by my maidenhead at twelve year old ...

I was your mother much upon these years
That you are now a maid ...

I have seen the day
That I have worn a visor and could tell
A whispering tale in a fair lady's ear ...

Now old desire doth in his death-bed lie,
And young affection gapes to be his heir ...

This feeling for age-old process is perhaps caught up into a casual phrase of the Nurse's, a warm appreciation of the old man's unsubtle joke:

I warrant, an I should live a thousand years,
I never should forget it.

Involved with the husband's repetitions, one might say, is the rhythm of an existence unchanged in a thousand years. Under Juliet's particular gift, in the action that follows, for saying 'Ay' to a situation, lies any small child's easily observed habit of hopefully saying, 'Yes' to anything; and under that – so the Nurse's speech suggests – lies a resilience and resurgence in nature itself.

All in all, there is considerable density of reference in the Nurse's speech. And this density is not in itself affected by the explanation we find for it: whether we choose to talk of a tissue of inexplicit conceptions within the mind of the artist himself, or whether we like to think of it as some more conscious artistry that expects a more conscious response, does not matter. The degree of deliberation that ever exists on Shakespeare's part does not seem a fruitful critical issue: it contains too many questions impossible to answer. What one can say is that the Nurse's speech presents an image of Juliet's past that happens to contain, or that contains with a purpose, a premonitory comment on her future. It alerts and reminds the audience of what is to come as do the far more formally deployed curses of Margaret in *Richard III*. But here an interesting and important complexity occurs. Margaret's curses are choric and impersonal in function: she speaks almost as Clio, the Muse of History. But the Nurse is a character in a romantic tragedy, and approaches the impersonal only in so far as a fool may. The degree of impersonal truth in her account remains a lively question. To ask whether the natural is true might have seemed in itself a not unnatural question to an Elizabethan; for Edmund, who made Nature his Goddess, was an unnatural bastard who played his brother and his father false. Both the Nurse and her vision of things are (we might say) true but not necessarily trustworthy. It is for this reason that one may call her account 'the Nurse's story'; something that offers fascinating and rich glimpses of the centre of the play from an angle that is an angle merely. She presents the play's major subjects and events – love and death – in an innocent and natural language, that of earthquakes and weaning and a fall backward. In her first story the earthquake comes out of the summer heat randomly, but not meaninglessly, for the catastrophe has scale – is a date in nature: and so with love and death. A weaning is a stage, from milk to the stronger meat of existence; so also with love and death, if we take it that it is the death of Eros in agape, and of youth in manhood which is in question. In her second reminiscence, the old man's joke reduces the complicated interwoven events of the play to a 'fall backward': and in the phrase, a childish accident, Adam's maturing sin, sexuality, and tragic death are all involved. In the connotations of the phrase, a child's innocence and an age-old blame blend with the potent romantic and erotic myth of love and death as inseparable companions, and make it startlingly harmless: romanticism grows into 'something childish but very natural'.

Through 'It stinted, and said "Ay" ' significance and appropriateness move, as through the whole of the Nurse's speech; and they are of a kind whose resonances are not easily pinned down. The action that follows certainly pins down the Nurse: what she comes down to is a randy and treacherous advocacy of bigamy. In this light we can look back and find her account of things, for all its humanity, lacking in full meaning and dignity. The Nurse's sense of 'need' (' 'Twas no need ... To bid me trudge') does not cover a large enough human span, and the old man's consolations (' 'A was a merry man – took up the child') are clearly slightly outgrown even by an intelligent three-year-old. And yet something remains to be said. If we find some difference between the vision of *Romeo and Juliet* and that of Shakespeare's more mature tragedies, this difference might be in part put down to the effective predominance in the former of 'the Nurse's story'. Her speech establishes a natural milieu in which earthquake and weaning, a fall and a being taken up so balance that the ill effects of either are of no importance; and in so far as what she says relates to the rest of the play, it helps to suggest that the same might be true of love and death. And there seems to be a peculiar echo of her procedure in all the rhetorical doublings and repetitions of the play and especially in the paradoxes of the love and death speeches. The play's structural doublings, too, are curious, and perhaps deserve to be more often noted than they are. Romeo loves twice, once untruly and once truly; Juliet dies twice, once untruly and once truly. In any such doubling there is a point of contrast (the first love and death were illusory, the second real) but there is bound to be in implication a point of similarity also: if the first was mere game, so may the second be. Whatever the relation of the two in terms of logic, when acted out the doubled events create an imaginative equivalence.

This sense of a final equilibrium in which there is recompense for loss is in fact established as early in the play as possible, in its Prologue: which closes its doubling and paradoxical account of the feud with

> The which if you with patient ears attend,
> What here shall miss, our toil shall strive to mend.

By the end of the play it is possible to have a stubborn expectation, against all rationality, that love and death are going to 'cancel out', that Romeo and Juliet have been merely 'Sprinkled with blood to make them grow'. The image is horticultural (and is used by Bolingbroke at the end of *Richard II*). Such an image is not wholly inappropriate to a play in which Romeo lightly accuses the Friar of telling him to 'bury love' and the Friar sharply answers

> Not in a grave
> To lay one in, another out to have.

The expectation that the young lovers will 'rise again' is fairly equivo-cally met. Their survival owes more to art than to nature: they are no more than golden statues. Yet *Romeo and Juliet* is one of the first of Shakespeare's many plays whose peculiar quality is to make distinc-tions between art and nature seem false: 'the art itself is nature'. It is perhaps no accident that Mercutio and the Nurse, the play's fool and natural, turn out to be the most fertile of storytellers.

From Barbara Everett, *Young Hamlet: Essays on Shakespeare's Tragedies* (Oxford, 1989), pp. 109–23.

NOTES

[Barbara Everett's analysis of the Nurse's speech in Act I, scene iii and her role in the play as a whole illustrates at least two of the more general theo-retical points made by other writers in this volume. First, it bears out the idea that character in a play by Shakespeare depends on construction and on narrative function rather than simply revealing a personality indepen-dent of the rest of the plot. The Nurse is constructed mainly out of lan-guage, since her speech is entirely different from any other character's, and this suggests a particular point of view on the action not held by others. Her multiple functions are seen mainly in relation to the other women characters, Juliet and Lady Capulet. It is she who establishes, for example, the importance of Juliet being fourteen, that it is an early age for the rapidly maturing experience she is about to undergo; and she is also given muted premonitions that Juliet's life will not be long. In many ways the Nurse is the only character other than Romeo who *values* Juliet as an inde-pendent, growing person with a past, since she seems to have had more close and continuing contact with her since birth than even Juliet's own mother. In this sense she allows the audience to value Juliet in the same way, as still close to childhood but on the threshold of marriage. Secondly, Everett illustrates the point made by Joseph Porter, that in a Shakespeare play the apparently liminal or marginal character can provide vital com-mentary on the central action in ways that more involved characters cannot. The Nurse is seen to have a uniquely detached perspective, and si-multaneously she broadens the cultural scope of the play to take in the 'cere-monies' like weaning, and natural processes like earthquakes. Ed.]

1. These remarks are indebted to Peter Laslett's discussion of the relatively late age of puberty and of marriage in Elizabethan bourgeois society in his valuable sociological study *The World We Have Lost* (1965).

9

Eloquence and Liminality: Glossing Mercutio's Speech Acts

JOSEPH A. PORTER

As Mercutio crosses the threshold from Brooke into Shakespeare he acquires not only a brother, a friendship, and a death but also a distinctively eloquent and vividly characteristic voice. To the extent that he stands outside the main plot, neither affecting it nor being affected by it until his death, mere language has a particular prominence with him. As is well known, Mercutio is a landmark in Shakespeare's early development of characterisation in distinctive speech, and much of the impressionistic admiration (as well as some of the disapproval) he has elicited has been for his speech. Harbage[1] speaks of his 'matchless exercise in verbal cameo-cutting and imaginative fooling', Holland[2] of his 'puns, rhymes, jokes, set-speeches, and other masks', and Snyder[3] of the fact that 'speech for him is a constant play on multiple possibilities: puns abound because two or three meanings are more fun than one'. With pragmatic, or speech-act, analysis we may uncover some more of the nature of what Mercutio does with words.[4]

Pragmatics, the study of speech acts – of verbal action and 'the relation between linguistic signs and their users[5] – derives from the now classic first-generation investigations of J. L. Austin, and also of H. P. Grice and J. R. Searle,[6] and has been extended, elaborated, and refined in a large number of second-generation studies – as early as 1978 Verschueren[7] lists over fifteen hundred. A speech act ('illocutionary act' in Austin's alternative terminology) is an act performed in speech, such as asserting, denying, naming, or thanking.

As Austin observes in his pioneering *How to Do Things with Words*,[8] speech acts may generally be inexplicit (i.e., have inexplicit illocutionary force), as when I say, 'I wasn't there', or explicit (having explicit illocutionary force), as when I perform the same act explicitly by saying 'I deny that I was there'. In the latter case the act is called a 'performative'.[9] In addition to explicitness, many other features of speech acts have been studied, such as directness, commitment on the speaker's part, and relative authority of speaker and hearer. Austin used such features as the basis for a taxonomy of illocutionary force dividing speech acts into five large families; a number of other taxonomies more or less resembling his have been proposed since.

The theory and study of speech acts has come to be called pragmatics, the term formed in parallel with the traditional levels of linguistic analysis, phonetics, syntactics, and semantics. Pragmatics includes not only the (taxonomic or other) study of discrete speech acts but also Gricean conversation analysis of strings of speech acts. Pragmatic conversation analysis concerns itself with global speech acts (composed of a number of separate illocutions), manifold speech acts (whose simultaneous discrete components may be directed to different hearers), and with such features of conversation as control and uptake. Pragmatic conversation analysis thus resembles sociolinguistic discourse analysis, and the two may be combined, as in Burton.[10]

The 'pragmatic space' in which speech acts exist has for its dimensions the distinguishing features of the acts.[11] This space may be conceived of as absolute and Newtonian, but for a literary text, and especially for a play, it seems more reasonable to posit a relativistic space, one determined and successively modified by the speech acts it contains.

Many literary texts have by now been discussed or analysed pragmatically. Speech acts in Shakespeare have been discussed by Fish and Porter, and in passing by Pratt, Elam, and Dubrow.[12] The discussion here assumes those studies as part of its context, as it does the large evolving body of pragmatic theory, particularly of Austin, Searle, and Grice in the first generation and G. Leech, Bach and Harnish,[13] and D. Burton in the second. Since pragmatic discriminations tend to be fine-grained, the first part of this chapter stays close to the text, especially Mercutio's four speaking scenes: I.iv,

II.i, II.iv, and III.i. Therefore, in the next few pages in particular it may be useful to have a text of the play at hand.

The servants in the opening scene of *Romeo and Juliet* establish the play's initial public, male, pragmatic space as one of edgy quarrel-someness in which the salient kinds of speech acts are insults, challenges, and defiances, and in which the nicest calculations are carried out with respect to kind of illocution and degree of uptake – 'take it in what sense thou wilt' (l. 25) – and directedness – 'No sir, I do not bite my thumb at you, sir, but I bite my thumb, sir' (ll. 47–8).

This pragmatic space of Verona's streets undergoes two large modulations in the first scene. At the entrance of the Prince with his train (l. 78) the space grows heavily hierarchical and formal. All stand silent to hear the sentence of their prince, to which no reply is permissible. Then, after Escalus exits, the verbal action becomes comparatively intimate though still public in Benvolio's conversations with all three Montagues. By the end of the scene the play's dominant pragmatic space has been established. Under the variations lie obvious constants, such as the fact that virtually all of the action is performed by males more or less in public. The three varieties of this pragmatic space recur through the play, of course – the hierarchicalised one only at III.i and the last scene, but the other two repeatedly.

The play's other (and as it were tonic) main pragmatic space appears in the third scene. This is the withdrawn, private female and domestic space of the Capulet household, and of the marriage of Romeo and Juliet, which stands in a certain dialectical opposition to the dominant space. While my concern is not to treat what may be called Juliet's space at any length, it does figure as a determinant for what follows about the space that may be called Mercutio's. For, if Tybalt embodies the public world's narrow irritability, Paris its decorousness, Benvolio some of its fraternal support, and Romeo some of its honour, then that world's most illustrious representative is Mercutio. As ready as Tybalt to take offence, Mercutio seems more admirable inasmuch as the honour he dies defending is a friend's rather than his own. In the somewhat more retired space of his comradeship with Romeo and Benvolio, his high spirits make him generally more appealing than his friends. As embodied in speech acts the two sorts of behaviour are closely related. Giving the lie, scorning, and mocking shade easily into friendlier kinds of jesting and ropery, and the preposition Sampson withdraws in his careful admission of thumb biting reappears naturally enough in Romeo's characterisation of Mercutio's speech action: 'He jests at scars that never felt a wound' (II.ii.i).

Having been mentioned in the guest list in I.ii, Mercutio makes his first appearance in I.iv with Romeo and Benvolio immediately before the festivities at the Capulet house. Benvolio, who has been Romeo's confidant heretofore, now begins that recession by which he eventually slips unheralded out of the play. Here he has four speeches with a total of thirteen lines, one light chiding addressed to Romeo and then another to Mercutio, and each of the two remaining speeches addressed to both of his companions.[14] Benvolio thus provides a lightly ceremonial and retiring sanction for the most vigorous friendship in the scene. His presence would matter even if he had no lines. The first-person plurals of Romeo and Mercutio include him in their reference, and some of what they say may be understood as partly addressed to him. Even when one of the two main speakers addresses the other by name – 'Nay, gentle Romeo, we must have you dance' (I.iv.13), 'Peace, peace, Mercutio, peace. / Thou talk'st of nothing' (ll. 95–6) – still what is said seems to assume Benvolio as audience. Indeed it is of structural significance that the parties to the most highly charged pair-bond never appear alone together, while each does appear alone with Benvolio.

The spirited dialogue of Mercutio and Romeo in scene iv sets Mercutio's character and continues the characterisation of Romeo as it establishes a good deal of the dynamics of their relation for the action to follow. Through the play of witty question, challenge, and response weaves a pattern of answering imperatives – '**Rom.** Give me a torch' (l. 11), '**Mer.** Give me a case' (l. 29) – and denials – '**Mer.** Nay, gentle Romeo' (l. 13), '**Rom.** Nay, that's not so' (l. 44) – that, together with the easy movement back and forth between the pronouns of address 'thou' and 'you', establish an essential equality and even fraternity between the two men.

Within that fraternity substantial differences appear. The basic roles the two men play here in I.iv and through II.iv, in scenes together and apart, exhibit many traces of Brooke's name's catalysis of the god in Shakespeare's mind. In I.iv Mercutio, through and under the verbal play, delivers much the same exhortation and offer of assistance as did Mercury to Odysseus and to Aeneas: end your infatuation. The resonance with Virgil's Mercury in particular is amplified by the 'Rome' in Romeo, and fainter Trojan-Roman overtones sound in the names Paris and Juliet.[15]

These basic roles for the two friends mean that, through the badinage, Mercutio is essentially active and Romeo reactive or passive. Mercutio's exhortation, 'be rough with love' (l. 27), his essential one and his weightiest here despite its contextual wit, embodies the hortatory mode characteristic here and below of Mercutio's address to his friend. Playful as these direct or indirect exhortations are – 'Nay, gentle Romeo, we must have you dance' (l. 13); 'borrow Cupid's wings / And soar with them above a common bound' (ll. 17–18); 'Prick love for pricking' (l. 28); 'Take our good meaning' (l. 46) – and each perhaps of negligible importance alone, together they contribute an urgent pressure to everything Mercutio says. Romeo by contrast characteristically replies that he is unable to comply with his friend's exhortations – he won't dance, don't ask him – and his most urgent words, 'Peace, peace, Mercutio, peace' (l. 95), urge not action but its cessation.

Mercutio himself is rough with love in this scene, virtually equating it with excrement (l. 42). Here as later his opposition is only to love and not at all to sexuality, he being one of Shakespeare's most engagingly bawdy characters. The servingmen at the beginning of I.i have engaged in some rough bawdy, and in I.iii the Nurse has introduced a lighter touch of bawdy into the female conversation, but the conversation between Romeo and Benvolio before I.iv has been chaste as the fair Rosaline, with indeed only a single direct reference to sexuality despite the fact that nearly all their talk is of young women.[16] But here, in reply to Romeo's 'Under love's heavy burden do I sink' (l. 22), Mercutio begins to administer the moly of bawdy: 'And, to sink in it, should you burden love – Too great oppression for a tender thing' (ll. 23–4). Mercutio continues with the bawdy language here and in the next two scenes, making it usually, as in its introduction, a kind of witty play into which he has some success drawing both his friends.

Another of Mercutio's salient characteristics, named memorably twice after his death (III.i.120, 163) but apparent almost from his first words, is a certain impatient scornfulness. In I.iv it shows in his dismissive 'What care I / What curious eye doth quote deformities?' (ll. 30–1) and in the irreverence of his talk about love. There is an air of dismissal also about Mercutio's change of subject at line 29. Soon after the three companions enter, discussing the speech they will not have delivered, Romeo brings the conversation around to his own love, the subject of his and Mercutio's first wit-sally. Then at line 29, in the middle of one of his own speeches, Mercutio in effect concludes discussion of Romeo's lovesickness by asking for a visor. Benvolio seconds the change of subject (ll. 33–4), but Romeo must talk more of his distress, whereupon Mercutio delivers a light rebuke, 'Tut' (l. 40), and a particularly unattractive figure for Romeo's predicament (ll. 40–3).

Roughly the middle third of the scene consists of Mercutio's longest single speech, a key one for his characterisation as is generally acknowledged. It is also a key for some of the significances to be developed here. I return to it in the following pages, but some initial points may be made immediately.

Inasmuch as the Queen Mab speech is prompted by Romeo's mention of his dream and is itself both about dreams and dreamlike, it may be that behind the fairies' midwife stands the classical deliverer of dreams. Inasmuch as this uncanny speech seems to catch everyone including the speaker unaware, it may be that what we have is a kind of possession of Mercutio by the god. Or, to put the matter differently, it may be that here the god looms through the man. If so, the face he presents is more disturbing than in the first part of the scene. And in the chill forebodings that darken the end of the scene there may be traces of Mercury's role as psychopomp. Indeed parts of the speech itself may come from beyond the grave inasmuch as Shakespeare seems possibly to have added to it after writing Mercutio's death.[17]

The first touch of foreboding appears in the interchange leading into the speech, where Romeo gives his undisclosed dream as the reason ' 'tis no wit' to go to the masque. There may be a touch of disdainful fastidiousness in Mercutio's 'Why, may one ask?' (l. 49), an interrogative embedded in an interrogative, with the distance and formality of the pronoun echoing similar qualities in the 'sir' five lines earlier. The half-line with which Mercutio checks Romeo's recounting of his dream, 'And so did I [dream]' (l. 50), then becomes the more decisive by virtue of its pronoun, as does his next, 'That dreamers often lie' (l. 51), by virtue of its rhyme.

The Queen Mab speech itself is notable as an example of failure to observe several of the conversational maxims that fall under Grice's 'cooperative principle':[18] 'Make your conversational contribution such as is required, at the stage at which it occurs, by the accepted purpose or direction of the talk-exchange in which you are engaged.' In particular Mercutio here infringes on the maxims of quality, 'Try to make your contribution one that is true', relation, 'Be relevant', and manner, 'Be brief (avoid unnecessary prolixity)',

Mercutio's conspicuous flouting of these maxims raises the possibility of what Grice calls 'conversational implicature', the conveyance of unstated information by exploiting infringements of the cooperative principle.[19] The possibility seems especially worth considering in the context of talk about what pragmaticists term speaker-meaning (versus utterance-meaning) in Mercutio's 'I mean sir' (l. 44) and 'Take our good meaning' (l. 46) with Romeo's follow-up 'And we mean' (l. 48).

The speech does seem to carry Gricean implicatures that can in principle be worked out. I return to the task below, but already a part of the implicated message has been broached. For Mercutio here is doing what he did less spectacularly above at line 29: he is changing the subject away from Romeo's woes. A part of what the speech implicates, then, would seem to be something like 'Please stop crying out loud, for crying out loud', at least in its beginning. As the speech continues, Mercutio seems carried away by it, so that Romeo's interruption (addressing Mercutio by name for the first time, as if to call him to himself) is like the breaking of a rapture. And whatever conversational implicature was present appears lost on Romeo as he says 'Thou talk'st of nothing' (l. 96).[20]

Mercutio assents 'True, I talk of dreams' in a remarkable speech, his last in the scene. Echoes of Mercury appear in the final four lines about the wind as well as in the mention of dreams. The cold hands Shakespeare found in Brooke have here been transmuted into the frozen bosom of the north. There is a bit of an echo of

> O'er ladies' lips, who straight on kisses dream
> Which oft the angry Mab with blisters plagues
> Because their lips with sweetmeats tainted are
> (ll. 74–6)

in

>   the wind, who woos
> Even now the frozen bosom of the north
> And, being anger'd, puffs away
>   (ll. 100–2)

which increases Mercutio's association with a dangerous supernatural or inhuman vindictiveness that may itself derive partly from Mercury. And in the entire speech, with its 'vain fantasy, / Which is as thin of substance as the air' and of the wind that 'puffs away from thence', there is a strong suggestion of Mercury's disappearance after his first meeting with Aeneas ('From lookers eyesight too thinnes he vannished ayrye'.[21] Well might Romeo's mind misgive some consequence hanging in the stars.

While Mercutio speaks of language or speech rather often, and mentions several specific speech acts, he performs only three speech acts explicitly, as performatives.[22] Two of these, 'I tell ye' (II.iv.iii) and 'I warrant' (III.i.100), serve for passing emphasis, but the third receives considerable emphasis itself. This is the conjuring he performs in jest in his second scene, II.i. There, when Mercutio and Benvolio enter looking for Romeo, and Benvolio urges 'Call, good Mercutio' (l. 5), Mercutio bursts out with one of his typical verbal extravagances, first naming the act, 'Nay, I'll conjure too' (l. 6), then performing it inexplicitly, 'Romeo! Humours! Madman! Passion! Lover! / Appear thou' (ll. 7–8), and then, when the act proves unsuccessful or 'unhappy' in Austin's term ('He heareth not, he stirreth not, he moveth not', l. 15), naming the act again, 'the ape is dead and I must conjure him' (l. 16), and performing it again, this time explicitly in a performative:

> I conjure thee by Rosaline's bright eyes,
> By her high forehead ...
> That ... thou appear to us.
> (ll. 16–21)

Benvolio interjects, 'And if he hear thee, thou wilt anger him' (l. 22) – and of course the withdrawn Romeo does overhear – and Mercutio in reply names his act thrice more, twice with the same name, 'conjur'd' and 'conjure', and once with the phrase 'My invocation' (ll. 26, 29, 27).

As Gibbons points out, with the ritual of conjuration there is a possibly unique conjunction of naming and summoning, the two primary kinds of speech act called calling: 'Mercutio burlesques the ritual summoning of a spirit by calling it different names; when the right one is spoken the spirit, it is supposed, will appear and speak'.[23] Hence Mercutio here puts his distinctive stamp, jesting and supernatural, on two of the play's main bodies of speech act.

The importance of naming is generally acknowledged, the lovers being star-crossed first and primarily in their names Montague and Capulet,[24] and name-calling acting as a fuse for Verona's disorders. Mercutio's quinquepartite nomenclature of Romeo, then, is a direct anticipation of Juliet's 'wherefore art thou Romeo?' of a mere sixty-eight lines later, also overheard by the man in question. But calling as summoning also figures importantly in the play at large, including stage directions,[25] and it figures in the way Juliet's balcony scene answers this scene of Mercutio's. Mercutio's Mercurian message is that Romeo should stay with, or come back to, the world of male comradeship. In II.i, with that world represented onstage by Mercutio and Benvolio, Romeo overhears Mercutio summon him and does not comply. In II.ii, after overhearing Juliet offer herself to him in apostrophe, he does come forward. The play seems both to authorise and to regret Romeo's choice as its disastrous consequences unfold.

Those consequences seem to be enfolded in the very nature of Mercutio's performative conjuration. In I.iv Mercutio has already shown himself something of a conjurer as he invokes Queen Mab for his friends. And just as there his 'fragile constructions ... cannot altogether conceal ... a destructive, arbitrarily malicious "animus" ',[26] so here a fair amount of aggression is apparent beneath the high jinks. In Benvolio's opinion Mercutio's jesting mention of Rosaline's 'quivering thigh, / And the demesnes that there adjacent lie' (ll. 19–20) will anger Romeo if he hears. Mercutio, pleading innocuousness in reply, proceeds still further with the bawdy and personal. Romeo does overhear and, so far as we can tell, Benvolio's prediction proves inaccurate, but the scene invites us to consider whether that prediction might not have been more on target had Mercutio made light with Juliet's name instead of with Rosaline's. In any case a flickering Mercurian aggressiveness animates not only Mercutio's references to Rosaline but also his treating the flesh-and-blood Romeo as a spirit to be invoked: 'The ape is dead and I must conjure him' (l. 16).

After the balcony scene[27] and Romeo's morning meeting with Friar Laurence, Mercutio and Benvolio enter at II.iv. Mercutio is still asking where the devil this Romeo should be. Here in particular Mercutio anticipates Hotspur whose scorn of the perfumed lord sent by Henry to demand prisoners (*I Henry 4* I.iii.45–65) echoes Mercutio's scorn of Tybalt's fighting by the book. When Mercutio has divined that Tybalt's letter to Romeo is a challenge, and Benvolio has opined that Romeo will answer it, Mercutio's 'Any man that can write may answer a letter' (l. 10) makes a pragmatic joke reprised in Hotspur's witty mistaking of Glendower's boast about calling spirits (*I Henry 4* III.i.50–2).[28] As Gibbons notes, by 'answer it' Benvolio means 'accept the challenge', while Mercutio pretends to take him to mean 'reply to the letter'. Mercutio thus adopts as a ploy the behaviour Romeo in I.ii and Benvolio seemingly in the next line exhibit inadvertently toward him; that is, not taking the speaker's good meaning. The good meaning of Mercutio's wilful misprision here would seem to be to call Romeo's valour into question, as he does more directly in his next speech (where once again in Mercutio's ominous jesting the lovesick friend has died).[29]

After some seventeen lines of Mercutio's witty denigration of Tybalt's fencing and speech, Romeo enters for the wild-goose chase of wit with Mercutio who, supposing his moly or some other to have cured his friend, ends the sally with a good-hearted congratulatory welcome back into the fraternity, coupled with another of his vigorously unattractive figures for love:

> Why, is not this better now than groaning for love? Now art thou sociable, now art thou Romeo; now art thou what thou art, by art as well as by nature. For this drivelling love is like a great natural that runs lolling up and down to hide his bauble in a hole.
>
> (ll. 88–93)

The ironies are rich. Far from being cured, Romeo is more deeply in love than before, betrothed, and with arrangements made for the secret marriage. And then far from groaning or drivelling, he is inspirited enough by the secret match with Juliet to cry a match (l. 70) with Mercutio in the wit-capping. These ironies seem to me to work for the most part to build and enlarge our sympathy for Mercutio in his welcome to Romeo. As we watch the addressee hang back from any immediate reply, while Benvolio interjects 'Stop there, stop there' (l. 94), on which Mercutio seizes for a bit of largely phallic bawdy wit-capping with him, we may also – depending on how Romeo's silence is performed – feel some rueful sympathy for him in the awkwardness of the moment.

The entrance of the Nurse and Peter in II.iv provides more silence for Romeo, while Mercutio jests with the Nurse. She stands as something of a female analogue to him, as is generally recognised, and as is suggested in the echo of Mercutio's earlier request for a visor to hide his own visage in his remark to Peter about the fan, 'Good Peter, to hide her face, for her fan's the fairer face' (ll. 106–7).[30] After the rapid interplay that follows, containing Mercutio's memorable figure for the hour, his mockery of the

Nurse's erroneous taking of Romeo's words to her, and his singing, he exits with Benvolio.

There follows the play's most extended discussion of Mercutio's speech, three speeches by Romeo and the Nurse with codas of a kind in Peter's 'I saw no man use you at his pleasure' (l. 154) and the Nurse's second 'Scurvy knave' (l. 159). The denigration in what Romeo says,

> A gentleman ... that loves to hear himself talk, and will speak more in a minute than he will stand to in a month
>
> (ll. 144–6)

seems designed to smooth ruffled feathers, but it may also contain a grain of truth. The length of the Queen Mab speech, for instance, could be taken as supporting evidence for the first clause, which seems indeed to have been used as a warrant for some performances of the entire role, such as Barrymore's in the 1936 film. Still, Mercutio's pleasure in the wild-goose chase of wit with Romeo seems as much at his friend's talk as at his own, so that Romeo's slight here may seem unfair and ungenerous.

Romeo's second and more surprising clause exhibits the momentarily pervasive bawdiness Mercutio has left in his wake. Romeo's bawdy seems conscious, and Gibbons assures us that Peter's is also[31] although I see no reason it has to be. As for the Nurse, while Gibbons is surely right that 'she *unintentionally* expresses indecencies through unfortunate choice of words'[32] he seems inconsistent in rejecting her 'And he stand to [anything against me]' from Quarto I, which could be said as innocently as 'suffer every knave to use me at his pleasure'. The Nurse has a further bit of unwitting bawdy here that depends directly on Mercutio. The vexation comes from him in her 'I am so vexed that every part about me quivers' (ll. 158–9), and so too does the bawdy deriving from her unknowing echo of his conjuring by Rosaline's 'quivering thigh, / And the demesnes that there adjacent lie' (II.i.19–20). The echo is the more conspicuous given that 'quiver' is infrequent in Shakespeare, appearing only once in each of four other plays and *The Rape of Lucrece*.

The Nurse instigates the interchange by asking Mercutio's identity for the second time in the scene. Earlier when she asks the man himself, Romeo replies riddlingly, giving her only the first syllable of the name she asks for, 'One ... that God hath made, himself to mar' (ll. 114–15) and she, as if she can almost hear the name

herself, repeats 'By my troth it is well said; "for himself to mar"'
(l. 116). Now, asking again (and again in vain) for the man's identity, she herself uses the syllable, 'I pray you, sir, what saucy merchant was this?' (l. 142), unwittingly giving Mercutio another light
trace of the patron god of merchants.

Mercutio leaves ribaldry aside in his final scene (III.i), but not witty
jesting. In his mockery of Benvolio for a quarrelsomeness they both
know is more rightly attributable to Mercutio himself, in all his
play with Tybalt's name and with his own mortal wound, we see
the same sensibility as in his preceding scene, and similar verbal
action. There are echoes from earlier scenes as well. The dismissive
'What care I/What curious eye doth quote deformities' from his
first scene here echoes first in his reply to Benvolio's announcement
of the advent of the Capulets, 'By my heel, I care not' (l. 36) and
'Men's eyes were made to look, and let them gaze' (l. 53).
Mercutio's oath, sworn by a part of his body peculiarly charged by
his resonances with Mercury, is a scornful capping of Benvolio's
'By my head'. Mercutio's next oath, 'Zounds' (l. 48), is far more
impassioned, and with the same oath in his dying words (l. 101) he
reaches 'a peak of tension'[33] in a sequence of oaths stretching back
through all four of his speaking scenes.

In this last of Mercutio's scenes his speech acts constitute four
large movements with an intermission in the middle. After the
initial characterisation of Benvolio as a quarreller (ll. 1–36) comes
Mercutio's first interchange with Tybalt (ll. 37–58), in which he
vents some of the scorn for the man we have seen him express
earlier to Benvolio. The fiery Tybalt, as is generally noticed, exer-
cises restraint as Mercutio guys and challenges in speech bristling
with imperatives – 'Couple' (l. 39), 'make' (l. 40), 'look' (l. 46), 'go'
(l. 57), and first-person pronouns (ll. 39, 45, 46, 47, 54[2], 56) – in
twelve lines that, in the context of Mercutio's first twenty-five
lines to Benvolio with no imperatives and only four first-person
pronouns,[34] manifest the aggressiveness Tybalt brings out in
Mercutio.

Mercutio's aggressiveness of course has a strong phallic compo-
nent deriving from his previous bawdiness and from the play's
other sword–phallus linkages, as well as more distantly from
Mercury's phallicism. Zeffirelli, as may be remembered, embodies
some of this in the staging of Mercutio's 'Here's my fiddlestick'.
There may even be a subtextual image of the phallic roadside herm
in the combination of Mercutio's fiddlestick with Benvolio's 'We

talk here in the public haunt of men ... Here all eyes gaze on us' (ll. 49–52) and Mercutio's 'Men's eyes were made to look, and let them gaze. / I will not budge for no man's pleasure, I' (ll. 53–4).

Pragmatically the most interesting moment in this part of the scene may be the transition from Mercutio's 'Could you not take some occasion [for blows] without giving?' (l. 43) to Tybalt's reply, 'Mercutio, thou consortest with Romeo' (l. 44). For one thing, Tybalt here shows that he knows Mercutio by name. More importantly, the force of what he says is open to interpretation to an unusual degree. While he could be answering Mercutio's question indirectly, he could also be returning to the subject of the 'word with one of you' (l. 38) he requests at the beginning of the interchange; that is, presumably Romeo's whereabouts.

After the intermission of Romeo's appearance and Tybalt's challenge with Romeo's refusal to take it up, Mercutio in his third large pragmatic movement of the scene delivers his disapproval of Romeo's pacifism in the first words he speaks, 'O calm, dishonourable, vile submission' (l. 72). If they are addressed to Romeo they are Mercutio's only words to him in this part of the scene, even though Romeo pleads, 'Gentle Mercutio, put thy rapier up' (l. 83), and then exhorts both him and Tybalt to forbear and twice calls them both by name. Mercutio ignores his friend, addressing first one challenge and then a longer and more insulting one to the reluctant Tybalt, and then inviting the swordplay to begin.

The first sentence of the fourth and final movement of Mercutio's speech action, 'I am hurt' (l. 91), has a brevity uncharacteristic of him, which may show his pain or his quickly dawning cognisance of the severity of the wound. And the brevity, together with the naked simplicity of the language and the absence of any vocative indicator, makes the sentence look as if Mercutio may be talking to himself as much as to anyone else.

Immediately – and the immediacy manifests much about the workings of Mercutio's mind here – he addresses Romeo, for the first time since 'vile submission', with his malediction. Three more times in the lines that follow, including his final words in the play, Mercutio makes the same transition, from the gravity of his own condition to the curse. The repetition makes the retributive nature of the curse very clear, and Mercutio's uncanniness and access to the supernatural make his curse alone, even without his death, seem to draw down the consequence yet hanging in the stars. After the first utterance of the malediction Mercutio returns to the subject of his wound, now taking cognisance of its mortality, 'I am sped.' Then in 'Is he gone, and hath nothing?' he addresses a third subject to which he also returns, Tybalt.

The initial incredulity of Benvolio and Romeo heightens audience sympathy for Mercutio and may help create an effect of clairvoyance for everything he has said and done in the play. The incredulity may create sympathy for Benvolio and Romeo as well, with its suggestion of a childlike inability to believe the worst. Benvolio's near-quotation, 'What, art thou hurt?' in particular may produce that effect, and its intimate pronoun serves as a foil for the relentless new distance in the 'you' with which Mercutio addresses Romeo, in the maledictions and also at lines 99, 104, and 105.

Mercutio addresses one further subject in addition to the main ones as he breaks off his fulminations against Tybalt to ask Romeo 'why the devil came you between us? I was hurt under your arm' (ll. 104–5), recounting the action prescribed in the unusually detailed stage direction '*Tybalt under Romeo's arm thrusts Mercutio in*' (l. 89, in Q1 only), and strongly suggesting that Romeo is to blame for Tybalt's blow having hit home. Romeo's reply, 'I thought all for the best' (l. 106), depending on how it is delivered may have some of the same childlike air as Benvolio's last question. However much or little explanation, excuse, or self-justification is given to the line, it seems addressed to Mercutio, and at least in part an answer to his question. Yet Mercutio seems not to take Romeo's statement as meriting any acknowledgement at all as he addresses his next words to Benvolio by name, 'Help me into some house … Or I shall faint' (ll. 107–8). The meanings of 'house' in lines 107 and 108 are so different that the chime, if noticed, may seem the sort of homonymy we routinely ignore. It functions, though, to suggest that such shelter and safety as exists in Verona is in bourgeois familial structures, out of the reach of a figure like Mercutio.

In his last words Mercutio does finally address Romeo, with the curse, followed by an explicit assignment of blame for his death to the Montagues and Capulets – 'your houses, / They have made worm's meat of me' (ll. 108–9) – a reaffirmation of the mortality of the wound and finally a contracted version of the curse, 'Your houses!' (l. 110).

Almost immediately the chronic reporter Benvolio recounts these events with some elaborations and discrepancies. There may be an echo of Brooke in the hand with which, Benvolio says, Mercutio has beat cold death aside. Benvolio's quotation of Romeo (l. 167) is inaccurate[35] but he describes the key tableau faithfully:

Romeo ...
... 'twixt them rushes; underneath whose arm
An envious thrust from Tybalt hit the life
Of stout Mercutio.

(ll. 166–71)

Thus for the third time the play emphasises Romeo's immediate part in Mercutio's death.

Mercutio's speech acts, then, constitute a characteristic manifold in significant contrast with that constituted by the speech acts of such other characters as Romeo and Benvolio, and full of resonances with Shakespeare's received Mercury. In the pragmatic space as it develops around Mercutio, Romeo describes his own situation and laments it, begs off dancing and play with words and swords but takes part in the latter two in response to Mercutio and Mercutio's death, protests the love he bears the furious Tybalt, and, with Juliet, wonders at her beauty and vows his love to her. All the while Benvolio notably reports what has happened, and also manifests his good wishes in mild suggestions to attend the festivity or to retire from the hot street.

   Mercutio's speech acts differ eloquently. He urges, exhorts, and prods his friends, in jest and in earnest. He turns aside from the matter at hand in riddles he knows the answers to and also in the oracular account of Queen Mab that carries him away. He invokes Romeo, shrugs off the regard of others, challenges Romeo and Benvolio in jest and to wit-combat and Tybalt in earnest to mortal swordplay, and finally curses his friend and his friend's love. Mercutio's essential subtextual address is to Romeo, and it is a Mercurian summoning away from love to the fellowship of men, guarded with warnings of the consequences of not heeding. Although Mercutio stays in the dark about precisely why his friend shrugs off the summons, he dies with accurate enough knowledge that the ancient grudge has been complicated by love across the lines. And Mercutio's malediction, extending to the love as to the grudge, and past Rosaline to Juliet, punishes all.

'ABOVE A COMMON BOUND'

After Mercutio's last exit assisted by Benvolio Romeo speaks immediately of him in soliloquy, giving him the first three of the series of encomiums in obsequy that extends through the remainder of the scene:

> This gentleman, the Prince's near ally,
> My very friend, hath got this mortal hurt
> In my behalf.
>
> (III.i.111–13)

So begins what may be called Mercutio's exit limen, or threshold; that is, the space between his last appearance onstage and the last direct references to him in the play, at V.iii.75.[36] It answers his entrance limen, the space between the first reference to him, when he is named with his brother Valentine in the guest list at I.ii.68, and his first appearance onstage at I.iv.S.D., but it contains almost the entire second half of the play, with several important references to him beginning with this one, as well as other sorts of echo. Indeed as an exit limen for so important a character Mercutio's seems unprecedented in Shakespeare. It also, by the way, seems paralleled only by the titular hero's exit threshold in *Julius Caesar*, unless we include thresholds extending across more than one play, as with Richard's in the Lancastrian plays. The play with the most similar structure is, not surprisingly, *The Winter's Tale*, where Mercutio's exit limen is reprised in a happier key by the offstage 'death' and long absence from the play's action of Hermione, in whose name we glimpse the same god as in Mercutio's. Since that liminal god himself presides over boundaries and thresholds, it is peculiarly and deeply right that Mercutio's exit limen should be so long, or, to put it slightly differently, that his vigorous presence in the first half of the play should be answered by as long an absence. That absence itself grows vigorous by virtue of Romeo's seemingly gratuitous mention of Mercutio in the play's last scene, and for other reasons that will be touched on below, so that in fact Mercutio has a kind of immanence through the second half of the play. The effect begins with the exit of the mortally wounded Mercutio aided by Benvolio, which shares some of the uncanniness of Mercury's abrupt disappearances 'too thinnes ... ayrye' as in Stanyhurst's *Aeneis*.

Romeo continues, in the soliloquy that becomes apostrophe, to exhibit the changed perception of his position in the state of affairs, a changed perception brought about by Mercutio's death-in-progress. His reputation is stained with Tybalt's 'slander' and

> O sweet Juliet,
> Thy beauty hath made me effeminate
> And in my temper soften'd valour's steel.
>   (ll. 115–17)

This strikingly sexist account of the effect of female beauty could almost have come from Mercutio himself.

Benvolio the reporter then enters with the news of what has happened offstage, beginning with the half-line that has introduced Juliet's balcony soliloquy shortly before:

> O Romeo, Romeo, brave Mercutio is dead,
> That gallant spirit hath aspir'd the clouds
> Which too untimely here did scorn the earth.
>   (ll. 118–20)

Other features link the two moments, including a trace of the Mercury-angel wind-god 'inter terram et caelum currens'. It appears in Romeo's apostrophe to Juliet as 'angel ... winged messenger' (II.ii.26–8), and here it recurs in the second and third lines, especially the second with its three wind images and the powerful phonetic chime between two of them. That chime sets up a phonetic resonance for 'scorn', here first attributed to Mercutio – heretofore in the play scorn has been named only by Tybalt, and erroneously attributed to Romeo. Mercury however has displayed scorn repeatedly, indeed more clearly than aspiration. The image of aspiring the clouds, and even the word aspire, manifest Mercutio's Marlovianness. Here we may note a certain amount of apotheosis in Benvolio's account, to which his encomiums 'brave' and 'gallant' contribute.[37]

Benvolio's report is amplified in the remainder of the scene: in Romeo's 'Mercutio slain' (l. 124) and his 'Mercutio's soul / Is but a little way above our heads' (ll. 128–9); in the Citizen's 'he that kill'd Mercutio? / Tybalt, that murderer' (l. 139); in Benvolio's own 'brave' (l. 147), 'bold' (l. 161), and 'stout' (l. 171), and his new information that Mercutio is the Prince's kinsman (l. 147); in the Prince's own two references (ll. 184, 191), especially his second, 'My blood for your rude brawls doth lie a-bleeding' (which like the Citizen's remark works to exonerate Mercutio); and in Montague's 'Romeo ... was Mercutio's friend' (l. 186).

This amplification keeps Mercutio very much present in the mind of the audience through the eighty-eight lines of the scene that follow his final exit, and so prepares for his continuing subliminal presence through most of the rest of the play. When Romeo in the Capulet tomb identifies the man he has killed as 'Mercutio's kinsman' (V.iii.75), the reference seems not gratuitous; rather it comes with a kind of naturalness or even inevitability, invoking a presence already immanent among the present and imminent corpses, a presence reactivated seven lines before by the 'conjuration'.

That presence is immanent because we miss Mercutio; we want him in the final scene, more perhaps than we want the actually present and named Paris and Tybalt, more than we want the other major absent characters, Benvolio and the Nurse (whose absence goes unmarked by any reference to either of them and may go unremarked by an audience), and certainly more than we want Lady Montague, the only other absent character referred to.[38] The explicit references just discussed have kept the absent Mercutio present in our minds, and so have other sorts of echo, such as the phonetic echo in the line with which the Prince closes Mercutio's death scene, 'Mercy but murders' (l. 99). And we may see a trace of Mercutio in IV.ii. When Capulet begins the scene by handing a guest list to a servant with the command 'So many guests invite as here are writ' (IV.ii.1) he enacts a reprise of Mercutio's introduction into the play. Moments later Mercutio's shadow falls over Capulet's impulsive and disastrous decision to advance the marriage day from Thursday to Wednesday – *mercredi*, Mercury's day.

The aubade of Romeo and Juliet, III.v, provides a good example of Mercutio's immanence. Juliet's claim that the daylight is a meteor exhaled by the sun to be a torchbearer (l. 14) recalls not only the wind and breath associated with Mercutio but also Romeo's denial of his friend's request, 'Give me a torch, I am not for this ambling' (I.iv.11). Mercutio also inheres in traces of the god Mercury who seems almost to hover over the scene, to effect the lovers' separation in one of the god's own liminal hours, the dawn, and to send the hero on the road. Traces of Mercury are associated with the lark and with the daylight. The lark is 'herald' (l. 6) and it sings 'harsh discords' (l. 28) with an echo of the words of Mercury at the end of *Love's Labour's Lost*, and the image of the severing clouds and day 'tiptoe on the misty mountain tops' (l. 10) echoes Mercury's skimming the clouds and pausing on Mt Atlas, as in *Aeneid* 4.

In addition to his posthumous presence in traces like these, Mercutio is immanent through his exit limen because his death occurs offstage. Any number of factors may have been involved in

Shakespeare's decision to remove Mercutio's death from our view. It gives Romeo a moment alone onstage (except for servants) to deliver the soliloquy expressing his dawning awareness of the gravity of the situation. And then possibly the actor playing Mercutio needed to exit so that he could change and re-enter thirty-two lines and a swordfight later as the Prince, in which case, by Meagher's principles of economy and recognition reference to Mercutio would inhere in everything the Prince does and says, including the last words of the play.[39]

Whatever its other effects, Mercutio's offstage death fixes Mercutio in a boundary region between life and death, or elevates him above that boundary. In all fictions including 'reality' the more attractive a person the more likely we are somewhere in our minds to treat reports of his or her death as greatly exaggerated. Some genres accommodate real or apparent resurrection more readily than others. While resurrections and recoveries such as those of Philoclea,[40] Guyon, Arthur, and Amoret[41] are the staple of narrative romance, deaths in English Renaissance drama before 1595, in particular that written by Shakespeare, tend to be final. But Mercutio's peculiar offstage demise, coupled with his earlier access to the supernatural and the quality of the references to him and echoes of him through his exceptionally long exit limen, place his death under a kind of erasure, giving it an uncanny trace of Mercury's ascension from the earth to the vaulty heaven, or the whisper of a promise not fulfilled until the answering *The Winter's Tale*.

In Mercutio's onstage presence too, before he crosses the mortal boundary into his long exit threshold, he embodies the liminality of the Mercury who presides over the wild border regions, the herm who stands by the roadside to guide a wayfarer or a *romeo*. Boundaries – that of the ancient feud, those of gender and generation, those between night and day and life and death – crisscross Mercutio's play, and much of its action transpires at such Mercurially liminal times and sites as dawn, the city walls, the garden and balcony, the interurban road, and the entrance to the tomb. Above all others Mercutio before his death manifests this liminality in his behaviour, as when he turns aside from his companions as if rapt in his talk of dreams, fantasy, and the wind that, in Benvolio's words, 'blows us from ourselves' (I.v.104).

Mercutio's social structures are themselves textbook examples of the liminal as expounded by Van Gennep, Turner, and others.[42] As with that stage in rites of passage and initiations when the initiates have left behind old social affiliations, and perhaps names, without yet having assumed new ones, so that they live together for a time outside the ordinary dwelling area, in radical equality and strong bondedness, so with the trio of Benvolio, Romeo, and Mercutio.

The avatar of this world is Mercutio. He summons Romeo back to it with his conjuration, and he works to hold both his friends in it with the verbal play he initiates and leads with both of them, and with his scorn of the love that ends in marriage and, in the Queen Mab speech, of adult occupations. But Mercutio's eloquence is for nought: Benvolio slips away, Romeo falls in love and marries, and the mortally wounded Mercutio is left to curse. As the form of his curse shows, a subtext of his concluding situation, at least in his understanding, is an *in trivio* Mercury without any *romei* to direct. They have all retreated to the shelter of their houses, which he curses for being houses. And since the Montagues and Capulets stand opposed, and since their opposition (combined with an individual attraction across the hostile boundary) is the cause of Mercutio's death, he has in a sense at last traded places with Romeo in the triad with Juliet. Now standing between them, Mercutio curses them and their houses because he is destroyed by them. Thus in Mercutio's final tragic configuration the liminal has become central, the god of the wild border region has become god of the agora.

THE HISTORICAL MOMENT

These matters of eloquence and liminality, of locution and location, ramify massively in Shakespeare's 1595 London. Here my aim is no more than to aerate a bit of accumulated sediment by suggesting some of the larger social, political, and cultural issues Shakespeare and his audience address consciously or not through the person of Mercutio.

Shakespeare's own career to 1595 had been governed by a rich interplay of periphery and centre, and happy and unhappy eloquence. Whatever the lost years contain, during them if not before, the realm of discourse widened and Stratford, once securely central among its surrounding farms and villages, was displaced and revealed as comparatively peripheral to London. And yet as we all know from the subsequent career, and as indeed may be apparent in the works through *Romeo and Juliet*, the displacement was never unequivocal or irrevocable. Nor could it have been quite whole-hearted or guiltless. Nor are the movements at issue those of one man alone, but rather they are those of whole classes of the best and brightest provincials drawn to London, drawn away from lives mapped out for them by the dominant feudal order of the provinces, and drawn to more speculative futures by the emergent capitalism of the capital. In the comparative insulation of *Romeo and Juliet* Mercutio stands like a lightning rod for the social forces at play, and opposed charges run up and down him. From the provincial vantage he is the son become extravagant outsider, cursing the secure provincial houses by his very departure for a rented room in London; and he is also a kind of presiding spirit of the town centre, with his bawdry and folklore and his life in the public haunt of men. From the vantage of the capital he consorts with sons of the bourgeoisie, entertaining them with his mercantile sauciness, but at the same time he is the kinsman of the County Paris and of the Prince, and so allied to the residual aristocratic social construct of honour. About this last allegiance, with Mercutio as later with Hotspur, Elizabethan social divisions and contradictions are especially apparent, as the play both necessitates the death and at the same time regrets and even in a sense denies it.

The primary effective means for Shakespeare's displacement of Stratford to the periphery seems to have been the eloquence of the playwright and narrative poet. As we know, while by 1595 he had achieved notable financial success with both sorts of writing, and recognition for both as well as (probably already) for his sonnets, internal strains, disjunctions, and contradictions in that success (variously exhibited in the changing tone of the dedications of the narrative poems, in the anti-theatrical sonnets, and in the metadrama of some of the plays) were reproducing similar stresses in the society at large, and were on the point of necessitating resolution.

That resolution, we know, would be the abandonment of non-dramatic verse and the decisive consolidation of interest and allegiance in drama. But even without the hindsight of the later career it might be possible to see contradictions between non-dramatic poetry and drama, between patronage and the rewards of the marketplace, between flattering the selected aristocrat and flattering the heterogeneous theatregoing public, in *Romeo and Juliet*, and to see portents of the resolution. Mercutio is surely dramatic to the lyric of the lovers. Carried away into his one extra-dramatic moment, the Queen Mab speech, he seems to try to escape from it as it continues by subverting it from within, piling incongruity on incongruity and exhibiting a more and more alarming misogyny, as if gnashing his teeth and beating against the lines until Romeo rescues him. By contrast the lovers' lyricism gives even their 'dramatic' interchanges with each other some of the stability of non-dramatic verse. Their kind of eloquence culminates in the aureate immobility celebrated in the play's concluding lines. Mercutio's culminates in ... what? Liminal persistence, a memory and a promise, the whisper of an increasing allegiance to the more marginal genre, the more questionable and ephemeral one that flies its flags in the margins of the city.

The city of London itself is liminal in a still widening realm of discourse. Hints along the way in the provincial schools could scarcely have prepared for the full weight of realising in London that the centre is elsewhere after all, the city of cities is in another country and irremediably anterior besides. Various kinds of frontal assault on the fact are possible, including the preliminary acknowledgement of setting one's first tragedy, *Titus Andronicus*, there. As we know, that strategy grows increasingly powerful – indeed preemptive – in the career after 1595. Still more powerful, it might be argued, is the more characteristic strategy of finding direction by indirection out, the liminal method. It works in *Romeo and Juliet* to suggest that there is life beyond Rome, a dramatic eloquence on the periphery.

From Joseph A. Porter, *Shakespeare's Mercutio: His History and Drama* (Chapel Hill, NC, 1988), pp. 100–21.

NOTES

[Just as Mercutio in the play threatens to steal the show from the lovers because of his powerful interventions and early death, so he threatens to unbalance this collection in his favour since he has two whole essays to himself – Joseph Porter's and Jonathan Goldberg's. However, it is true that the character is important. Mercutio has been constructed in relation to the plot to show the deadly consequences of the family feud in a more social sphere than the lovers' closed circle – his line 'A curse o' both your houses' encapsulates the whole play in one line – and he has been given some of the most memorable passages. The great actors have always been attracted to this role rather than Romeo's, for these reasons (see the film *Shakespeare in Love* for a modern and amusing example). We can justify the two essays in a different way, since they make equally illuminating points about the play as a whole. Porter makes three general contributions. First, he shows that, Mercutio is a poet's construction, and in this case the building-blocks are 'speech acts', in the technical terminology taken from the study of pragmatics in linguistics. Although Porter happens to apply this approach to Mercutio, there is no reason why it cannot be used to analyse the speech acts of other characters. Secondly, Porter complements Barbara Everett in giving a detailed demonstration that an apparently marginal character who is not directly involved in the love-plot can make a big difference to our understanding of the central action, simply by supplying an oblique and 'liminal' commentary. He does in fact connect Mercutio and the Nurse in this structural sense, and makes liminality a Shakespearean stylistic signature, deriving from his provincial roots. In his book, Porter even gives to the otherwise unglorified Apothecary his moment of critical fame as a poor man who must earn his living. This volume does not include a consistently Marxist essay but if such a one were to be written it would focus on characters like this (see Brecht, essay 7). Thirdly, Porter provides detailed insight into the functions of Mercutio's presence in relation to the play as a whole. Quotations are from the Arden edition, *Romeo and Juliet*, ed. Brian Gibbons (London, 1980). Ed.]

1. Alfred Harbage (ed.), *William Shakespeare: A Reader's Guide* (New York, 1963), p. 145.

2. Norman Holland, 'Shakespeare's Mercutio and Ours', *Michigan Quarterly Review*, 5 (1966), 115–23, pp. 118–19.

3. Susan Snyder, '*Romeo and Juliet*: Comedy into Tragedy', *Essays in Criticism*, 20 (1970), 391–402, p. 395.

4. While there is substantial consensus about a great deal in the field of pragmatics, there have also been enough disagreements for Charles Altieri (*Act and Quality: A Theory of Literary Meaning and Humanistic Understanding* [Amherst, MA, 1981], p. 69) to write in 1981, 'This field is now in turmoil'. Some of the turmoil is simply a function of the field's youth, size, and diversity. As the newly formed International Pragmatics Association announced: 'Today, pragmatics is a large, loose, and disorganised collection of research efforts ... their contribution to our understanding of human verbal communication often does not reach its fullest potential as a result of the emerging theoretical, methodological, and terminological diversity' ('Announcements', *Journal of Pragmatics*, 10 [1986], 53). In addition, the form of J. L. Austin's *How to Do Things with Words*, ed. J. O. Urmson (Oxford, 1962), as we have it, has invited contradictory

readings and attributions. It is a posthumous, sometimes fragmentary series of lecture notes, and it includes a sort of dialogic sequence of provision and revision. Hence for instance, Deirdre Burton [see note 10 below – Ed.] pp. 37ff. is able to attribute to Austin the distinction between performatives and constatives without going on to explain that Austin introduces the distinction only to collapse it as untenable. See also Joseph A. Porter, 'Pragmatics for Criticism: Two Generations of Speech Act Theory', *Poetics*, 15 (1986), 243–57.

5. Geoffrey N. Leech, *Explorations in Semantics and Pragmatics* (Amsterdam, 1980), p. 2.

6. Austin, *How to Do Things with Words*; H. P. Grice, 'Logic and Conversation', in *Speech Acts*, ed. Peter Cole and Jerry L. Morgan (New York, 1975); J. R. Searle, *Speech Acts: An Essay in the Philosophy of Language* (Cambridge, 1969), and *Expression and Meaning: Studies in the Theory of Speech Acts* (Cambridge, 1979).

7. Jef Verschuren, *Pragmatics: An Annotated Bibliography* (Amsterdam, 1978).

8. Austin, *How to Do Things with Words*.

9. Speech act theorists for the most part use the word performative to mean 'illocutionarily explicit speech act'. But in the work of some pragmaticists, and still more in the work of some literary critics and theoreticians, performative simply means speech act. The confusion grows directly out of ambiguity resulting from Austin's dialogic exposition.

10. Deirdre Burton, *Discourse and Discourse: A Sociolinguistic Approach to Modern Drama Dialogue and Naturally Occurring Conversation* (London, 1980).

11. Leech, *Explorations*, p. 114.

12. Stanley E. Fish, 'How to do Things with Austin and Searle', *Modern Language Notes*, 91 (1976), 983–1025; Joseph A. Porter, 'Pragmatics for Criticism: Two Generations of Speech Act Theory', *Poetics*, 115 (1956), 243–57; Mary Louise Pratt, *Toward a Speech Act Theory of Literary Discourse* (Bloomington, IN, 1977); Keir Elam, *Shakespeare's Universe of Discourse: Language-games in the Comedies* (Cambridge, 1984); Heather Dubrow, *Captive Victors: Shakespeare's Narrative Poems and Sonnets* (Ithaca, NY, 1987).

13. Leech, *Explorations*; Kent Bach and Robert M. Harnish, *Linguistic Communication and Speech Acts* (Cambridge, MA, 1979).

14. The first speech generally given to Benvolio may in fact be Mercutio's, as Capell suggested. The speech acts involved, the diction, and the scorn make it sound more like Mercutio (see Brian Gibbons [ed.], *Romeo and Juliet*, Arden edn [London, 1980], I.iv. 1n).

15. See Donald Cheney, 'Tarquin, Juliet, and Other *Romei'*, *Spenser Studies*, 3 (1982), 111–24.

16. Rosaline will not be besieged by loving terms nor assailed by eyes, 'Nor ope her lap to saint-seducing gold' (I.i.212). While not bawdy, the line is enough of a surprise for Gibbons (p. 93n) to comment at length, and not altogether persuasively, when he suggests that 'we may suppose his [Romeo's] immaturity has allowed the conceit to get out of hand'.

17. See Sidney Thomas, 'The Queen Mab Speech in *Romeo and Juliet'*, *Shakespeare Survey*, 25 (1972), 73–80.

18. Grice, 'Conversation', pp. 45–6.

19. See Grice, 'Conversation', and Bach and Harnish, *Communication*, pp. 165–72.

20. Michael Goldman, *Shakespeare and the Energies of Drama* (Princeton, NJ, 1972), p. 37, contrasts 'arias' given in company such as the Queen Mab speech with the isolated ones of Romeo and Juliet. One of Queen Mab's accoutrements, incidentally – 'Her chariot is an empty hazelnut' (l.59) – carries a reference to the element mercury. 'One of the most widespread uses of quicksilver has been to afford protection against the Evil Eye, "spells" and related misfortunes. ... A typical example ... said to have been in practice since the middle ages, is to hollow out the kernel of a hazelnut and replace the contents with quicksilver. The amulet is to be hung around the neck, placed under the bedpillow or under the threshold of the door. ... Hazelnuts ... are frequently used as adjuvants to quicksilver' (Leonard J. Goldwater, *Mercury: A History of Quicksilver* [Baltimore, MD, 1972], p. 26). Mercutio returns to the subject of hazelnuts when he tells Benvolio 'Thou wilt quarrel with a man for cracking nuts, having no other reason but because thou hast hazel eyes' (III.i.18–20). Hazelnuts are mentioned only once elsewhere in Shakespeare, in conjunction with the only other appearance of the word 'hazel' ('hazel-twig', *The Taming of the Shrew*, II.i.255).

21. Richard Stanyhurst, trans. *Richard Stanyhurst's Aeneis* (Leyden, 1582), sig. L2v.

22. By my count Mercutio has fifteen explicit references to speech acts apart from his three performatives. Five are his references to conjuring in Act II, scene i. In addition he mentions asking (I.iv.49, II.i.98), prayer (I.iv.87), swearing (I.iv.87), challenging and answering (II.iv.8,10), jesting (II.iv.63, 65, 78), and calling (III.i.58).

23. Gibbons, *Romeo and Juliet*, p. 124n.

24. European hereditary surnames manifest a late medieval and Renaissance bourgeois familial impulse opposed to much of what Mercutio represents. The Normans brought the comparatively new practice to England, where the first hereditary English surnames are

recorded in the Domesday Book (1086). While much has been written about the history of hereditary familial nomenclature, and about the histories of particular surnames, so far as I know the phenomenological or Foucauldian archaeology that would probe the evolution to any depth has yet to be done. 'Arden', incidentally, is one of the earliest English hereditary surnames (P. H. Reaney, *The Origin of English Surnames* [London, 1967], p. 302).

25. *'One calls within: "Juliet"* ', I.v.142 S.D.; *'Paris offers to go in and Capulet calls him again'*, III.iv.11 S.D. The second appears in Q1 but not in Q2–4, F. The word appears in only eight Shakespearean stage directions, twice in *Romeo* and once in six other plays. The word is frequent in the text of *Romeo*, and summoning with or without the word 'call' happens a number of times without stage direction, as at III.v.64–5.

26. Edward Snow, 'Language and Sexual Difference in *Romeo and Juliet'*, in *Shakespeare's Rough Magic: Renaissance Essays in Honor of C. L. Barber*, ed. Peter Erickson and Coppélia Kahn (Newark, DE, 1985), 191n13.

27. The balcony scene answers the mock conjuration in ways beyond that already noted. The discussion of what to swear by (II.ii.107–16) answers Mercutio's talk of conjuring by parts of Rosaline. And, as George Walton Williams has drawn to my attention, Mercutio's mocking 'Cry but Ay me!' (II.i.10) is answered by the first words Romeo hears Juliet speak from the balcony, 'Ay me' (II.ii.25). Nor are the echoes of Mercutio from Act II scene i alone. Romeo's apostrophe (ll.26–32) to Juliet as 'a winged messenger of heaven' (l.28) not only invokes Mercury as angel but also in imagery and vocabulary strikingly echoes Mercutio's children of an idle brain speech discussed above.

28. See Joseph A. Porter, *The Drama of Speech Acts: Shakespeare's Lancastrian Tetralogy* (Berkeley, CA, 1979), p. 58.

29. How is it we know that Mercutio hasn't really misunderstood Benvolio? Perhaps because assuming he had would entail his seeming more lacking in common sense than we are willing to grant even though Benvolio seems willing to grant it. Mercutio's linkage with writing here and in the Capulet guest list, by the way, evinces a trace of Mercurian graphism. It may be objected that all four young men – the three friends and Tybalt – are linked to written messages on both occasions. However, Mercutio alone here uses the word 'write', doing so in a sentence without mention of the other three men, so that his linkage with writing is stronger than theirs. The situation brings him into the margins of the play's later fateful missives.

30. Gibbons, *Romeo and Juliet* (p. 105n) cites 'To see him walk before a lady, and to bear her fan' (*Love's Labour's Lost*, IV.i.144) for the

custom of carrying a fan. In some nineteenth-century productions, as in the silent film version of 1908, the fan is made oversize for comic effect. Just possibly the fan Venus gives Mercury as a pledge in Peele, *The Araygnement of Paris* (I 584), could have figured in Shakespeare's creation of the Nurse's fan. The Nurse and Mercutio are analogous in their bawdiness and fondness for oaths, their serving as advisers to the titular heroes, and even their names, 'Angelica' standing to 'Mercutio' as 'angel' to 'Mercury'. The parallelism mustn't be pushed too far though. Where Mercutio achieves a kind of apotheosis in his death, the Nurse compromises herself pretty thoroughly in the last half of the play.

31. Gibbons, *Romeo and Juliet*, pp. 152–3n.

32. Ibid., p. 147n.

33. Frances A. Shirley, *Swearing and Perjury in Shakespeare's Plays* (London, 1979), p. 101.

34. Line 36, Mercutio's last to Benvolio in the scene's first large movement, 'By my heel, I care not', would bring the total of first person pronouns there up to six if taken as part of that movement; I rather consider it transitional for, while it is addressed to Benvolio, it clearly manifests some of the hostile scorn Tybalt rouses in Mercutio. Line 54, 'I will not budge for no man's pleasure, I', with its striking placement of the pronouns and late-as-possible caesura, exhibits some of the tragic and lonely egotism that reappears mutatis mutandis in Coriolanus's '... like an eagle in a dovecote, I Fluttered your Volscians in Corioles. / Alone I did it' (*Cor.* V.vi.113–15).

35. See Sigurd Burckhardt, *Shakespearean Meanings* (Princeton, NJ, 1968), pp. 162–3.

36. A general dramaturgic theory of characters' limens or thresholds could be useful. It would need to take into account not only cases like Mercutio's, where reference to the character precedes his first entrance and follows his last exit, but also cases with no entrance or exit limen, where no reference precedes or follows the character's appearance onstage, and perhaps – though this raises problems – negative limens. The theory might take into account a given limen's comparative fullness (or emptiness) of reference to the character. Mercutio's exit limen, for instance, especially in its beginning, seems comparatively full of reference to him. The theory could also be made to handle interliminal or subliminal spaces between a given character's onstage appearances.

37. 'Brave' and 'gallant', both favourite terms of approbation for Shakespeare, share a high degree of etymological obscurity. If the hypothesis that gallant is from an adaptation of an Old High German word for wandering or going on pilgrimages (*Oxford English Dictionary*, s.v.) is correct, there is a suggestion (probably unavailable to Shakespeare) of Mercutio's becoming one of the *romei* himself here. 'Gallant' is one of the notable links between Mercutio and Hotspur.

38. According to John C. Meagher in 'Economy and Recognition: Thirteen Shakespearean Puzzles', *Shakespeare Quarterly*, 35 (1984), 7–21, Lady Montague and the Nurse must both be absent in the final scene because their actors are present in other roles. Meagher bases his theory on the seemingly required doubling of roles imposed on Shakespeare by the size of his troupe, and on what he takes to be Shakespeare's exploitation of that limitation in his metatheatric use of the audience's presumed recognition of actors playing doubled roles. Because Lady Montague's absence creates too obvious an asymmetry to be ignored, Shakespeare has Montague announce her death on the spot 'rather lamely' (p. 12). But 'one abrupt demise is enough; having eliminated Lady Montague explicitly, it would not be diplomatic for Shakespeare to try to get by with killing the Nurse through an analogous grief' (p. 12). Meagher holds that we in fact do miss the Nurse in the final scene. And see note 39 below. In Q I, incidentally, Benvolio is mentioned in V.iii.36.

39. Meagher, ibid., p. 13, has Mercutio doubled with Paris, but other arrangements are feasible. Mercutio's doubling with the Prince would 'explain' the peculiar offstage death. Booth offers no more compelling reason for it. But Mercutio's exit to die offstage followed shortly by the Prince's entrance does suggest that the roles of Mercutio and the Prince might have been doubled, or perhaps 'tripled', since he asks us also to entertain the possibility that the same actor might have played Paris, an admitted improbability given the necessary legerdemain with Paris's body in Act V scene iii to permit the Prince's entrance in the same scene. While the proposed tripling would provide a pleasing reflection of the kinship of the three characters, Stephen Booth in *'King Lear', 'Macbeth', Indefinition, and Tragedy* (New Haven, CT, 1983) offers no more compelling reason for it. But Mercutio's exit to die offstage followed shortly by the Prince's entrance looks more like an accommodation to doubling than anything else in the play.

40. Sir Philip Sidney, *The New Arcadia*, ed. Albert Feuillerat (1912, repr. Cambridge, 1963), pp. 485–8.

41. Edmund Spenser, *The Faerie Queene*, 2.8, 3.5, 3.12.

42. See Arnold Van Gennep, *The Rites of Passage* (1901, trans. Monika B. Vizedom and Gabrielle L. Caffe [Chicago, 1960]) for the three stages of rites of passage (i.e., separation, margin or limen, and reaggregation) and Turner, 'Betwixt' and *Ritual*, for an expansion of liminality to a border region incorporating some of Van Gennep's stage of separation, and for the liminal society: 'The liminal group is a community or comity of comrades' ('Betwixt', p. 100). David Bevington, *Action is Eloquence: Shakespeare's Language of Gesture* (Cambridge, MA, 1984) uses Turner notably: Victor Witter Turner, 'Betwixt and Between: The Liminal Period', in *Rites de Passage* (1964, repr. ch. 4 in *The Forest of Symbols: Aspects of Ndembu Ritual* [Ithaca, NY, 1967] and *the Ritual Process: Structure and Anti-Structure* (Chicago, 1969).

10

Romeo and Juliet's Open Rs

JONATHAN GOLDBERG

Over the past twenty years, *Romeo and Juliet* has become the Shakespeare play assigned to more US high school students than any other. *Julius Caesar* has been usurped; the sexual revolution has replaced the civics lesson. Yet, given the conservative nature of most high school curricula, one can only assume that the play is taught in formalist terms (the young vs the old, night vs day, love vs society, etc.) and toward a valuation of a kind not limited to high school lesson plans. Typical in this regard might be these sentences from Brian Gibbons's 'Introduction' to his Arden edition of the play (1980): 'The lovers are from the outset withdrawn in an experience of sublime purity and intense suffering which renders them spiritually remote from other characters and the concerns of the ordinary world. The single clear line of ideal aspiration in love is set against the diversified complex intrigues which proliferate in the ordinary world, and contact between the two has tragic consequences.'[1] In such an estimation (it recurs as the thesis in the thirty-five pages of his 'Introduction' given over to – ominously – 'The Play'), Gibbons would seem to be doing little more than echoing the closing lines of the play, in which the prince intones, 'never was a story of more woe / Than this of Juliet and her Romeo' (V.iii.308–9) as his response to the offer of Montague and Capulet to raise a monument to the dead pair of lovers:

> **Mont.**   For I will raise her statue in pure gold,
>   That whiles Verona by that name is known,

> There shall no figure at such rate be set
> As that of true and faithful Juliet.
> **Cap.**   As rich shall Romeo's by his lady's lie,
> Poor sacrifices of our enmity.
>
> (V.iii.298–303)

Predictably enough, Gibbons finds in this moment that the 'artifice of eternity' (p. 74) is being erected, the statues symbolising for him 'the alchemical transmutation of worldly wealth, property, earth, into the spiritual riches of the heart and the imagination' (p. 76).

In such estimations of the 'purity' and transcendentality of their love, and, by extension, of Shakespeare's art, mystifications are set up to obscure what can as easily be read in the lines: that the corpses of Romeo and Juliet continue to have a social function, indeed that they make possible the union of the two opposing houses; moreover, this is as long lasting as the name of the city in which their monument is erected, while the material value of the statues, insisted upon as Montague and Capulet vie in their offers, is tied to that contingent temporality, to a future that cannot be predicted or controlled however much these grasping and still rival-rous fathers would do so. Reading the lines this way, one can hear them echoing against the concerns in the play, voiced over and again, about the possibility that names and words might be un-moored and uncontrollable, subject to accidents and to determina-tions that no artifice of eternity can secure. One could also see that the three men speaking at the end of the play are bent upon secur-ing the social [order] through the dead couple, and one could extend this back to the entire play, reading the love of Romeo and Juliet as imbricated in rather than separated off from 'ordinary' life. The idealisation of the lovers, to be brief, serves an ideological func-tion. The marriage of their corpses in the eternal monuments of 'pure gold' attempts to perform what marriage normally aims at in comedy: to provide the bedrock of the social order. Or, to speak somewhat more exactly, the heterosexual order.

Yet, what is solidified in this final set of gestures is indicated just before, when Capulet offers his hand to Montague and calls him 'brother' (l. 295). For, to speak more exactly, what the ending of the play secures is a homosocial order,[2] and it is that configuration that continually triangulates the relation of Romeo and Juliet, adding in every instance a third term that gives the lie to the shelter of their love. Romeo and Paris as possible husbands, still fighting over the body of Juliet in the final scene of the play; Capulet and

Paris as the patriarchal couple trading Juliet between them; Romeo
and Tybalt as enemies and yet as lovers, joined and divided by
Juliet. The functioning of the patriarchy (the 'brotherhood' of
Montague and Capulet at the end of the play, the surrogate sonship
that extends from Capulet to Paris), as well as its misfunctioning (if
rivalry and enmity are that – an easily disputed point), is tied to the
love of Romeo and Juliet. Indeed, what makes their love so valuable
is that it serves as a nexus for the social and can be mystified as
outside the social. The sexual revolution replaces the civics lesson
indeed: with the myth of love as a private experience the personal is
disconnected from the political.

One would think, therefore, that feminist criticism that has
engaged the play would speak against the formalist project that I
have conveniently fetched from the account offered by Gibbons; to
a certain extent it has, and valuably, by excoriating patriarchal violence in the play. But it too dreams of the ideal world that Gibbons
imagines. I take as typical the opening sentences of Coppélia Kahn's
discussion of the play: '*Romeo and Juliet* is about a pair of adolescents trying to grow up. Growing up requires that they separate
themselves from their parents by forming with a member of the opposite sex an intimate bond which supersedes filial bonds.'[3] This
seems ready for high school use; the play is translated effortlessly
into modern (at any rate 1950s) terms. The tragedy of the play
implied in these opening sentences has to do with the failure of
Romeo and Juliet to grow up into the mature couple that has separated itself from parental bonds. Mystified, thereby, is the fact that
at the end of this ideal trajectory lies the transformation of the
couple into its parents; what they rebel against is also what they
become. These blandly descriptive sentences reek of prescriptive-
ness, most notably when growing up is allowed, indeed required to
have, a single heterosexual trajectory. How far this might be from
Romeo and Juliet the term 'homosocial' has already begun to
suggest, and Kahn's rewriting of the play to suit her normalising
plot couldn't be clearer. For rather than breaking the filial bond,
Romeo and Juliet re-ensure it; it is the brotherhood of Montague
and Capulet that they secure. And such would have been the case
too had the play been the comedy Kahn desires, in which boys
would arrive at manhood free of the phallic aggression and fear of
women that deform the patriarchy, for even in this benign state
they would not leave behind the institutional site of marriage upon
which patriarchy rests. Were the social order to work properly,

Kahn implies, it would effortlessly produce heterosexuality. Shakespeare, she believes, critiques patriarchy because it does not make growing up easy; his art is on her side.

In the pages that follow, I do not seek to enlist Shakespeare for the projects of a formalist and heterosexist agenda, but rather, following Eve Kosofsky Sedgwick, to suggest that the homosocial order in the play cannot simply be reduced to a compulsive and prescriptive heterosexuality; that sexuality in the play cannot be sheltered from sociality; that sexuality in the play cannot be found enshrined in an artifice of eternity because neither the social work that the play performs nor the play itself (a formalist phantasm) can be thought of in those terms.

Accounts of the sort that I have been invoking rest upon the value of the love between Romeo and Juliet, treating it as a unique manifestation, the locus of all kinds of intensities and transcendentalities (the perfection of the individual and, concomitantly, of the work of art). So doing, critical estimations could be said to follow a path that the play itself marks out, for, at the opening of the play, Romeo is in love, but not, as it happens, with Juliet, rather with Rosaline, and from the opening of the play, Romeo is being solicited to forget her and pass on to some more responsive object. The critics, that is, manage to do what Romeo is told to do. 'Forget to think of her' (I.i.223), the peace-mongering Benvolio counsels his friend – his 'fair coz' (I.i.205) – a lesson he reiterates in less than exalted terms: 'Tut man, one fire burns out another's burning' (I.ii.45). It is a lesson Romeo learns; to Friar Laurence's worried query, 'Wast thou with Rosaline?' Romeo replies, 'I have forgot that name, and that name's woe'. 'That's my good son' his 'ghostly father' returns (II.iii.40–3): Benvolio and Friar Laurence have been preaching Romeo the same sermon, a lesson in forgetting that, at least in the first scene of the play, Romeo protests that he cannot learn, a lesson which, once accomplished, involves, arguably, the very transformation that Benvolio counsels, not so much a forgetting as a replacing, a substitution. Seen in that light, Juliet as replacement object is inserted within a seriality rather than as the locus of uniqueness and singularity. The play offers reasons to think about the relationship in these terms, not least when Juliet on the balcony ponders Romeo's name and likens it to the rose that remains itself whatever it is called (II.ii.38–49). Is Juliet that rose, and, thereby, Rosaline renamed? What would the consequences be of thinking of her as the newest avatar of Rosaline in the play?

What, moreover, would follow from the other identification implied in Juliet's lines, one which locates Romeo in the place of the rose, and thus also in Rosaline's place? At the very least, a recognition that desire might not be determined by the gender of its object, that the coupling of Romeo and Juliet is not a unique moment of hetero-sexual perfection and privacy but part of a series whose substitu-tions do not respect either the uniqueness of individuals or the boundaries of gender difference.

These implications can be read from the start, in Benvolio's gentle solicitations of his 'fair coz'; as the play opens, Benvolio knows where to find Romeo because he shares with him a like con-dition, 'measuring his affections by my own' (I.i.124), keeping his distance as Romeo keeps his, weeping at his sorrows, displaying thereby a 'love ... that ... / Doth add more grief to too much of mine own' (ll.186–7); one heart vibrates to the other's:

> **Romeo** Dost thou not laugh?
> **Ben.** No coz, I rather weep.
> **Romeo** Good heart, at what?
> **Ben.** At thy good heart's oppression.
> **Romeo** Why such is love's transgression.
>
> (I.i.181–3)

'Love's transgression' here refers indifferently to the effects of Rosaline upon Romeo, dividing him from himself, and the affec-tion, the love of Benvolio for him, marked as it is, at once, by the strongest indications of identification and distance. His counsel, that Romeo forget Rosaline, is tantamount to a desire for him to re-member himself and his friend; his counsel to replace Rosaline with some other flame is undertaken in the belief that a happy Romeo would be a happier companion.

The situation with Rosaline can't help but recall the initial se-quence in Shakespeare's sonnets, where the sonneteer urges the young man to marry in order to further solidify bonds between men. In those poems, as Sedgwick astutely observes, the woman is barely present, no more than the conduit for firming up the patri-archy and guaranteeing the young man's place within a social order in which all the most heavily invested relations are those between men. The woman in these poems is no one in particular, simply anyone whom the young man would marry, and she poses no threat to the men or to the love that the sonneteer proffers. Rosaline would seem to be in much the same situation; she has no lines in the play and if she ever is onstage – at the ball at the Capulet's to which she has been invited, for example – her presence is unmarked and unremarked. Benvolio's desire that Romeo replace Rosaline with some more willing young woman seems to operate within the assumption that such a woman could occupy the position of the woman in sonnets 1–17, a nonentity that would guarantee that Romeo fulfilled his debt to society and yet remained available for the comforts of friendly solicitations. Such assumptions, it might be supposed, are at play too when Friar Laurence breathes a sigh of relief that his 'son' has not transgressed with Rosaline, and he hastens to legitimate the relation with Juliet by arranging their marriage. If these plans presume a smooth transition from one love to another, they also make clear that from the start Romeo's condition is not one in which love exists in the privatised domain to which commentators assign it. Romeo's absence is remarked by his parents as the play begins; his friend's counsels make clear that love affects their relation too; and Friar Laurence moves quickly to legitimise the relationship through the institution of marriage.

In this context it is worth noting that Romeo's initial oxymoronic descriptions of love are occasioned by the signs of the street fight that opens the play; that is, he reads his emotional state as the reflection of the public brawl. This is only to say from another vantage point that love, from the start of the play, is implicated in the social, not separate from it. Thus if, from one vantage point, it might appear that in moving from Rosaline to Juliet, Romeo moves from an unproblematic love to a disruptive one, the plot of replacement would seem rather in either case to recognise the sociality of desire. The difference between Romeo's two loves – of comfort and despair? – is crossed from the start, and both loves work to secure and to disrupt the social; both loves are 'transgressive'. Both loves are forbidden, a fact made clear when we recall the moment when Rosaline is first named in the play; her name appears on the list that Romeo reads of those invited to the Capulets' ball; she is Capulet's 'fair niece' (I.ii.70). 'My only love sprung from my only hate' (I.v.137): Romeo may be, for Juliet, her first transgressive desire, but she is, for Romeo, the second in his pursuit of forbidden loves. When Juliet delivers her speech about Romeo and the name of the rose, she inserts him into the series in which she already participates as Romeo's substitute love, a new Rosaline with a different name (it is worth noting that the Rosaline figure in Shakespeare's source has no name).

Placing him in her place, however, Juliet follows a textual track marked out earlier. For while it is arguable, as I have argued, that the negotiations around Rosaline resemble those in the initial sequence of Shakespeare's sonnets, one moment in which those poems are recalled might suggest that the configuration is not quite the one I have already described. Romeo's complaint about Rosaline is that she is unresponsive, chaste as the moon; refusing to be 'hit / With Cupid's arrow' (I.i.206–7), she is armed against love, even against 'saint-seducing gold' (l. 211): 'O she is rich in beauty, only poor / That when she dies, with beauty dies her store' (ll. 213–14). These are recognisable complaints from the initial sonnets, but there they are directed at the young man who threatens by a kind of usury to make waste. These charges are laid at Rosaline as well in the lines immediately following those quoted above, when to Benvolio's query, 'Then she hath sworn that she will still live chaste', Romeo replies, 'She hath, and in that sparing makes huge waste'. In these respects Rosaline duplicates the young man who seems to have a patent on a beauty that the sonneteer cannot imagine located anywhere but in him and a progeny of young men who will duplicate and keep forever in circulation his unmatchable beauty.

> Looke what an unthrift in the world doth spend
> Shifts but his place, for still the world injoyes it
> But beauties waste hath in the world an end,
> And kept unusde the user so destroyes it.[4]

If Rosaline is, in this respect, in the place of the young man of the sonnets, the connection is furthered by her name, for it is possible to suspect that in the sonnets her name is his; in the very first poem he is named 'beauties *Rose*' (I.ii). Hence, when Juliet ponders the name of the rose – a name that might as well be hers or his – her lines operate in this sphere of gender exchange too.

On the one hand this could explain why the figure of Rosaline is so unthreatening in the play, how easily Romeo's grief over her can be incorporated in homosocial relations; she is so little a woman that she might as well be a man, so little a woman that all she does is to consolidate relations between men and serve as a conduit for them. Yet before one endorses this reading, one would also have to add: she is a forbidden love, as much as Juliet is, and as threatening too. If, that is, Rosaline, and the infinite replaceability of the rose, intimate the smooth workings of a homosocial order that gives

women a place only in order to erase them, the transgressive danger
spied in this love – even if it is between men and so secured – is
what the period might call *sodomy*. Moreover, that transgression –
of alliance, of the ties of the patriarchal organisation and distribution of property and entitlements – while usually thought to occur
between men, can also take place between a man and a woman.
Locating Rosaline as the young man, in short, might as easily place
her in the sphere of the homosocial as in the space of less contain-
able and less socially approved desires. It's here that one might
suspect that the name of the rose – like the name Rosaline as it
travels in Shakespeare's plays to characters in *Love's Labour's Lost*
and *As You Like It*, where Rosalind's other name, of course, is
Ganymede – plots a trajectory from the fair young man to the dark
lady. For it is of course the case that the threatening sexuality that
the dark lady represents – outside marriage and promiscuous and
dangerous to the homosocial order – is closer to sodomy than
almost anything suggested in the poems to the young man. Yet one
must think of these sets of poems in a complementary and displaced
relationship rather than, as in Joel Fineman's account, as marked by
the uncrossable diacritical markings homo and hetero.[5] Just as the
threat to Romeo's masculinity that Juliet represents when he declares himself effeminised by her – valour's steel gone soft
(III.i.111–13) – might be read not only within the dynamics of the
dark lady sonnets (Juliet assuming Rosaline's guise in that transformation), but also as suggesting another movement across gender: if
Romeo is feminised by her, she perhaps is masculinised. Hence, at
the moment when Romeo spies Juliet on the balcony, he declares
that the sun has replaced the moon; the moon earlier is Rosaline's
celestial counterpart, mythically allying her to Diana. Is the sun,
then, male, and is Juliet Romeo's Apollo? Such a question returns
us to the position of Rosaline as fair young man and to the possibility that Juliet's gender is equally destabilised, and thereby leads us
to ponder desires that are not governed by the gender of objects
and which are not allied to the formations of gender difference as
the homo / hetero divide imagines them.[6]

Such a way of reading the play is anathema to heterosexualising
readings of *Romeo and Juliet* and of Shakespeare in general. Thus,
when Janet Adelman, for example, declares that the tragedy begins
at the moment in which Romeo announces his effeminisation ('O
sweet Juliet, / Thy beauty hath made me effeminate / And in my
temper soften'd valour's steel' [III.i.115–17]) because it signals the

breakup of male–male relations in the play, solidified by their aggression toward and fear of women, this marks a tragedy that she regards as inevitable when comedy takes the form of male bonding or, worse, as it seems in Adelman's account, when male bonding can extend itself to the transvestite actor.[7] In those instances, Adelman opines, Shakespeare's plays indulge in the supposition 'that one need not choose between a homosexual and a heterosexual bond' (p. 91), a belief that she terms a fantasy that stands in the way of maturity and male development, which must culminate in heterosexuality. Otherwise, the plays might suggest 'the fantasy that the relationships [with transvestite actors] are simultaneously homosexual and heterosexual – a simultaneity that threatens to become uncomfortable when, for example, in *As You Like It* we hear that Orlando has kissed Ganymede-Rosalind' (p. 86). We, it is presumed, don't like it, and the reason seems to be that anything other than heterosexuality is repellent.

However much arguments like Kahn's or Adelman's expose the misogyny of Shakespeare's play, their enforcement of heterosexuality and gender difference belies energies in the plays that cannot be reduced to the erasure of women. For if one thinks of Rosaline or of Juliet assuming the place of men, or of Romeo taking up a feminine position, those differences only read invidiously within the logic of a compulsory heterosexuality. When Rosaline is imagined as hoarding herself, and refusing to open her lap to gold, she is, like the young man and like the dark lady, imagined as sexually autonomous and sexually self-fulfilling. Insofar as Juliet takes up the position of Rosaline, their difference is marked by a single word. The woman who says no has become the woman who says yes; 'Ay' is Juliet's first reported word (I.iii.43), her first word in the balcony scene (II.ii.25), and the locus of her subjectivity is her assent to desire, her active solicitation of sexual experience (see, in this respect, her play on 'Ay' and 'I' in III.ii.45–51). When she thinks about having sex with Romeo, she imagines cutting him up into little pieces (III.ii.21–5); whether this marks her as (in the favoured terms of Kahn's analysis) phallically aggressive or not, it suggests that the diacritical markings of gender are transgressed in the play, something to be seen as well earlier in the same soliloquy, in which the solicitation of night, a maternal figure, is transformed into the scene of an enactment of a 'strange love' (III.ii.15) in which Romeo first is night and then lies 'upon the wings of night / Whiter than new snow upon a raven's back' (ll. 18–19). In this 'purification' and masculinisation of her beloved not only has he become – as she was – the brightness of day, but he also takes Night from behind; strange sex indeed.

It is, of course, arguable that the transgressions of gender that masculinise Juliet (or Rosaline) participate in misogyny (either by way of erasure or by excoriating active sexuality, as occurs most often in the play through attacks on the nurse), but this move across gender also allows a subject position for women that is not confined within patriarchal boundaries. That is to say, it is only by seeing the energies in the plays that are not dictated by a compulsory heterosexuality and gender binarism that one can begin to mark their productive energies. In the case of *Romeo and Juliet*, as I have been suggesting, this means to put pressure on the heterosexualising idealisation of the play and on the magical solution it arrives at over the corpses of the young lovers. It is, in short, to make them available for forbidden desires that really do call patriarchal arrangements into question. Readings of the plays, written from whatever position, that seek to enforce a compulsory heterosexuality must be complicit with the domestication of women and with the scapegoating of men (often by palming off the ills of heterosexuality on homosexuality). Such readings need to be opposed, and not merely on ideological grounds; hetero- and homosexuality are profound misnomers for the organisation of sexuality in Shakespeare's time. As this essay has been suggesting, gender and sexuality in *Romeo and Juliet* do not subscribe to the compulsions of modern critics of the play.

So much Juliet's lines on the name of the rose prompt us to think, especially, as I have been suggesting, in the identifications across gender that they allow, and for the ways in which they open trajectories of desire that cross gender difference. If the rose is most literally Rosaline's name respelled, it is, with only the slightest metaphorical force, Juliet's as well, since she is not only Romeo's newest rose, but is herself locked within 'orchard walls ... high and hard to climb, / And the place death' (II.ii.63–4), a dangerous flower to be plucked, dangerous, as I have been suggesting, and as this description does too, because the desires she represents are closely allied to forbidden sexual acts more usually thought of as taking place between men. Juliet is most explicitly a flower when she has apparently been taken by death. 'The roses in thy lips and cheeks shall fade' (IV.i.99), Friar Laurence tells her, and this is what her father sees; 'the sweetest flower of the field' (IV.v.29), he tells her husband-to-be, has been taken already, not, as is the case, by Romeo, but by death: Death has 'lain with thy wife. There she lies / Flower as she was, deflowered by him' (ll. 36–7). Such imaginings of the sexual act as taking place in the wrong place ('the place death') and with the wrong partner only further the sense that the sexual field in which desire operates in the play is the forbidden desire named sodomy. The ungenerative locus of death allies the sexual act to the supposedly sterile and unreproductive practice of usury associated with the young man and with Rosaline's self-hoarding and waste, themselves as suggestive of sodomy as they are of masturbatory activities as well.

If the living-dead Juliet is the flower deflowered, the usual deformations of the signifier that works to make these connections in the play – the name of the rose – find a further point of transformation (of nominal difference and identification) at her funeral. Friar Laurence orders rosemary to be strewn on her supposed corpse (IV.v.79) and the stage direction at line 96 suggests that it is done: '*Exeunt all but the Nurse and musicians, casting rosemary on Juliet.*' Juliet's living-dead status could be taken to prevaricate in bodily terms between the generative and ungenerative desires whose paths cross each other in the play; much as she has and has not been deflowered by death, her union with Romeo is, from the end of the second act of the play, legitimated by marriage and continues to summon its allure from the unspeakable terrain of sodomy. If, in her balcony speech, Juliet joins herself to Romeo through the name of the rose – the name that connects them both through the cross-gendered figure of Rosaline as well – at her funeral the name has been transformed to rosemary. But this too has been anticipated by the vagaries of the signifier, or so the nurse reports in lines that seem to have misheard the balcony declaration and to send those lines about the rose along the route to the rosemary cast upon Juliet:

> **Nurse** Doth not rosemary and Romeo begin both with a letter?
> **Romeo** Ay, Nurse, what of that? Both with an 'R'.
> **Nurse** Ah, mocker! That's the dog's name. 'R' is for the – No, I know it begins with some other letter; and she hath the prettiest sententious of it, of you, and rosemary, that it would do you good to hear it.
>
> (II.iv.202–8)

The circuit of desire moves through the letter R, linking Romeo, the rose, Rosaline, rosemary, and Juliet, whose name begins with some other letter but is not misspelled in this sequence, proper and improper at once like the name Rosemary attached by her to Romeo and through the rosemary to her living-dead body, or like the forbidden fruit (whose other proper name we will, in a moment, confront) that can be domesticated behind the orchard walls.

The nurse's lines deform the lovely alliteration of the letter R; she hears in it not only the growling of a desire that is less than transcendentally human – the bestial bark – but also something else. In his note on lines 205–6, Brian Gibbons allows Phillip Williams to complete the nurse's unfinished sentence: 'the Nurse just stops herself from saying the word *arse* – "with a somewhat unlooked-for show of modesty"'.[8] Another name for alliteration, apt here: assonance; another name for the movement of the letter R and the cross-couplings it allows, the *open Rs*. Gibbons goes where the nurse does not, immodestly allowing the unspeakable, and not just in the margins; the word is pronounced outside the garden walls as well:

> **Mer.**   If love be blind, love cannot hit the mark.
> Now will he sit under a medlar tree
> And wish his mistress were that kind of fruit
> As maids call medlars when they laugh alone.
> O Romeo, that she were, O that she were
> An open-arse and thou a poperin pear!
> (II.i.33–8)

The medlar, whose other name, open-arse, is this secret now pronounced, is a member of the rose family (check Webster's if you don't believe me).[9] Gibbons allows the open-arse into his text (it appears in no quarto nor in any early edition of the play), an instance, in which, as he puts it in the textual introduction of his edition, he has 'retained' an 'archaic' form (p. 25) unwarranted by his copytext.[10]

I don't want to be detained here by the textual crux of II.i.38, much as it would communicate with the other moment that has animated this discussion – the passage on the rose, which also has a famous textual problem around the very issue of the proper name or word which makes possible the open Rs of this text; or the nurse's assonance, available only in Q_2, a text of the play remarkable for its self-remarking textuality.[11] Rather, I would simply notice that in this scene Mercutio begins by conjuring Romeo, naming him by his proper – which is to say, entirely generic –

names: 'Romeo! Humours! Madman! Passion! Lover!' (II.i.7), and that when these (im)proper names fail to raise him, Mercutio tries a more (in)direct approach, naming him by calling him up in the name of Rosaline: 'In his mistress' name / I conjure only but to raise up him' (ll. 28–9). If the lines imagine Romeo rising to occupy this place, they deal at once in an identification between Romeo and Rosaline and with Romeo's desire for Rosaline. These meet in that conveniently open place that the Rs mark, the open-arse that also hits and deflects the mark (much as both Q_1 and Q_2 fail to deliver what Gibbons and most modern editions now allow Mercutio to say). Mercutio's lines about a blind love that does and does not hit the mark recall Benvolio's counsels earlier about the deflection of Romeo's desires from Rosaline (I.i.203–5), and they too suggest that the path of the deformations of desire away from her never leaves the spot that she marks, which is precisely the unnameable crossing here (in the modern text) not left blank or marked out or marked over. The locus of anal penetration, of course, is available on any body, male or female. Mercutio's conjuring also conjures him into the magic circle, an O that is not, as most commentators would have it be, the vaginal opening, for this is how Mercutio voices – through Rosaline – his desire for Romeo, his version, that is, of Benvolio's more benign voicing of the place she can occupy between men.[12] Mercutio is calling Romeo up for him, as he does throughout the opening acts of the play, a deflection of Romeo's desire from the unresponsive beloved, to one who, as much as Juliet later, wants to share a bed with Romeo (where Mercutio would lie is suggested by the solitary bed he goes home to, the 'truckle-bed' [II.i.39] that lies under one placed above it).

As Mercutio conjures up Romeo in his generic names, and then deflects those names through the name of Rosaline, he calls up his relationship to Romeo. The secret name of Romeo in the play, as Joseph Porter has convincingly argued, is Valentine, the otherwise non-existent brother of Mercutio named only in the list of those invited to the Capulet ball that the illiterate servant cannot read, and that Romeo does: '*Mercutio and his brother Valentine*' (I.ii.68).[13] It resonates (assonates) with another name down the list, '*Signior Valentio and his cousin Tybalt*' (l. 71). This second Valentine, as invisible elsewhere in the play as the first, participates in a cousinship that, like the brotherhood of Mercutio and Valentine, may name properly what cannot be said. This male couple resounds when Tybalt charges Mercutio with being Romeo's 'consort' ('Mercutio, thou consortest with Romeo. / **Mer.** Consort?' [III.i.44–5), and to Mercutio's dismay at Romeo's declaration a few lines later that he would rather make love than fight with Tybalt. Tybalt, after all, is someone that Mercutio characterises as ill-equipped to handle a sword; if Romeo is his man, as he declares (III.i.55), then, Mercutio opines, Romeo will follow him, taking him, it would seem, from behind. If Mercutio counsels Romeo to prick love for pricking (I.iv.28), it is, it appears, because he fears that his Valentine has received the 'butt-shaft' (II.iv.16) of love, that Rosaline, armed like Diana, has hit his mark, that the boy love has come to the depth of his tail and buried his bauble in that hole rather than in his (see II.iv.90–100). To return to the scene of conjuring, then, is to register Mercutio's rivalry for a place that anyone might occupy and to recognise his projection into Rosaline's place as his own, as his way, that is, of occupying the magic circle or owning, to vary the metaphor slightly, the desires named by the open Rs in the text.

That these desires can be named variously, and never properly, Mercutio's lines further intimate when the secret name is one that maids trade among themselves in private. Female secrecy is broached in those lines, and appropriated to a secret about transgression that does not respect gender difference. If there is, in this context, something to be said about the textual crux at II.i.38, it is perhaps best suggested by J. Dover Wilson's gloss in the Cambridge edition of the play (1955) on the reading that is adopted by Gibbons (and by a number of other editions, most recently by Stanley Wells and Gary Taylor in their 1986 Oxford *Complete Shakespeare*). Q_1, as noted above, has 'open *Et caetera*' at this point while Q_2 prints 'An open, or thou' (Div). Wilson argues that a compositor or scribal error is responsible for 'or' (as a misreading of manuscript 'ers', the presumption that leads Gibbons to 'retain' a reading not found in any printed text but assumed to have been in Shakespeare's hand). In writing his note on the crux, Wilson conveniently ignores the comma in Q_2 which might, like the unfinished sentence of the nurse's, indicate that Mercutio leaves unsaid what needs not be said (the alternative name for the medlar is about as available as anything, an open secret not to be said more openly). This allows him to dispose of the possibility that 'or' means 'or' rather than being a misread arse. 'He speaks', Wilson opines, 'of the fruits [the ripely rotten apple and the popping pear] as complementary not alternative so that "and" not "or" is required' (p. 151).

'And' introduces, anglice, the 'bad' Q_1 evasion of the more forth-rightly named Rs. For Wilson, this is what is proper and required at this spot, that her arse and his poperin complement each other. In other words, Wilson reads 'and' to mean 'or' (inserts 'and' in his text so that it does so) since 'or' might mean 'and'; 'or', were it to be there, might offer an 'alternative' that Wilson will not allow, the possibility that either member of the couple could assume either po-sition. This is perhaps the scandal that the whispering of the maids is about, or that can be heard as Juliet swallows the potion in order to get Romeo in the grave before Tybalt does ('O look, methinks I see my cousin's ghost / Seeking out Romeo that did spit his body / Upon a rapier's point! Stay, Tybalt, stay' [IV.iii.55–7]. In those lines Juliet assumes Mercutio's rivalrous position, while Tybalt functions for her – as he had for Romeo, and as he does earlier for Juliet in a scene that prevaricates over and also enforces the identity of her cousin and her lover (III.v.65–125) – as the switching point for an identification that breaches love and enmity, friend and villain, death and life, the open arse and the open grave of transgressively (un)productive desires. What these moments share – and they structure the trajectories of desire imagined in the play – is the recognition that anyone – man or woman – might be in the place marked by the open Rs of *Romeo and Juliet*.

From Jonathan Goldberg, '*Romeo and Juliet*'s Open Rs', from *Queering the Renaissance*, ed. Jonathan Goldberg (Durham, NC, 1994), pp. 218–35.

NOTES

[Jonathan Goldberg provides the second essay on Mercutio in this book, and he enters into sympathetic dialogue with Joseph Porter's approach. The book from which this essay comes is called *Queering the Renaissance*, and Jonathan Goldberg also wrote a book called *Sodometries*. Both titles indicate that he practises 'queer theory'. This ap-proach deals with understandings of sexuality and identity, but unlike feminism, for example, it sees gender as a fluid and indeterminate cate-gory that can encompass a range of 'politics of difference' based on sexu-ality. Inevitably, this will often mean in practice challenging the supremacy of heterosexuality. While Callaghan tends to suggest that *Romeo and Juliet* itself canonises heterosexuality, Goldberg suggests that this idealisation has been enshrined in criticism and teaching. There is, he suggests, another reading of the text itself available, the line of 'brotherhood' and 'surrogate sonship' and other male–male relationships. This text, Goldberg argues, is given complexity by the presence of Mercutio. If we see Romeo's relationship with Juliet as not transcendent but as part of a potential series of substitutions for Rosaline, then his relationship with Mercutio, and Mercutio's feelings for Romeo, become sustained and central to the play's presentation of sexuality. Goldberg examines much detail in the play's imagery that supports a gay reading, arguing that it is 'only by seeing the energies in the plays that are not dictated by a compulsory heterosexuality and gender binarism that one can begin to mark their productive energies'. Quotations from the Arden text, *Romeo and Juliet*, ed. Brian Gibbons (London, 1980). Ed.]

1. Brian Gibbons (ed.), *Romeo and Juliet* (London, 1980), p. 70. All citations are from this edition. For further evaluations of this edition, see my review of it in *Shakespeare Studies*, 16 (1983), 343–8 and Stanley Wells's review in *TLS*, 4030 (20 June 1980), 710. G. Blakemore Evans in his New Cambridge edition of the play (1984) devotes pp. 16–20 to 'language, style and imagery' in familiar formalist terms.

2. I take the term from its usage by Eve Kosofsky Sedgwick, *Between Men* (New York, 1985), and in the pages that follow depend upon her arguments throughout the book as well as their particular application to Shakespeare in the chapter 'Swan in Love'.

3. Coppélia Kahn, 'Coming of Age in Verona', reprinted from *Modern Language Studies*, 8 (1977–78), 5–22 in Carolyn Ruth Swift Lenz, Gayle Greene, and Carol Thomas Neely (eds), *The Woman's Part* (Urbana, IL, 1980), pp. 171–93.

4. 1609 text quoted from *Shakespeare's Sonnets*, ed. Stephen Booth (New Haven, CT, 1978), 9.9–12.

5. Joel Fineman's account in *Shakespeare's Perjured Eye* (Berkeley, CA, 1986) compulsively reproduces this distinction – even claiming for Shakespeare nothing less than the invention of 'the poetics of heterosexuality' (p. 18), yet, as he moves to take up the issue of cross-coupling, and with it the phenomena of the pricked prick and the cut cunt (see, e.g., pp. 275 ff.), as he terms them, the difference between hetero- and homosexuality is breached. Nonetheless, the mode of breaching is by the route of castration and thus operates under the aegis of the oedipal and thereby within the heterosexualising argument that allows for difference only under that rubric.

6. Work on the historicity of gender that would lend support to these suppositions would include Stephen Greenblatt's 'Fiction and Friction', in *Shakespearean Negotiations: The Circulation of Social Energy in Renaissance England* (Oxford, 1988), esp. pp. 73–86; Thomas Laqueur's *Making Sex* (Cambridge, MA, 1990); and Ann Rosalind Jones and Peter Stallybrass, 'Fetishizing Gender:

Constructing the Hermaphrodite in Renaissance Europe', in Julia Epstein and Kristina Straub (eds), *Body Guards* (New York, 1991).

7. See Janet Adelman, 'Male Bonding in Shakespeare's Comedies', in Peter Erickson and Coppélia Kahn (eds), *Shakespeare's Rough Magic* (Newark, DE, 1985); pp. 80–1 are on *Romeo and Juliet*.

8. G. Blakemore Evans also cites Williams at this point in his New Cambridge edition, but then misunderstands the implications of the nurse's speech: 'Obviously she can't read or spell, and because of its rude associations she decides that "Romeo" and "rosemary" must begin with some other letter' (p. 115). The nurse, however, registers that she stops herself from saying a word that sounds like it begins with an R but doesn't; Evans's swipe at the nurse's illiteracy displaces, one suspects, his discomfort at the associations implicated in the nurse's assonance.

9. I'm grateful to Natasha Korda for pointing this out to me as well as to a set of notes she prepared on the crux in Mercutio's lines which has helped me think through the points argued here.

10. For a glance at this 'retention' (anal?) and its supposed restoration of an original unavailable in any text that might claim to be close to a Shakespearean original, see Random Cloud, 'The Marriage of Good and Bad Quartos', *Shakespeare Quarterly*, 33 (1982), 430–1. For a defence of the properness of this scandalous reading by the modern editor who first printed it in his 1954 Yale edition of the play, see Richard Hosley, 'The Corrupting Influence of the Bad Quarto on the Received Text of *Romeo and Juliet*', *Shakespeare Quarterly*, 4 (1953), 21. Hosley would rather have *open-arse* than allow his text to be 'contaminated' by the 'bad quarto', Qr, which reads 'open *Et caetera*' (Dir) at this spot.

11. For pursuit of the crux about the name of the rose, up to the point engaged in this essay, I refer the reader to an earlier essay of mine, ' "Whats in a name? that which we call a Rose": The Desired Texts of *Romeo and Juliet*', written for and delivered at the 1988 session of an annual conference at the University of Toronto on editorial and textual matters and forthcoming in the volume of papers from that meeting, *Crisis in Editing: Texts of the English Renaissance*, ed. Randall McLeod. In that essay I call into question the usual supposition that of the two quarto editions of the play, Q_1 (1597) is simply a 'bad quarto' (shaped by the memories of actors and the imposition of non-authorial materials), while Q_2 (1599) is authoritative and derived from Shakespeare's hand; rather, I suggest, both texts arise from a theatrical milieu of continual revision and rewriting, and no modern text of the play can fail to consult both or can easily adjudicate differences between the two texts or, as often happens, when Q_2 offers more than one version of the same set of lines, in the hope of arriving at final or

original authorial intention. I argue that intentionality was never so limited.

The crux involved in II.i.38 will be unravelled in the discussion that follows; in Q₁ the line alludes to an 'open *Et caetera*' (Dir), which, were one to take that script as depending solely on stage performance, would mean that this reports the line as spoken (i.e., as speaking and possibly evading speaking more forthrightly), though it is also possible to regard the *Et caetera* either as a way of naming otherwise what need not be named any more forthrightly or as an evasion of more direct naming supplied by the printer and not following what the actor actually said.

At this point, Q₂ reads 'open, or,' (Div), and, it is assumed, as I discuss below, that 'or' represents a misreading by the compositor of Shakespeare's hand ('ers' is assumed to have been in the manuscript); the notion that 'arse' was once really in the text or spoken on stage is not quite so easily made, however, since the comma in Q₂ might indicate that a pause, and not a word, was offered at this spot. Again, one faces the dilemma of whether an unsaying said more than the more forthright reading offered by Gibbons; whether the lines in each earlier text have been censored, and if so, by whom; what, if anything, was actually spoken by the actor at this point; or, indeed, whether there was one way in which this line ever was delivered. Or, finally, whether this massive textual problem does not also correspond to the very nexus of the utterly unspeakable / absolutely commonplace nature of anal sex, in this instance dictated by all the proprieties surrounded by the supposed unbreachable difference between the allowable spheres of male–male intimacy and the excoriated one called sodomy, or between the supposition that the only 'good' sex performed by male–female couples is procreative and conducted under the auspices of marriage, everything else being capable of being called, once again, sodomy.

12. I follow Joseph Porter here, who argues in *Shakespeare's Mercutio* (Chapel Hill, NC, 1988) that the lines 'involve the idea of Mercutio's taking Rosaline's place not only as conjurer but also as container of Romeo's phallus' though I do not follow him in wishing to make this the 'fleeting apparently subliminal trace of sexual desire on Mercutio's part' (p. 157) since that assumption implies that homoerotic desire must operate within the regimes of a closet that, I think, more appropriately might be seen as part of the modern apparatus of sexuality with its markers of homo- and heterosexuality. Since these desires are not distinguished and their boundaries are more fluid in Shakespeare's time, there is no need to make them unavailable, which locating homo-eroticism as subliminal does. On pp. 160–2, Porter ably dismantles the heterosexualising readings of this moment, in which even an open-arse is read as a figure for female genitalia, the most extraordinary of such instances perhaps being that of Eric Partridge, *Shakespeare's Bawdy* (London, 1990 [1947]): ' "An open *et-caetera*" must here mean "an

open arse". Yet my interpretation of Shakespeare's "open *et-caetera*" as "pudend" is correct, for the opening clearly refers to the female cleft, not the human anus. With the human bottom regarded as involving and connoting the primary sexual area, compare the slangy use of *tail* for the human bottom in general and for the female pudend in particular' (pp. 101–2). While Porter valuably insists that Mercutio's lines are about sodomy, his concession that 'of course the sodomy is heterosexual' (p. 161) could be seen as complicit with the heterosexualising of Partridge and other commentators on the line precisely because it differentiates homo- and heterosexual sodomy. The acts are not so distinguishable; moreover, the conceptual range of the term sodomy in the period does not heed the hetero / homo distinction, as Alan Bray makes clear as a starting point in his discussion in *Homosexuality in Renaissance England* (London, 1982), p. 14. My arguments above about a transgressive sodomy, and its link to cross-gender relations, seek to void this diacritical marker, and the move seems to me important both because it takes account of the history of sexuality but also insofar as it opposes the ways in which the distinction of homo- and heterosexual sodomy was mobilised in the US Supreme Court decision in *Bowers* v. *Hardwick*, which denied any fundamental constitutional right for acts of so-called 'homosexual sodomy' while guaranteeing the legality of the act for heterosexuals.

13. See Joseph A. Porter, 'Mercutio's Brother', *South Atlantic Review*, pp. 49 (1984), 31–41, and the fuller development of the argument in *Shakespeare's Mercutio*, pp. 1–10, 145–63.

Further Reading

The listing concentrates on works published in the 1980s and 1990s, following the orientation of the New Casebooks series. Since critics don't often obediently fall into some consistent 'school', no attempt is made to classify them according to their approaches. If the essay is consistently from a particular point of view, it is usually obvious from the title. Works from which essays in this collection are extracted are not listed here. An excellent bibliography is supplied by Sasha Roberts in her monograph on *Romeo and Juliet* for the Writers and Their Work series, from which essay 8 is extracted. A whole volume of topical essays is *Shakespeare Survey*, 49 (1996), ed. Stanley Wells – individual articles are listed below.

RECENT SINGLE-VOLUME EDITIONS

Andrews, John F. (ed.), *Romeo and Juliet*, The Everyman Shakespeare (London: J. M. Dent, 1993).

Blakemore, Evans G. (ed.), *Romeo and Juliet*, The New Cambridge Shakespeare (Cambridge: Cambridge University Press, 1992; first publ. 1984). Especially good on history of performance, and contains a shortened text of the source, Arthur Brooke's *The Tragicall Historye of Romeus and Juliet*.

Colman, Adrian, *Romeo and Juliet*, The Bell Shakespeare (Sydney: Science Press, 1994). A new and expanding series of scholarly editions, with a lot of information about the play's performance history in Australia.

Gibbons, Brian (ed.), *Romeo and Juliet*, The Arden Shakespeare series 2 (London: Routledge, 1994). Mainly useful for detailed notes; contains a shortened text of the source, Brooke's *The Tragicall Historye of Romeus and Juliet*.

CASEBOOKS AND COLLECTIONS PUBLISHED AFTER 1990

Andrews, John F. (ed.), *Romeo and Juliet: Critical Essays* (London: Garland Publishing, 1993).

Cookson, Linda, and Bryan Loughrey (eds), *Romeo and Juliet*, Longman Critical Essays (Harlow: Longman, 1991).

Halio, Jay L. (ed.), *Shakespeare's 'Romeo and Juliet': Texts, Contexts, and Interpretation* (Newark and London: Associated University Press, 1995).

Porter, Joseph A. (ed.), *Critical Essays on Shakespeare's 'Romeo and Juliet'* (New York: G. K. Hall, 1997).

Scott, Mark W. (ed.), *Shakespearean Criticism*, vol. 5 (Detroit: Gale Research, 1987). A large amount of criticism through the centuries – rather large and expensive for individuals but belongs in libraries.

Williamson, Sandra L. and James E. Person, Jr, *Shakespearean Criticism*, vol. 11 (Detroit, New York and London: Gale Research, 1990). Useful collection of theatre reviews of significant productions.

WORKS ON *ROMEO AND JULIET*

Andreas, James, 'The Neutering of Romeo and Juliet', in Robert P. Merriz and Nicholas Ranson (eds), *Ideological Approaches to Shakespeare: The Practice of Theory* (Lampeter: Edwin Mellen Press, 1992), pp. 229–42.

Bassnett, Susan, 'Wayward Sons and Daughters: *Romeo and Juliet, A Midsummer Night's Dream* and *Henry IV Part 1*', in *Shakespeare: The Elizabethan Plays* (London: Macmillan, 1993), pp. 57–71. Feminist reading.

Bijvoet, Maya C., *Liebestod: The Function and Meaning of the Double Love-Death* (New York and London: Garland, 1988). This book looks unpromising but in fact contains excellent material.

Bly, Mary, 'Bawdy Puns and Lustful Virgins: The Legacy of Juliet's Desire in Comedies of the Early 1600s', *Shakespeare Survey*, 49 (1996), 97–109.

Bullough, Geoffrey, *Narrative and Dramatic Sources of Shakespeare* (London: Routledge and Kegan Paul; New York: Columbia University Press, 1957–75), vol 1. The standard edition of Shakespeare's sources: it is illuminating and interesting to witness Shakespeare's creative practice by comparing the source, in this case Arthur Brooke's *The Tragicall Historye of Romeus and Juliet*.

Calderwood, James L., 'Romeo and Juliet: A Formal Dwelling', in *Shakespearean Metadrama* (Minneapolis: University of Minnesota Press, 1971); repr. in Andrews, *Romeo and Juliet: Critical Essays*, pp. 85–117. 'Metadramatic' approach focusing on the issues of self-consciousness about 'naming' in the play.

Calderwood, James L., 'Unfathering in Romeo and Juliet', in *Shakespeare and the Denial of Death* (Amherst: University of Massachusetts Press, 1987), pp. 105–9.

Colaco, Jill, 'The Window Scenes in *Romeo and Juliet* and Folk Songs of the Night Visit', *Studies in Philology*, 83 (1986), 138–57.

Conrad, Peter, 'Romeos, Juliets, and Music' in *To Be Continued: Four Stories and their Survival* (Oxford and New York: Clarendon Press, 1995), pp. 47–94. Includes an entertaining account of operatic versions of *Romeo and Juliet*.

Davies, Anthony, 'The Film Versions of *Romeo and Juliet*', *Shakespeare Survey*, 49 (1996), 153–62.

Davis, Philip, 'Nineteenth-century Juliet', *Shakespeare Survey*, 49 (1996), 131–40.

Dollimore, Jonathan, *Death, Desire and Loss in Western Culture* (New York: Routledge, 1998), pp. 102–16. Draws on Kristeva's essay and develops its ideas.

Farley-Hills, David, 'The "Bad" Quarto of *Romeo and Juliet*', *Shakespeare Survey*, 49 (1996), 27–44.

Farrell, Kirby, 'Love, Death, and Patriarchy in *Romeo and Juliet*', in Norman N. Holland, Sidney Homan and Bernard J. Paris (eds), *Shakespeare's Personality* (London: University of California Press, 1989), pp. 86–102.

Foster, Donald W., 'The Webbing of *Romeo and Juliet*', included in the anthology ed. Joseph A. Porter (1997, see above).

Fowler, James, 'Picturing *Romeo and Juliet*', in *Shakespeare Survey*, 49 (1996), 111–29.

Gibson, Rex, ' "O, what learning is!" Pedagogy and the Afterlife of *Romeo and Juliet*', *Shakespeare Survey*, 49 (1996), 141–51.

Goldman, Michael, *Shakespeare and the Energies of Drama* (Princeton, NJ: Princeton University Press, 1972). Contains a brief and vigorous chapter on *Romeo and Juliet*.

Gurr, Andrew, 'The Date and Expected Venue of *Romeo and Juliet*', *Shakespeare Survey*, 49 (1996), 15–25.

Hapgood, Robert, '*West Side Story* and the Modern Appeal of *Romeo and Juliet*', *Shakespeare Jahrbuch*, 8 (1972), 99–112.

Hapgood, Robert, 'Popularizing Shakespeare: The Artistry of Franco Zeffirelli' in Lynda E. Boose and Richard Burt, *Shakespeare the Movie: popularizing the plays on film, tv, and video* (London and New York: Routledge, 1997), pp. 80–94.

Holderness, Graham, *Romeo and Juliet*, Penguin Critical Studies (Harmondsworth: Penguin, 1990).

Holding, Peter, *Romeo and Juliet: Text and Performance* (London: Macmillan, 1992).

Howard, Jean E., *Shakespeare's Art of Orchestration: Stage Technique and Audience Response* (Urbana and Chicago, University of Illinois, 1984).

Jorgens, Jack, *Shakespeare on Film* (Bloomington: Indiana University Press, 1977); repr. in Andrews, *Romeo and Juliet: Critical Essays*, pp. 163–76.

Kahn, Coppélia, 'Coming of Age in Verona', *Modern Language Studies*, 8 (1978), 171–93; repr. in *The Woman's Part: Feminist Criticism of Shakespeare*, ed. Carolyn Ruth Swift Lenz, Gayle Greene and Carol Thomas Neely (Urbana: University of Illinois, 1980), pp. 171–93; also repr. in Kahn's book *Man's Estate: Male Identity in Shakespeare* (1981); and in Andrews, *Romeo and Juliet: Critical Essays*, pp. 337–58.

Knowles, Ronald, 'Carnival and Death in *Romeo and Juliet*: A Bakhtinian Reading', *Shakespeare Survey*, 49 (1996), 69–85. Carnival and the grotesque in *Romeo and Juliet*.

Laroque, François, 'Tradition and Subversion in *Romeo and Juliet*', in Halio, *Shakespeare's 'Romeo and Juliet': Texts, Contexts, and Interpretation*, pp. 1–36.

Levenson, Jill L., *Shakespeare in Performance: Romeo and Juliet* (Manchester: Manchester University Press, 1987).

Levenson, Jill L., 'Changing Images of *Romeo and Juliet*, Renaissance to Modern', in Werner Habicht, D. J. Palmer, and Roger Pringle (eds), *Images of Shakespeare* (London: Associated University Press, 1988), pp. 151–62.

Levenson, Jill L., 'Shakespeare's *Romeo and Juliet*: The Places of Invention', *Shakespeare Survey*, 49 (1996), 45–55.

Levith, Murray J., *Shakespeare's Italian Setting and Plays* (Basingstoke: Macmillan, 1989), pp. 54–60.

Locatelli, Angela, 'The Fictional World of *Romeo and Juliet*: Cultural Connotations of an Italian Setting', in Michele Marrapodi, A. J. Hoenselaars, Marcello Cappuzzo, and L. Falson Santucci (eds), *Shakespeare's Italy: Functions of Italian Locations in Renaissance Drama* (Manchester: Manchester University Press, 1993), pp. 69–84.

Mahood, Molly M., *Shakespeare's Worldplay* (London: Methuen, 1957); repr. in Andrews, *Romeo and Juliet: Critical Essays*, pp. 56–72.

McCown, Gary M., ' "Runnawares Eyes" and Juliet's Epithalamium', *Shakespeare Quarterly*, 27 (1976), 150–70.

Mertner, Edgar, ' "Conceit brags of his substance, not of ornament": Some Notes on Style in *Romeo and Juliet*', in Bernard Fabian and Kurt Tetzeli von Rosador (eds), *Shakespeare: Text, Language, Criticism: Essays in Honor of Marvin Spevack* (New York: Olms-Weidmann, 1987), pp. 180–92.

Novy, Marianne, 'Violence, Love, and Gender in *Romeo and Juliet* and *Troilus and Cressida*', in *Love's Argument: Relations in Shakespeare* (Chapel Hill, NC: University of North Carolina Press, 1984), pp. 87–97; repr. in Andrews, *Romeo and Juliet; Critical Essays*, pp. 35–49.

Oz, Avraham, ' "What's in a Good Name?" The Case of *Romeo and Juliet* as a Bad Tragedy', in Maurice Charney (ed.), *'Bad' Shakespeare: Revaluations of the Shakespeare Canon* (London: Associated University Press, 1988), pp. 133–42.

Ozark Holmer, Joan, ' "Myself condemned and myself excus'd": Tragic Effects in *Romeo and Juliet*', *Studies in Philology*, 88 (1991), 345–62.

Ozark Holmer, Joan, 'The Poetics of Paradox: Shakespeare's versus Zeffirelli's Cultures of Violence', *Shakespeare Survey*, 49 (1996), 163–79.

Pasternak Slater, Ann, 'Petrarchism Come True in *Romeo and Juliet*', in Werner Habicht, D. J. Palmer and Roger Pringle (eds) *Images of Shakespeare* (London: Associated University Press, 1988), pp. 129–50.

Pearlman, E., 'Shakespeare at Work: *Romeo and Juliet*', *English Literary Renaissance*, 24 (1994), 315–42.

Porter, Joseph A., 'Marlowe, Shakespeare and the Canonization of Heterosexuality', *South Atlantic Quarterly*, 88 (1989), 127–47.

Richmond, Hugh M., 'Peter Quince Directs *Romeo and Juliet*', in Marvin and Ruth Thompson (eds), *Shakespeare and the Sense of Performance* (London: Associated University Press, 1989), pp. 219–27.

Roberts, Sasha, *William Shakespeare: 'Romeo and Juliet'*, Writers and Their Work series (London: Northcote House and British Council, 1998).

Rowell, George, 'Mercutio as Romeo: William Terriss in *Romeo and Juliet*', in Richard Foulkes (ed.), *Shakespeare and the Victorian Stage* (Cambridge: Cambridge University Press), pp. 87–96.

Smith, Peter J., *Social Shakespeare: Aspects of Renaissance Dramaturgy and Contemporary Society* (London: Macmillan, 1995), pp. 125–35. A study of bawdy in the play.

Snow, Edward, 'Language and Sexual Difference in *Romeo and Juliet*', in Peter Erickson and Coppélia Kahn (eds), *Shakespeare's 'Rough Magic': Renaissance Essays in Honor of C. L. Barber* (London: Associated University Press, 1985), pp. 168–92; repr. in Andrews, *Romeo and Juliet: Critical Essays*, pp. 371–401.

Snyder, Susan, *The Comic Matrix of Shakespeare's Tragedies* (Princeton, NJ: Princeton University Press, 1979), pp. 56–70.

Snyder, Susan, 'Ideology and the Feud in *Romeo and Juliet*', *Shakespeare Survey*, 49 (1996), 87–96.

Stamm, Rudolf, *Shakespeare's Theatrical Notation: The Early Tragedies*, The Cooper Monographs 33 (Gesamtherstellung: Francke Verlag Bern, 1989), pp. 79–114.

Thomson, Leslie, ' "With patient ears attend": *Romeo and Juliet* on the Elizabethan Stage', *Studies in Philology*, 92 (1995), 230–47.

Traub, Valerie, *Desire and Anxiety: Circulation of Sexuality in Shakespearean Drama* (London: Routledge, 1992).

Urkowitz, Steven, 'Five Women Eleven Ways: Changing Images of Shakespearean Characters in the Earliest Texts', in Werner Habicht, D. J. Palmer, and Roger Pringle (eds), *Images of Shakespeare* (London and Toronto: University of Delaware Press, 1986), pp. 292–304.

Wallace, Nathanial, 'Cultural Tropology in *Romeo and Juliet*', *Studies in Philology*, 88 (1991), 329–44.

Watson, William Van, 'Shakespeare, Zeffirelli, and the Homosexual Gaze', in *Literature Film Quarterly*, 20:4 (1992), 308–25; repr. in Deborah Barker and Ivo Kamps (eds), *Shakespeare and Gender: A History* (London: Verso, 1995), pp. 235–62.

Watts, Cedric, *Romeo and Juliet*, Harvester New Critical Introductions to Shakespeare (London: Harvester, 1991). Useful book-length study of the play.

Wells, Stanley, 'The Challenges of *Romeo and Juliet*', *Shakespeare Survey*, 49 (1996), 1–14.

White, R. S., '*Romeo and Juliet*', in Stanley Wells (ed.), *Shakespeare: A Bibliographical Guide* (Oxford: Clarendon Press, 1990). Surveys older criticism of the play. Booklist complements this one, by referencing works before the 1980s.

Whittier, Gayle, 'The Sonnet's Body and the Body Sonnetized in *Romeo and Juliet*', in *Shakespeare Quarterly*, 40 (1989), 27–41.

SOME GENERAL WORKS

Adelman, Janet, *Suffocating Mothers: Fantasies of Maternal Origin in Shakespeare's Plays, 'Hamlet' to 'The Tempest'* (London: Routledge, 1992).

Bakhtin, Mikhail, *Rabelais and his World*, trans. Helene Iswolsky (Cambridge, MA: MIT Press, 1968).

Ball, Robert Hamilton, *Shakespeare on Silent Film: A Strange Eventful History* (London: George Allen and Unwin, 1968), pp. 217–18.

Belsey, Catherine, *Desire: Love Stories in Western Culture* (Oxford: Blackwell, 1994). Important book, though it does not deal with *Romeo and Juliet* specifically.

Ben-Amos, Ilana Krausman, *Adolescence and Youth in Early Modern England* (London and New Haven, CT: Yale University Press, 1994).

Bray, Alan, *Homosexuality in Renaissance England* (London: Gay Men's Press, 1982).

Bray, Alan, 'Homosexuality and the Signs of Male Friendship in Elizabethan England', *History Workshop Journal*, 29 (1990), 1–19.

Conrad, Peter, *A Song of Love and Death: The Meaning of Opera* (London: Chatto and Windus, 1987).

De Munck, Victor C., *Romantic Love and Sexual Behavior: Perspectives from the Social Sciences* (Westport, CT: Praeger, 1998).

De Rougemont, Dennis, *Love in the Western World* (New York: Pantheon (1956).

Dreher, Diane Elizabeth, *Domination and Defiance: Fathers and Daughters in Shakespeare* (University Press of Kentucky, 1986).

Gediman, Helen K., *Fantasies of Love and Death in Life and Art: A Psychoanalytic Study of the Normal and the Pathological* (New York University Press, 1995).

Grady, Hugh, *The Modernist Shakespeare* (Oxford: Clarendon Press, 1991). An important analysis of twentieth-century criticism of Shakespeare.

Hartnoll, Phyllis (ed.), *Shakespeare in Music* (London: Macmillan, 1964).

Haynes, Alan, *Sex in Elizabethan England* (Thrupp, Gloucestershire: Sutton Publishing, 1997).

Heinemann, Margot, 'How Brecht Read Shakespeare', in Jonathan Dollimore and Alan Sinfield (eds), *Political Shakespeare: New Essays in Cultural Materialism* (Manchester: Manchester University Press, 1985), pp. 203–30.

Kamps, Ivo (ed.), *Materialist Shakespeare: A History* (London: Verso, 1995).

Klein, Joan Larsen (ed.), *Daughters, Wives and Widows: Writing by Men about Women and Marriage in England, 1500–1640* (Urbana, IL: University of Illinois Press, 1992).

Lilar, Suzanne, *Aspects of Love in Western Society*, ed. Jonathan Griffin (London: Thames and Hudson, 1965), first published in French as *Le Couple* (Paris: Editions Bernard Grasset, 1963).

Orgel, Stephen, 'The Authentic Shakespeare', *Representations*, 21 (1988), 1–26.

Rothwell, Kenneth S. and Annabelle Henkin Malzer, *Shakespeare on Screen: An International Filmography and Videography* (New York: Neal Schuman Publishers, 1992). Indispensable reference work – much valuable information on films before 1990.

Rothwell, Kenneth S., *A History of Shakespeare on Screen* (Cambridge: Cambridge University Press, 1999).

Selden, Raman, *A Reader's Guide to Contemporary Literary Theory* (London: Harvester Wheatsheaf, 1989).

Shaughnessy, Robert, *Shakespeare on Film*, New Casebooks (London: Macmillan, 1998). Useful material, but oddly enough does not include an essay on film versions of *Romeo and Juliet*.

Stallybrass, Peter, 'Patriarchal Territories: The Body Enclosed', in Margaret Ferguson, Maureen Quirngan and Nancy Vickers (eds), *Rewriting the Renaissance: The Discourses of Sexual Difference in Early Modern Europe* (Chicago: Chicago University Press, 1985), pp. 123–42.

Stone, Lawrence, *The Family, Sex and Marriage in England, 1570–1700* (Harmondsworth: Penguin, 1977).

Tennov, Dorothy, *Love and Limerence: The Experience of Being in Love* (New York: Stein and Day, 1979).

Thompson, Ann, and Sasha Roberts (eds), *Women Reading Shakespeare 1660–1900: An Anthology of Criticism* (Manchester: Manchester University Press, 1997).

Wymer, Rowland, *Suicide and Despair in the Jacobean Drama* (Brighton: The Harvester Press, 1986). Chapter 6 is on 'Deaths for Love'.

Ziegler, Georgianna, ' "My Lady's Chamber": Female Space, Female Sexuality in Shakespeare', *Textual Practice*, 4 (1990), 73–90.

WEB SITES

http://www.romeoandjuliet.com/

http://www.ardenshakespeare.com/main/ardennet/ (Arden on the Internet)

http://www.folger.edu/welcome.htm (Folger Shakespeare Library)

Notes on Contributors

Catherine Belsey chairs the Centre for Critical and Cultural Theory at Cardiff University. Her books include *Desire: Love Stories in Western Culture* (1994) and *Shakespeare and the Loss of Eden: The Construction of Family Values in Early Modern Culture* (1999).

Bertolt Brecht (1898–1956) is the most internationally influential playwright and theatre theorist of the twentieth century. His best known plays are *The Caucasian Chalk Circle, The Threepenny Opera, The Good Person of Szechwan* and *Galileo*. An excellent introduction to his work is John Willett's *The Theatre of Bertolt Brecht* (third edn, 1967).

Dympna C. Callaghan is William P. Tolley Professor in the Humanities at Syracuse University. Her latest book is *Shakespeare Without Women* (1999).

Lloyd Davis teaches Renaissance literature and drama at the University of Queensland, where he is currently Director of Studies in the Faculty of Arts. He is the author of *Guise and Disguise: Rhetoric and Characterization in the English Renaissance* (1993) and the editor of *Sexuality and Gender in the English Renaissance: An Annotated Edition of Contemporary Documents* (1998), along with other essays and books in the areas of early modern studies, cultural studies and Victorian literature. He is the current editor of *AUMLA*.

Barbara Everett has held Fellowships and Lectureships at both Oxford and Cambridge, and is now Senior Research Fellow at Somerville College, Oxford. She has delivered both the Lord Northcliffe Lectures at University College, London, and the Clark Lectures at Trinity College, Cambridge. She has published on a wide variety of subjects. Shakespeare editions include *Antony and Cleopatra* (Signet), and *All's Well That Ends Well* (New Penguin). Her most recent books are *Poets in Their Time: Essays on English Poetry from Donne to Larkin* (1986), and *Young Hamlet: Essays on Shakespeare's Tragedies* (1989).

Jonathan Goldberg is Sir William Osler Professor of English Literature at Johns Hopkins University. His most recent book is *Desiring Women Writing: English Renaissance Examples* (1997).

Barbara Hodgdon is Ellis and Nelle Levitt Professor of English at Drake University and the author of *The End Crowns All: Closure and Contradiction in Shakespeare's History* (Princeton, 1991), *Henry IV, Part 2* in the Shakespeare in Performance series (Manchester, 1996), and *The Shakespeare Trade: Performances and Appropriations* (Pennsylvania, 1998). She is the editor of *The First Part of King Henry the Fourth: Texts and Contexts* (Bedford–St. Martin's, 1997) and of the forthcoming Arden 3 *Taming of the Shrew* as well as an Associate General Editor of Arden Online.

Julia Kristeva is a Professor at the University of Paris 7 – Denis Diderot. Her special interests are linguistics, semiology, psychoanalysis and twentieth-century literature. Among her works which have been translated into English are *Desire in Language: A Semiotic Approach to Literature and Art, Revolution in Poetic Language, Powers of Horror: An Essay on Abjection, New Maladies of the Soul, Time and Sense, Proust and the Experience of Literature*.

Joseph A. Porter, Professor of English at Duke, is the author of *The Drama of Speech Acts: Shakespeare's Lancastrian Tetralogy* and *Shakespeare's Mercutio: His History and Drama*, and the editor of *Critical Essays on Shakespeare's Romeo and Juliet*. He is currently editing the New Variorum *Othello*.

Kiernan Ryan is Professor of English Language and Literature at Royal Holloway, University of London, and a Fellow of New Hall, University of Cambridge. He is the author of *Shakespeare* (1989; 2nd edn, 1995; 3rd edn, 2000), and the editor of *King Lear: New Casebook* (1993), *New Historicism and Cultural Materialism: A Reader* (1996), *Shakespeare: The Last Plays* (1999) and *Shakespeare: Texts and Contexts* (1999). He is currently completing a study entitled *Shakespeare: The Comedies*.

Index

Adelman, J., 201–2
Aeneid, 183
Aeneis, 181
Anatomy of Melancholy, 13
Apologie of Raymond Sebond, 36
Arcadia, 11, 184
Arden of Faversham, 48
Arroyo, José, 136
Astrophil and Stella, 31, 71
Austin, J. L., 166, 167

Ball, Robert Hamilton, 20
Barrymore, John, 21, 176
Bataille, Georges, 13–14
Beatles, The, 22
Beauvoir, Simone de, 19, 118
Belsey, Catherine, 7
Bembo, Pietro, 34, 35
Bible, 7, 69
Bijvoet, Maya C., 24
Bogdanov, Michael, 141
Bonnie and Clyde, 24, 132
Branagh, Kenneth, 130
Brecht, Bertolt, 16–18
Brontë, Emily, 42
Brooke, Arthur, 29, 85, 94, 154,
    158, 166, 169, 180
Burton, D., 167
Burton, Robert, 13

Callaghan, Dympna, 15, 16, 20,
    40, 118
Carpaccio, 21
Castellani, Renato, 21
Castiglione, 34

Certeau, Michel de, 133
Changeling, The, 50
Coleridge, S. T., 33, 37
Colie, Rosalie, 50
Conrad, Peter, 8
Courtier, The, 34
Cuba, 23
Cukor, George, 21

Danes, Claire, 8, 22, 129–46
    passim
Dash, Irene, 118
Dean, James, 22, 136
della Francesca, Piero, 21
Dennis, C. J., 32
Derrida, Jacques, 55–9, 61, 65,
    89
Des'ree, 137, 138
di Lorenzo, Fiorenzo, 21
DiCaprio, Leonardo, 8, 129–46
    passim
Dickey, Franklin, 117
Dollimore, Jonathan, 34
Donne, John, 11, 32
Draper, J. W., 117
Dubrow, Heather, 167
Duchess of Malfi, The, 48, 50

écriture féminine, 19
Elam, Keir, 167
Evans, G. Blakemore, 65

Ferrand, Jacques, 49,
Fineman, Joel, 201
Fish, Stanley E., 167

Fisher, Helen, 6
Fitzgerald, F. Scott, 42
Ford, John, 48
Fowre Hymnes, 35
Fox Studios, 23
Freud, Sigmund, 10
Frost, David, 22

Gediman, Helen K., 10–13
Gibbons, Brian, 72, 83, 173, 174, 176, 194–6, 205, 206
Globe theatre, 3
Goldberg, Jonathan, 16, 20
Golding, Arthur, 35
Gouge, William, 103
Great Gatsby, The, 42
Greenblatt, Stephen, 31, 90
Grice, H. P., 166, 167, 171–2

Harnish, M., 167
Hazlitt, William, 5
Herbert, George, 42
Hodgdon, Barbara, 22
Homer, 57
Howard, Trevor, 21
Hume, David, 6
Hussey, Olivia, 8, 22

Jackson, Michael, 22
Jardine, Alice, 89
Johnson, Samuel, 118
Juliet's Desire, 21

Kahn, Coppélia, 118, 196, 202
Kennedy, Dennis, 134
Kermode, Frank, 106, 117
Kott, Jan, 21
Kristeva, Julia, 10, 16, 63, 99, 118
Kurosawa, Akira, 132
Kyd, Thomas, 28

La Dolce Vita, 132
Lacan, Jacques, 10, 58
Lane, Anthony, 139
Laqueur, Thomas, 49, 50
Laslett, Peter, 101
Lawlor, John, 117
Leech, G., 167

liebestod, 2, 10, 141
Los Angeles Times, 133
Love Is All There Is, 132
Luhrmann, Baz, 1, 20, 22–4, 129–46 passim

Macfarlane, Alan, 6
Margolyes, Miriam, 131, 138
Marlowe, Christopher, 83, 182
Marx, Karl, 17, 122
Matthews, Peter, 132
Metamorphoses, 35
Miami Beach, 23
Middleton, Thomas, 50
Milton, John, 42
Montaigne, Michel de, 36
Mooney, Michael, 102
MTV, 140

New Yorker, 132
Newman, Karen, 89, 90
Newsweek, 133

Of Domesticall Duties, 103
Ovid, 30, 35, 36, 37, 42, 50

Painter, William, 94
Paradise Lost, 42
Paris, Dave, 131
Perrineau, Harold, 138
Petite Palace of Pettie his Pleasure, 38, 40
Petrarch, 29, 30, 34, 37, 42, 50, 119, 120, 122
Pettie, George, 38, 40
Pisanello, 21
Plato, 30, 34, 35, 36, 37, 42
Porter, Joseph, 16, 20, 22, 87, 167, 206
Postlewaite, Pete, 131
Pratt, M. L., 167
Presley, Elvis, 22
Price, Leontyne, 138
Prince, 138, 139
Priscilla, Queen of the Desert, 132

Rabkin, Norma, 117
Rathbone, Basil, 21
Realm of the Senses, 79

Roberts, Sasha, 19
Rolling Stone, 136
Romeo and Juliet II, 21
Rougemont, Dennis de, 10, 68, 86
Royal Shakespeare Company, 138, 141
Runner, Joshua, 135
Ryan, Kiernan, 2, 18

Saint Matthew, 7
Saint Paul, 7
Saussure, Ferdinand de, 54
Searle, J. R., 166, 167
Second Sex, The, 19
Secret Sex Lives of Romeo and Juliet, The, 21
Sedgwick, E. K., 197
Sentimental Bloke, A, 32
Servants, The, 16–18
Shakespeare, William,
    Antony and Cleopatra, 1, 42, 48, 50, 116
    As You Like It, 9–10, 11, 201, 202
    Hamlet, 1, 37, 42, 77, 116
    Julius Caesar, 181, 194,
    King Lear, 1, 6, 116
    Love's Labour's Lost, 9, 201
    Macbeth, 1, 42, 116
    Merchant of Venice, The, 12, 48
    Midsummer Night's Dream, A, 1, 9, 11, 13, 38, 61, 76, 155
    Othello, 6, 9, 14, 42, 116
    Rape of Lucrece, The, 176
    Richard II, 164
    Richard III, 163
    Sonnets, 77
    Taming of the Shrew, The, 9
    Titus Andronicus, 187
    Twelfth Night, 9
    Two Gentlemen of Verona, The, 8
    Venus and Adonis, 36, 48, 50, 64
    Winter's Tale, The, 181, 184
Shakespeare in Love, 1
Shearer, Norma, 21
Sidney, Philip, 11, 31, 71, 184
Smith, Bruce, 105

Snow, Edward, 118
Spanish Tragedy, The, 28
Spencer, Lady Diana, 7
Spenser, Edmund, 35, 184
Stanyhurst, Richard, 181
Sternberg, Robert J., 6
Stockholder, Kay, 37, 95
Stone, Lawrence, 106–7
Symposium, 34

Tchaikowsky, 134
Tell-Trothes New-Years Gift, 101
Throne of Blood, 132
Tiepolo, 141
'Tis Pity She's a Whore, 48, 50
Titanic, 132
To Wong Foo, 132
Tragicall Historye of Romeus and Juliet, 37
Traviata, La, 13
Tristan and Isolde, 2, 10, 13, 24, 68, 77, 138
Tromeo and Juliet, 21, 132
Turner, V. W., 185

Van Gennep, Arnold, 185
Venora, Diane, 138
Verdi, 13
Verschueren, Jef, 166
Vietnam, 22
Village Voice, 139
Vindication of the Rights of Women, A, 19
Virgil, 183

Wagner, 23, 138
Webster, John, 48
Wells, Stanley, 43
West Side Story, 15, 21, 32, 131, 138
'When Doves Cry', 138, 139
Whetstone, George, 101
Whitaker, Virgil, 117
White Devil, The, 48
Whiting, John, 8, 22
Whittier, Gayle, 8, 29, 50
Wilde, Oscar, 14
Williams, Philip, 205
Wilson, J. D., 207

With Love, 132
Wollstonecraft, Mary, 19
Worthen, Bill, 130
Wuthering Heights, 42

Zaretsky, Eli, 88
Zeffirelli, Franco, 1, 21, 22, 131, 177
Zilborg, G., 13